ArtScroll Series®

Rabbi Nosson Scherman / Rabbi Meir Zlotowitz

General Editors

adapted by
Rabbi Moshe Gelbein
from the Hebrew
Mashal L'mah Hadavar Domeh

Published by
Mesorah Publications, ltd

משל
למה הדבר
דומה...

A MASHAL FOR EVERY OCCASION

RABBI YISRAEL BRONSTEIN

FIRST EDITION
First Impression ... March 2004

Published and Distributed by
MESORAH PUBLICATIONS, LTD.
4401 Second Avenue / Brooklyn, N.Y 11232

Distributed in Europe by
LEHMANNS
Unit E, Viking Industrial Park
Rolling Mill Road
Jarow, Tyne & Wear, NE32 3DP
England

Distributed in Australia and New Zealand by
GOLDS WORLDS OF JUDAICA
3-13 William Street
Balaclava, Melbourne 3183
Victoria, Australia

Distributed in Israel by
SIFRIATI / A. GITLER — BOOKS
6 Hayarkon Street
Bnei Brak 51127

Distributed in South Africa by
KOLLEL BOOKSHOP
Shop 8A Norwood Hypermarket
Norwood 2196, Johannesburg, South Africa

ARTSCROLL SERIES®
JEWISH PARABLES
© Copyright 2004, by MESORAH PUBLICATIONS, Ltd.
4401 Second Avenue / Brooklyn, N.Y. 11232 / (718) 921-9000

ISBN:
1-57819-317-6 (hard cover)
1-57819-716-4 (paperback)

Typography by CompuScribe at ArtScroll Studios, Ltd.
Printed in the United States of America by Noble Book Press Corp.
Bound by Sefercraft, Quality Bookbinders, Ltd., Brooklyn N.Y. 11232

↜ Table of Contents

Part 5: Divine Service

Examining the Fabrics / The Fire / The Appraiser / Between Israel and the Nations / The Inn / The King's Lodgings / The Difference Between One Guest and Another / The In-Laws / The Son's Punishment / The Advisors / Manager of the Estate / The Merchant Who Was a Spendthrift / *"His Pride Will Be Exalted With Glory"* / The Village Doctor / The Partnership / Compensation or Charity / A Free Gift / Penny After Penny / Hospitality to Guests / The Three Beloved Companions of the King / Foot Soldiers and Horsemen / *"I Have Set Hashem Before Me Always"*

The Apprentice / The Taste of Radish and Onion / The King's Two Gardeners / A Valid Reason / Eventually the Pennies Add Up / The Miser's Donation / The Lost Tool / The Reward for One Word / A Vessel of Exquisite Beauty / The Palace / The Work Tools / Delve in the Torah and Delve in it Again, For Everything Is in It / The Stores in the City / Everything is Contained Within It / The Torah of Earlier Generations / Torah Returns to Its Inn / On Condition to Fulfill / Man's Purpose / Choosing the Appropriate Profession / What to Ask For / The Watch

Prayer Without Proper Focus / Praying Daily / *"With His Soul He Brings His Bread"* / Preparation for Prayer / When Old Memories Are Rehashed / Instill Understanding in Our Hearts / The Request / Where Is His Focus Directed / Small Jars / The Giver of the Gift / A Boy's Weeping / A Favorable Request / In Former Years / How to Ask / A Proper Appearance / A House of Toothpicks / *"He Is The Healer of the Brokenhearted"* / Who Owes Whom? / The King's Seal / The Wanderer / A Prayer for the Public / Grab All That

Part 1

Faith and Trust in Hashem

◄§ Everything that Hashem Does is for the Best

A villager took a stroll through a big city and was unable to tear his eyes from its wondrous sights. Suddenly he came to the home of a professional tailor who was occupied with the production of fine garments and elegant overcoats for the royal household. As he stood in the doorway, the villager observed the tailor spread expensive silk fabric on the tables and lift a pair of scissors, intending to cut the material…

"Stop!" screamed the villager. "What are you doing? Why would you damage such expensive silk fabric?"

The tailor immediately realized that the nature of the man was unsophisticated. Nonetheless, out of the goodness of his heart, he politely explained his actions: "You should just know that I am not damaging in the least; rather, I am making improvements. This fabric will soon be transformed into an overcoat for the king!"

> There are times, said the Dubno Maggid, when we see a righteous person suffer, and the world asks in bewilderment, "Why was he deserving of such a harsh decree?" We must realize, however, that like the villager in the parable, we, too, are incapable of understanding that which we observe. We do not possess the intellectual capabilities that would allow us to comprehend Hashem's all-encompassing kindness. We do not realize that He is not destroying in the slightest; rather, He is making improvements.
>
> Everything that Hashem does is for the best!

◄§ The Lottery

With the pittance of pennies that he had amassed, a poor man set out and purchased a lottery ticket. The winning ticket was to be drawn in the big city, and an enormous sum of money was offered as first prize.

The poor man was struck by good fortune, as the first ticket chosen was none other than the one in his possession!

A feeling of jubilation pervaded the poor man's home and, swept away by the great joy, he and his many children erupted into a storm of dancing. They celebrated to such an extent, that their sounds of elation could be heard from outside their house.

"What could be the explanation behind the happiness in this unfortunate man's home?" wondered his neighbors.

When they were unable to find anyone who could present them with an explanation, the neighbors entered his house to see for themselves.

"What do you have to be so happy about?" asked his neighbors. "Why are you dancing?"

"I am a rich man," he responded, as he waved his lottery ticket before them. "This ticket won the grand prize!"

"So what?" challenged the neighbors. "At the present time you do not even have a penny to your name, and famine still resides in your home."

"You fools," replied the poor man. "What difference does it make that I do not have a penny? Now that I have won the lottery, it is as if the money is already in my pocket."

> A person who fulfills Hashem's mitzvos even in trying times, said the Chofetz Chaim, should feel true joy, for a great reward is awaiting him in the future. And even if it is not presently in his possession, it is similar to possessing the winning lottery ticket!

◆§ The Betrothal Feast

An extraordinarily wealthy individual sought a husband for his daughter. He set his sights on a particular young man, a budding Torah scholar who possessed sterling character traits. He was the most outstanding student in his yeshivah as well. There was just one problem — he came from a family of destitute paupers.

The wealthy man, however, disregarded the boy's poverty in favor of his many positive qualities, and his daughter and the young man were soon betrothed.

The wealthy man arranged a lavish betrothal feast befitting someone of his financial means. He instructed his servants – who readily complied — to adorn the tables with every imaginable delicacy and delight. Such a feast had seldom been seen!

He invited all of the distinguished members of the city to the feast as well. Even the ruler of the city exetended himself to attend in order to accord honor to the host.

The wealthy man had planned all of this with a specific motive in mind: to make an impression upon his future son-in-law, who would undoubtedly be dumbfounded by his father-in-law's exalted status.

But when the impoverished groom — who had lived his entire life literally starving for bread and had not eaten a decent meal in quite some time — entered the hall, he took scant notice whatsoever of the guests and the extravagant arrangement. Rather, he focused his entire attention on a straw basket that was filled to the brim with fresh rolls...

Following the festive celebration, the wealthy man discovered that his son-in-law was making inquiries regarding his prominent status and wealth.

Furious, the father-in-law approached the young man and exclaimed, "Now you are researching my standing? Why did you not attempt to investigate it when I displayed all of my honor before you at the betrothal feast, the likes of which neither you nor your fathers have ever seen...?"

> So it is with Hashem and the Jewish people, explained the Dubno Maggid. Hashem took us out of Egypt with a mighty hand and an outstretched arm, and demonstrated His strength — performing awesome feats which had never before been seen. Yet the Children of Israel paid no heed to the signs and wonders, as the verse states, "Our fathers in Egypt did not contemplate Your wonders" (Tehillim 106:7). Yet now we search for miracles and wonders in order to know His might?

⋙ From Where Will a Livelihood Come?

There are instances when a person hears a report that there are trying times in store, prices are expected to soar, etc., and his heart becomes filled with worry. How he will be able to earn a living and provide for his family? The Chofetz Chaim related an excellent parable regarding this matter.

There was an emperor who ruled with total dominion over many prosperous lands. His kingdom was replete with fertile and lush vineyards from which his subjects earned their livelihood. In short, they lacked nothing.

It once happened that several individuals plotted to overthrow the emperor. Their scheme was exposed, however, and before they had the opportunity to implement it, they were thrown into prison to await being tried on a charge of treason.

Prior to the trial, the emperor took a stroll in the palace garden. The garden was vast, showcasing fragrant flowers and blossoming fruit trees. Amid the trees was a small spring that flowed into several different streams. Swimming in these sparkling streams were schools of goldfish.

Suddenly, the emperor noticed a small songbird perched atop a tree. Its feathers were lovely, as was its melodious song.

He ordered his servants to capture the bird and place it inside a large cage. The cage was then placed in the great palace hall directly to the right of the throne. There the bird would gladden the emperor's heart by singing its extraordinary melodies.

The servants heeded the emperor's request.

When they brought the cage to the palace, one of the servants let out a sigh.

"Why are you sighing?" asked one of his friends.

"I am sighing," responded the servant, "because I feel compassion for this small bird. Have you not heard that a group of men were discovered having devised a scheme to overthrow the emperor? If that would ever occur, who would worry about this bird and take care of it? It would most certainly die of starvation..."

"That is why you are sighing?" laughed his friends. "Indeed, several men plotted the downfall of our glorious emperor who rules over many lands. But does that mean that there would not be found in the entire royal treasury the handful of seeds that is necessary to sustain a small bird?"

This applies to our own livelihoods as well, remarked the Chofetz Chaim. While there may be a rumor that prices will soar, does that mean that in the world of Hashem, the King of kings Who rules the entire universe, there will not be found the handful of "seeds" necessary to sustain us?

◄§ Servants' Labor

Sometimes, said the Dubno Maggid, it appears to an individual that he is trapped in a difficult predicament from which there is no escape. Let him not despair, however, for Hashem's salvation arrives in the blink of an eye and, on occasion, from the place from where he would have least expected it to come.

The Maggid asked, to what can this be compared? To a pauper, who must personally tend to each one of his daily needs. He cleans, cooks, organizes, and washes, all on his own.

A wealthy man, however, need not lift a finger, for he has a servant who does all that is necessary. When mealtime arrives, the servant sets the table and makes the necessary arrangements. He then goes to the kitchen and serves an assortment of delicacies. Following the meal, he clears the dishes and puts everything in order. Even after he has concluded the various tasks that pertain to the meal, he quickly turns his attention to the household chores that must be performed.

Then, continued the Maggid, there is a king, who has a massive staff of servants, so large that not one servant performs two different tasks. Rather, one servant is appointed over matters pertaining to food preparation and another over serving the food. A third servant is responsible for the horses' stables, while a fourth sweeps the king's courtyard. Each servant is assigned a particular chore.

Yet greater than them all is Hashem, the King of all kings, Whose kingdom is of such enormity that it is entirely unfathomable to any of His creations. Therefore, even if a situation appears hopelessly bleak, it is certain that Hashem, in His great mercy, will send salvation from an unexpected source, for Hashem has many agents to perform His bidding!

‿§ The Fruit of One's Labor

The Chofetz Chaim was once traveling on a train. In the railroad car was another Jew with whom he conversed throughout the trip.

"Tell me please, Reb Yid," asked the Chofetz Chaim. "Do you set fixed periods of time to study Torah?"

"Truthfully," answered the man, "I don't really have any time to spare, as I am a businessman, and the yoke of earning a living rests heavily upon my shoulders. From early morning until late at night I am busy with my work, and if I would not work as I do, a competitor would outdo me and impede upon my livelihood."

"You are mistaken," said the Chofetz Chaim. "I will illustrate the fallacy of your words for you with a parable:

A man traveled to the capital city to speak with the king's officers regarding an important matter. Seated in the railroad car, he grew impatient, as it appeared to be moving rather slowly. What did he do? He removed his coat, rolled up his sleeves, and with all his might, began to push the inside wall of the train…

" 'What are you doing?' asked the bewildered passengers.

" 'I know,' said the man, 'that when the horse hitched to my own wagon has difficulty ascending a mountain, I assist it by descending from the wagon and pushing... In this instance as well, I am pushing the car in order that it move faster.'

" 'You simple villager,' laughed the passengers. 'Do you truly think that your meager strength will be sufficient to move this powerful train, all the more so, when you are sitting inside?'

"So it is when it comes to one's livelihood," concluded the Chofetz Chaim. "Hashem, the King of all kings, worries about all His creations and sustains the entire world with His mercy. Do you truly think that as a result of your efforts you will increase your earnings?"

⋙ "Cast Upon Hashem Your Burden and He Will Sustain You"

There are times, noted the Dubno Maggid, that an individual is involved with a certain matter, and he gives much thought as to how to conduct himself — should he try this measure or perhaps persue an alternative option — expending considerable energy thinking and planning. A man must not forget, however, that everything comes from Hashem, Who ensures his existence and the fulfillment of all his endeavors, as the verse states, "Cast upon Hashem your burden and He will sustain you" (Tehillim 55:23).

This can this be compared to the poor man in the following story, noted the Maggid.

A poor man was trudging along the way, his bundles slung over his shoulder. Suddenly, a wealthy man riding in a magnificent stagecoach being drawn by two able-bodied steeds passed him by.

The wealthy individual saw the poor man on foot and took pity on him.

He instructed the driver to bring the coach to a halt, and invited the poor man to climb aboard with his belongings. Together they would travel to their individual destinations.

Overjoyed, the poor man climbed aboard the stagecoach, and the horses resumed their galloping.

After traveling for some time, the wealthy man noticed that his companion was sitting with his bundles laden upon his shoulder.

"Why don't you put your belongings down?" asked the wealthy man. "Are the bundles not heavy?"

"Indeed they are," sighed the poor man. "But I do not wish to weigh down the stagecoach."

The wealthy man had a good laugh. "Silly man," he exclaimed. "What is carrying you and your belongings at this very moment? Is it not the stagecoach?"

"Many designs are in a man's heart," (*Mishlei* 19:21), concluded the Dubno Maggid, but one must constantly recall that there is not even one action which is wrought by the power of man; rather, everything comes from Hashem alone.

⋖ঌ *Trust in Hashem Is the Foundation of the Entire Torah*

The Torah testifies regarding Avraham Avinu, "And he trusted in Hashem, and He reckoned it to him as righteousness" (*Bereishis* 15:6).

Why, asked the Chofetz Chaim, was it specifically Avraham's trust in Hashem that was reckoned to him as righteousness? After all, Avraham Avinu fulfilled the entire Torah!

From here we see, said the Chofetz Chaim, that trust in Hashem is more important than anything else and is the very foundation of the Torah.

This can be compared, continued the Chofetz Chaim, to a man drowning at sea, who suddenly spots a tree within reach. Which part of the tree does he lunge for? Not the branches, for they will break under his weight; rather, he grabs the roots of the tree…

Trust in Hashem, the Chofetz Chaim exclaimed, is similar to the strong roots of a tree, which are the basis and foundation of the entire tree…

The Tailor

In a certain city lived a tailor who was renowned for his expert craftsmanship. Noblemen and barons visited his home regularly, bringing their fine garments. The tailor never disappointed anyone. Time and time again, he consistently created stunning overcoats and elegant clothing that were amazing to behold. His fame continued to spread, until word of his talents reached the king's palace.

The king had the tailor summoned and informed him that from then on he would be employed in the king's courtyard. He would be personally responsible for sewing all the clothing for the palace staff. The king invited him to dwell in the servants' quarters, and ensured the tailor that he would provide for both him and his family. In addition, he would pay the tailor handsomely, guaranteeing him a generous monthly salary.

Elated, the tailor packed up his belongings and moved into his new home in the king's palace.

Some time afterwards, the tailor fell ill and lost his eyesight, leaving him unable to sew. He sought the assistance of the finest doctors available, and they concocted several medications for him. The treatments slowly took effect, but after spending such an exorbitant amount of money in order to procure medical assistance he was eventually left penniless.

Requiring additional medications but unable to afford them, his wife suggested that he sell his sewing machine, in order to purchase the medicines that he needed.

"Absolutely not!" shouted the tailor. "I may not presently be able to sew, but the king, nonetheless, acts kindly towards me and displays understanding for my predicament, as he realizes that I will soon be able to work again. However, if I sell my sewing machine, it is a sign that I am no longer a tailor… What will I do then?"

The same thing applies to the Jewish nation. While we may no longer serve Hashem in the ways that the earlier generations did, we nevertheless, trust in Him with all our hearts — for the Name of Hashem is proclaimed over us, and we remain servants of the King of all Kings!

◄§ Guaranteed Reward

In a small town lived a destitute pauper and his large family. The pauper suffered terribly at the sight of his young children asking for bread and being turned away empty-handed. He pondered the situation and decided to travel to a big city; there he would hire himself out to perform whatever form of work came his way. He would then support his family with the little money that he earned.

The pauper traveled to a nearby city and found work as a servant in the house of one of the wealthier men in the area.

He went about his task faithfully, and his master generously compensated him for his dedication. After several years, the pauper had amassed a significant sum of money, and he decided that it was time to return home.

On his way home, he was assailed by a band of thieves, who stole the money he had worked so hard to earn…

With little choice in the matter, he returned to the wealthy man's home and once again hired himself out as his servant. A kind-hearted individual, the wealthy man listened to his loyal servant's sad story and took pity on him. He then made him the following promise: "Work for me now, and when you wish to return home, I will compensate you accordingly. However, this time I will serve as a personal guarantor for your money. If, Heaven forbid, you are robbed once again, do not hesitate; rather, return to me, and I will replace whatever was stolen from you!"

The pauper thanked the wealthy man profusely and was amazed at his kindliness.

> So, too, exclaimed the Dubno Maggid, with regard to the Jewish people: Hashem promised our forefathers that their off-spring would be like the dust of the earth and the sand of the shores. Yet that which the verse states, "Then He established it for Yaakov as a statute, for Yisrael as an everlasting covenant" (*Tehillim* 105:10), is Hashem's guarantee that despite the fact that later generations may not at all deserve to witness the ful-fillment of this promise, Hashem will fulfill it nevertheless.

◆§ Hashem Controls the World

Shortly before a train departs from a busy train station, said the Chofetz Chaim, it is customary for the conductor to blow a whistle. Upon hearing the whistle, crowds of people rush to take a seat on the train that will shortly depart.

Yet there are others who bide their time and board the railway cars only after they hear the second whistle, which indicates that departure is imminent.

By the time the third whistle has been sounded, not a passenger remains on the platform, and the train commences its journey.

A simpleton errs, continued the Chofetz Chaim, by believing that the conductor who blows his whistle is the director of all the train's operations. For the truth is that he is no more than a minor official. The one who is actually in charge of the train sits in his of-fice and dispenses orders to his subordinates. They, in turn, dispense orders to their subordinates, and so on, until word reaches the conductor who subsequently blows the whistle.

> So it is with this world, concluded the Chofetz Chaim. There are those who believe that kings and officials are at its helm. The truth is, however, that there is a far superior authority, and

everything is in the hands, as it were, of Hashem, the King of kings. It is He and not anyone else Who is the true controller of the world.

❧ Achieving the Goal

A guest arrived at a well-known restaurant and told its owner that he would be residing in the city for a number of days. He requested that a portion of meat be sent each day of his stay.

When the time came for him to eat, he was disappointed to discover that he had been sent a portion of vegetables instead of the portion of meat that he had requested.

The man approached the owner of the restaurant and claimed that he had been deceived, since he had paid for meat and received cucumbers instead…

A similar event occurred to a merchant who was accustomed to purchasing silk fabric from a wholesaler. He would then visit merchants throughout the city and sell the silk for a substantial profit. On one occasion, without his prior knowledge, he was given velvet instead of silk. Despite the fact that he had not received the fabric he had requested, he nonetheless managed to earn a hefty profit selling the velvet.

The merchant would certainly not be disgruntled, for as long as he is able to earn his usual profit, what difference does it make to him whether he sells silk or velvet?

So, too, is a man's life in this world, explained the Dubno Maggid. When an individual desires to live a life of indulgence, he is terribly distressed when suffering comes his way, for instead of pleasure he received anguish.

This does not apply to *tzaddikim*, however, who make perfection of the soul their one and only purpose in life. That being the case, if they are struck by suffering, they accept it lovingly, for it, too, is a step towards the achievement of their ultimate goal.

ᴥ§ The Request of a Simple Soldier

Each and every individual must pray and beseech Hashem that the honor of His kingdom be increased in the world. That should be our highest priority.

The Chofetz Chaim gave a parable of a king who went to inspect the state of his troops. The king observed that his soldiers were undyingly loyal to his service, and this earned them much favor in his eyes.

"Request anything that you wish from me," said the king to his soldiers, "and I will grant it to you."

"Your Highness," said one of the soldiers. "You should know that I serve you with all my heart and soul. I therefore request that you provide me with my meals each and every day."

"You fool!" laughed his friends. "Are your meals — as well as the meals of the other soldiers — not already given to you automatically from the king's treasury? Even without asking for it, you will be provided for…"

> So it is with our own sustenance, concluded the Chofetz Chaim. We beseech Hashem to provide us with our livelihood, but we completely forget that it is unnecessary to do so, as Hashem concerns Himself with the needs of all His creations anyway.
>
> Instead, we must request that Hashem increase His honor and the honor of Torah in the world!

ᴥ§ The Wealthy Brother

A pauper had a brother who lived in a distant land. One day, the pauper heard that his brother had risen to great prominence. He had grown extremely wealthy and had been appointed one of the king's officers. The pauper was ecstatic upon hearing of his brother's good fortune.

"Why are you so overjoyed?" wondered his friends. "Has your brother given you something for which you asked him? Why, the two of you live very far away from each other, so how will you benefit from your brother's wealth? What's more, even if you exert the effort to make the journey and request that he improve your predicament, who's to say that he won't just slam the door in your face?"

"You are correct," responded the pauper. "Yet I am still happy that my brother is wealthy, and it is ten times better for me than had he been poor. If I indeed decide to journey to him and request his assistance — perhaps he will assist me, perhaps not. However, if he were poor — there would not be the slightest chance of him extending me any help whatsoever…"

> How a Jew must rejoice that he has a G-d, exclaimed the Dubno Maggid! As it states: "Great is our Lord and abundant in strength" (*Tehillim* 147:5). Additionally, the verse states, "Hashem, in Your might the king rejoices, and in Your salvation how greatly does he exult" (*Tehillim* 21:2).

❧ Hashem's Ways Are Concealed from Man

> Many people ask, remarked the Chofetz Chaim, "Why do we see the wicked living lives of wealth and luxury, while great *tzaddikim*, on the other hand, live with suffering, poverty and hardship?"
>
> The Chofetz Chaim answered:

To what can this be compared? To a man who visited a certain shul one Shabbos. He watched curiously as the *gabbai* called up various members of the congregation to recite blessings over the Torah. First he called a Kohen who was seated on the last bench in the shul. Next he called a Levi who was seated on a different bench, and a Yisrael who was seated on yet another bench. All in all, seven *aliyos* were dispensed, each one to a member seated in a different section of the shul.

"Why don't you just choose seven men from the same bench?" the visitor asked the gabbai.

"My dear sir," responded the *gabbai*, "you have been here for just one Shabbos and have therefore not seen the schedule that I use to dispense *aliyos*. If, however, you prayed here regularly, you would see that I follow a specific order, and each member of the shul is called up when it is his turn…"

> So it is with this world, concluded the Chofetz Chaim. Man is but a visitor here, his life span short and fleeting. He is therefore incapable of grasping the order and accounting with which Hashem guides His world. He must know, however, that there is both judgment and a Judge Who controls the world!

✑§ A Hopelessly Bleak Situation

A wealthy man had an only son whom he desired to see enter the world of business. He therefore gave him a large sum of money and instructed him to open a business.

The son did as his father had instructed, but as he was naïve and mild mannered, other businessmen easily took advantage of him. Far from being successful, his business was failing by the day.

When the son realized just how dismal his predicament was, he turned to his father for help. His father, however, was far from sympathetic, and he scolded him angrily, "Why do you turn to me?" he yelled. "Did I not provide you with ample funds to support yourself? Indeed, your business has not yet closed down; go to work and turn to me only when you are left with nothing."

Some time later, a fire erupted in the city, decimating the homes that stood in its path. The fire gained strength, blazing mercilessly, and the residents were finding it difficult to extinguish. The fire soon drew within close proximity to the son's business and his friends shouted out to him, "You must hurry! Quickly lend a hand, lest your business go up in flames and be totally consumed!"

"On the contrary," exclaimed the son. "Let it go up in flames! That way I will be left with nothing and will be able to return to my father and request his assistance…"

> As long as man lives according to the precepts of nature, explained the Dubno Maggid, Hashem does not offer him any supernatural assistance. However, when all of the natural paths to salvation are no longer available, even if it appears to an individual that he has been totally decimated by misfortune and he does not know where help will come from, he should know that it is specifically at that moment that salvation is closest!

❧ Why Do the Righteous Suffer?

> There are those who wonder, remarked the Chofetz Chaim, why there are *tzaddikim* who live in dire poverty and at times suffer greatly. Why, they ask, do the righteous suffer?
> The answer, said the Chofetz Chaim, can be explained by way of a parable:

A wealthy man had an only son whom he loved dearly. On one occasion, the son became ill, and his physicians were unable to find a remedy.

Everyone had just about given up hope, when an expert doctor from a distant land appeared on the scene and healed the child.

"Take great care," said the doctor to the boy's father, "that not a morsel of meat enter this boy's mouth – for it is meat that will harm him the most."

The father followed the doctor's instructions and kept a cautious eye on his son.

On one occasion, the wealthy man's business dealings forced him to travel far away. He therefore instructed his servants to heed the doctor's orders and to carefully watch over the child.

It was not to be, however. For, one day, the young boy entered the kitchen and was tantalized by the fragrant aroma of a meat dish. Unable to control himself, he snatched a piece of meat, stuffed it into his mouth, and ran outside.

That same day, the son began to feel ill, and it was not long before his ailment returned as before.

Upon returning home and finding his son bedridden, the father immediately set out for the doctor and pleaded with him to cure his son once more. "I give you my word," said the father, "that I will no longer travel from my home; rather, I will take good care of my son..."

The doctor agreed and healed the boy. Some time later, the father arranged a large *seudas hoda'ah* (lit. a feast of thanksgiving) to which he invited all of his acquaintances. The tables were laden with a variety of meat dishes; the father, therefore, understandably removed his son from the dining room, so that he would not be tempted to eat as before...

Not realizing that the father was only acting for his son's benefit, the guests misconstrued his true intentions. "Such a cruel man," they thought to themselves. "We are all dining on these meat dishes, and he forces his darling son to leave the room..."

> There are times, said the Chofetz Chaim, that Hashem punishes *tzaddikim*, and we are unable to comprehend the reason behind it. We must believe, however, that the poverty and deprivation that a *tzaddik* endures is soley intended for his benefit!
>
> "The Rock! — perfect is His work, for all His paths are justice; a God of faith without iniquity, righteous and fair is He" (*Devarim* 32:4). All of Hashem's deeds are truthful and fair!

ᴥৡ *Ruler of the City*

A king had an esteemed and beloved minister who served him with the utmost devotion. The king valued the minister's faithfulness and, as a gift, granted him complete control over a small city. Everything would be carried out according to the minister's command, and he would be the recipient of all the taxes as well.

Some time later, one of the men in the kingdom demonstrated extraordinary allegiance to the king. Desiring to reward him for his loyalty, the king granted him a special certificate that exempted him from paying taxes for the rest of his life.

The man eventually chose to live in the small city that had been granted to the minister.

As he had been exempted from paying taxes, he resided in the city but did pay any taxes.

Having been summoned to court for his apparent misdemeanor, the man displayed the certificate that had been signed with the king's signet ring and which exempted him from paying any taxes.

Seeing the certificate, the minister responded, "You would certainly be correct," he said, "if you would have been living in one of the king's cities. But this city is under my dominion alone and not the king's, and his certificate is of no use to you here. You must therefore pay your taxes like everyone else…"

> One who trusts in Hashem, explained the Dubno Maggid, is constantly aware that even though he may be receiving assistance from another, the person is merely a messenger. Hashem has arranged everything.
>
> But if a person places his faith in another individual, believing that he is the one responsible for his benefit or detriment — it is an indication that he does not fully recognize that everything is in the control of the Creator.

⋗ *The Storekeeper and the Thieves*

In a certain city lived a very wealthy man whose large general store was the source of livelihood for both him and his family. One night, a band of thieves broke into the store and stole massive amounts of merchandise as well as a significant sum of money from the cash register.

The storekeeper expended much effort in collecting the remaining merchandise from his store, and also the items that had been sitting in his warehouse for years. With considerable resilience, he opened a new business. While the store was certainly smaller than the previous one, he nevertheless managed to earn enough to live.

Some time later, however, thieves broke into this store again, this time leaving him with nothing...

Left with no other choice, the man sold his wife's jewelry and opened a small store in which he sold inexpensive household items. Misfortune struck soon after, however, as thieves surreptitiously entered his store and stole the few items that he had in stock.

The man was now left penniless...

What did he do? He borrowed a small sum of money from his friends and purchased some merchandise. Goods in hand, he went from town to town and city to city, knocking on doors and trying his best to make a sale.

He was walking home one day, with a few copper coins jingling in his pocket. Suddenly, a merciless thief riding on a strapping steed stopped him and demanded that he hand over everything in his possession...

The man began to weep bitterly and begged the thief not to take his money, so that he could afford to buy bread for his family. But the cruel thief ignored his pleas, snatched his bundles and money, and then galloped away into the nearby forest.

The man watched the thief as he rode further and further away. Suddenly, the thief rode into the branch of a willow tree and toppled from his horse...

Sprinting over to the thief, the man saw that this heartless individual had received his just desserts — he was no longer alive...

Rummaging through the thief's belongings, the man discovered a valuable treasure — precious gems and pearls — hidden within the folds of his saddle.

He took the treasure and ran to his house. Shortly thereafter, he regained his former status as a wealthy man; in fact, he was even wealthier than he had been before!

> It is forbidden, said R' Nachman of Breslov, for an individual to succumb to his suffering. Rather, let him turn his eyes to the Merciful One and continuously beseech Him for mercy. When the time is right, all of the good that he had previously will be restored to him, and it will be even greater than before.

⋑ "The Righteous Will Walk in Them" (Hoshea 14:10)

A drunken man sat in a tavern and gulped down his usual share of wine. Suddenly, he began to scream, "Jews! Save yourselves! Evacuate this tavern as it will soon collapse!"

The drunken man's words provided the other patrons with a hearty laugh. "Now wait just a minute," they cackled. "Why would this tavern collapse? It is built rather sturdily and its foundations are solid!"

"Just look, and you will see," he responded heatedly. "Each time I take a step, I stagger — sometimes to the right and sometimes to the left. This is a clear indication that the tavern is unstable and on the verge of collapse..."

One of the men stood up from his chair, walked back and forth, and then exclaimed, "See for yourself, you drunkard. I am walking straight without stumbling in the slightest. The reason you fall is because you are drunk and your head is spinning..."

> "For the ways of Hashem are straight" exclaimed the Dubno Maggid. "The righteous will walk in them and sinners will stumble over them!" (*Hosea* 14:10).

❧ One Who Trusts in Hashem

R' Nachman of Breslov related a story about a man who constantly placed his trust in Hashem:

A king sat on his throne and thought to himself, "There is no one like me in all the land, for I am a great king and ruler of the entire land. My storehouses are well stocked and I have not a worry in my heart."

Desiring to confirm this, the king disguised himself as an ordinary person and set out into the city.

Evening had fallen as the king walked through the alleyways, listening to the conversations that were emanating from within the houses. Indeed, from within each home he heard a conversation that centered on a particular worry: This one's roof had a leak, this one did not have a sufficient livelihood, another person's wagon had lost its wheel, while his neighbor did not own a wearable garment...

Suddenly, the king arrived at a rather unexceptional and poor-looking home. A small light shone through the window, and the pleasant sound of singing could be heard issuing from within.

The king drew close to the window and peered inside. He saw a set table laden with food and drink. Seated around the table was a family who appeared incredibly happy, and the head of the household was singing joyously, his face radiant...

The king knocked on the door and when it was opened, he was warmly invited in. He then asked the father to tell him what he did for a living. The father related that he was an expert at repairing old and damaged vessels. Every day, he said, people bring him vessels to repair and, with Hashem's kindness, he earns six gulden. He then returns home in good sprits and his wife prepares delicacies for the family.

When the father finished speaking, the king — who had not revealed his true identity — rose and left.

The following day, the king declared that under no circumstances were any old vessels to be brought in for repair. Anyone violating this command would be meted out the severest of penalties!

Despite the realization that he had lost his source of livelihood, the man did not despair. Rather, he went out into the street, wholeheartedly trusting in Hashem that He would provide him with an alternate means of earning a living.

Shortly thereafter, he spotted a gentleman chopping wood. He offered to hew the wood in his stead, and the man happily agreed. In this manner, he managed to earn six gulden on that day as well.

That evening, the king disguised himself once more and headed towards the man's house in order to see if a feeling of sadness prevailed there. How surprised he was when he noticed the light shining through the window and heard singing filling the home.

The king ascertained that the father had earned his money chopping wood. He quickly returned to his palace and the next day declared that it was forbidden for an individual to hire another man to chop his wood...

When the man woke that morning and he discovered that he had once again been deprived of a livelihood, he did not despair; rather, he hired himself out as one of the royal guards.

He received a spotess uniform along with a polished sword and was placed on guard alongside the king's palace.

Towards evening, the man dislodged the metal blade from the sword and replaced it with a wooden one that he had fashioned. He placed the wooden sword into his sheath, and his action went unnoticed. He then pawned the metal sword in exchange for six gulden...

When the king arrived at their house that evening, his amazement knew no bounds, for the family was feasting as they did each and every day. The king questioned the father, and the father — unaware of his visitor's true identity — innocently revealed what he had done to obtain the money...

While on guard the next day, the man was summoned to immediately appear before the king. When he stood opposite the throne, the king informed him that a traitor to the kingdom had been apprehended and was sentenced to death by sword. The king requested that he employ his sword in carrying out the verdict...

The man attempted to plead with the king, but it was of no use — the king was adamant that he and only he execute the traitor.

When the traitor was brought before the king, the man who trusted so wholeheartedly in Hashem stood up and announced, "Gentlemen! In the name of the king I am prepared to put this traitor to death. However, if he is indeed blameless, a miracle will occur and this sword will be transformed into one of wood!" The man drew his sword from its sheath and to everyone's astonishment, it was indeed made of wood…

The king, who was the only one who understood what had transpired, took great delight in the man's cunning and allowed him to return home in peace.

◆§ The Amazing Doctor

There lived a prominent ruler who had suffered from illness and poor health throughout his entire life. One day, the ruler heard that there was an expert doctor residing in a distant city who was known to be capable of curing every type of illness.

The ruler hurriedly sent the doctor a letter offering him to come and live in the palace. As compensation, he would receive a handsome monthly salary in addition to the generous living expenses that he would be afforded.

The doctor agreed and quickly moved into the ruler's palace. From then on, he healed whichever illnesses the ruler contracted.

In the same city lived a wealthy man who hated the ruler vehemently. In his desire to harm him, he sent a letter to the doctor inviting him to reside in his home. In exchange, he guaranteed to pay him many times more than the ruler did. The doctor would not hear of it, however, and refused the offer.

One day, the wealthy man encountered the doctor and expressed his amazement at his rejection of his proposal.

"Why would you not accept my offer?" asked the wealthy man. "Would you not earn far more money in my home?"

"Yes, indeed," responded the doctor. "But you see, in the ruler's home I am treated like a king. Since he recognizes my talents and needs my services around the clock, he is careful to treat me honorably. But in your house," concluded the doctor, "I will wander around like an unemployed individual and will not merit being treated respectfully at all..."

> By recognizing Hashem's kindness towards us at every waking moment, said the Dubno Maggid, and by arriving at the understanding that we are constantly in need of His mercy, we thereby increase His honor!

◆§ The Dowry Proffered the Rich Man's Son

A parable is drawn to a rich man who had an only son. The son was a *talmid chacham* who spent his entire day in yeshivah, studying Torah and serving Hashem. His wealthy father supported him and his family, providing them with both food and clothing.

When the son's daughter became of marriageable age, the son met with a *shadchan* (matchmaker) who made various proposals. From all of the young men that were mentioned, one appealed to him; the *shadchan* therefore hastened to arrange a meeting between the parents.

"How much of a dowry will you be providing your daughter?" asked the father of the *chasan*.

"With Hashem's help," replied the rich man's son, "I intend to provide my daughter with three thousand rubles."

"His words do not excite me in the least," whispered the father of the *chasan* to the *shadchan*. "For I know that he does not have so much as a *perutah* to his name, and all that he possesses is but a free gift from his father. That being the case, there is no guarantee that he will make good on his promise...

"Now, had I heard a similar promise directly from the mouth of his rich father — that would have been a different story!"

Man, explained the Dubno Maggid, does not so much as lift a finger unless it has been decreed from Above. He can neither harm nor benefit his fellow man unless it is the will of Hashem – Man's strength is in his mouth alone!

⋙ *The Captain*

On one occasion, the members of the congregation in Pittsburgh met with their esteemed rav, R' Shimon Zevitz. Their conversation revolved around upholding the main tenets of faith and religion.

"You must know," said the Rav, "that when it comes to matters regarding faith in Hashem, one must not compromise in any way whatsoever.

"To what can this be compared?" he continued. "To a gigantic ship sailing the sea. The captain steers the ship and keeps his eyes fixed on the compass in front of him, knowing quite well that if he deviates even one degree, he will be driven completely off course and will not reach his destination. He will simply drift aimlessly in the midst of the sea…

"One who deviates — however slightly — from the fundamentals of faith," concluded R' Zevitz, "will ultimately be led completely astray…"

⋙ *The Farmer*

A story is told about a city dweller who visited the village for the first time in his life. Looking around, he noticed a farmer plowing his field with a plow strapped to two powerful horses. He stared in amazement and could not believe what he was seeing. "Why is the farmer destroying the land?" he wondered. "And besides, how will he benefit from digging furrows in the dry earth?"

His astonishment grew even more when he realized that subsequent to "destroying" the land, the farmer was now scattering wheat kernels over the surface.

"This farmer must have lost his mind," thought the man to himself.

Several weeks later, however, the man noticed that stalks of wheat had grown in the field. He now understood that these stalks of wheat must have been the farmer's goal from the outset. Not much time had passed, however, when the farmer went out onto the field with a sickle in hand and cut down all of the wheat he had toiled so painstakingly to grow…

"This I simply cannot understand," exclaimed the man to himself. "After having labored to such a degree in order to grow these beautiful stalks of wheat — he cuts them down with a sickle?"

His curiosity continued to increase until he saw the farmer load the wheat harvest onto his wagon and transport it to the mill. There it was ground into white flour and eventually baked into fresh bread.

It was only then that the man understood the true intentions of the farmer!

> So it is with man in this world, explained the Dubno Maggid. There are times when man does not understand that which he sees, and his heart is filled with wonderment. This is due only to his lack of understanding and limited perspective. If, however, he were able to view the entire creation as a whole, he would arrive at a realization of just how extraordinary Hashem's providence truly is.

Part 2

Fear of Heaven

✍ Losing One's Way

When a person travels in an old, rickety wagon harnessed to an aged horse that can barely manage to pull it, the prospect of losing his way does not represent much of a threat to anyone but himself. Therefore, if he realizes that he has lost his way, he simply returns to the highway.

This is not the case, however, if the one traveling is a wealthy businessman who has twenty huge wagons filled with heavy merchandise. If he loses his way, there is potential danger to the many who follow him. For the grooves caused by his laden wagons will be noticeable, and they will mistakenly believe it to be the correct one. As a result they will lose their way just as he did…

> When a simple man sins, said the Dubno Maggid, he must mend his ways and return to the upright path. This is not the case, however, when the sinner is a great man to whom others look for guidance. For then the damage wreaked is far more severe, as those who stray subsequently will assume that their misdeeds are correct and noble, and he will have caused the masses to stumble.

✍ The Ruler's Entourage

A distinguished ruler was traveling with his family at the head of a massive entourage. When they reached the crossroads, the ruler spotted a pleasant looking inn, and — feeling the pangs of hunger and fatigue — ordered everyone to stop traveling and take up lodging for the night.

When the entourage entered the inn, the innkeeper hurried to serve them, dividing them up into two separate groups: The ruler and his family were led to a magnificent room that was adorned with plush carpets and featured a fireplace blazing with a warm and pleasant fire. Clapping his hands, the innkeeper signaled to his workers to set the table, and within a matter of moments they served delicacies — roasted duck, stuffed fowl, and fine wine — that were fit for a king.

Afterwards, the rest of the entourage, which included the servants, coachmen, and charioteers, were led into the kitchen at the back. There they sat at a large, bare, wooden table and were served stale bread and potato broth in clay bowls.

When they were preparing to take leave of the inn, the innkeeper presented an itemized bill, which included the cost of the ruler's meal as well as that of his entourage's.

> Man, explained the Dubno Maggid, is the ruler over all of his limbs. He must know and remember well that when the time comes, he will be required to pay for all of their actions!

৵ৢ A Flaw in the Garment

A pauper saved one *perutah* after another until he amassed just enough money to cover the expenses for the upcoming holidays.

Money in hand, he went out into the city square in order to purchase a few of the items that he needed for the holiday. He wandered around until he noticed a merchant selling fine—looking clothing. One of the garments caught his eye, and the pauper inquired as to its cost. The price being quite reasonable, he handed over all of his money and took possession of the garment. The pauper then hurried home with not a *perutah* remaining in his pocket.

Upon entering his rundown home, he showed his wife the garment he had purchased. Taking one look at it, she burst into a fit of screaming. "What did you do?" she yelled. "So you craved a garment for the holiday? On what will you make *Kiddush* — on the garment?"

Realizing that he had made a grave error, the pauper asked his wife for advice as to how he could rectify the situation.

"Go back to the merchant," said his wife, "and tell him that you found a flaw in the garment. Then request that he return your money!"

The pauper ran to the clothing stand, and while huffing and puffing, told the merchant, "Please return my money. I have found a defect in the garment that you sold me, and I do not wish to purchase it."

The merchant returned his money without saying a word.

"Why did you give the man his money?" asked the astounded customers who were standing nearby. "You should have simply given him an unflawed garment in its stead!"

"I am a veteran merchant," he responded, "and I can easily perceive the nature of a customer. This pauper did not want a garment at all; rather, he only desired that his money be returned to him. Just look at the first words he said when he approached me – 'Return my money.' Only afterwards did he tell me that he had found a defect in the garment.

"Had I exchanged the garment for a different one, he would have immediately found a defect in the new garment as well."

> There are two types of individuals, remarked the Dubno Maggid, who attempt to clarify the reasons behind the *mitzvos*. The first one truly fears Heaven and wishes to improve his performance of *mitzvos* by understanding their reasons. The second, however, wishes only to discover a flaw in the *mitzvos*. To such a person we do not respond, for he will only look for ways to discover new flaws.

❧ "Those who Hate You, O Hashem, I Hate Them" (Tehillim 139:21)

In a certain city lived a man who was renowned for his sterling character traits. He never lost his temper, not even toward someone who had intentionally angered him. Rather, he consistently retained a serene demeanor.

On one occasion he returned home only to find a thief in the midst of a burglary.

The man picked up a stick and, in a state of absolute fury, struck the thief until he fled from the house, battered and wounded.

"We're surprised at you," his friends told him afterwards. "After all, you've never become so enraged. What suddenly inspired you to change your behavior and beat the thief so furiously?"

"You're making an error," he responded. "The truth is that when others offend me, I do become angry. Yet I am, nonetheless, able to make light of the offense. On this occasion, however, I felt compelled to display my anger in order that the thief should not return to my house a second time."

> In *Tehillim* (139: 21,22), exclaimed the Dubno Maggid, it states, "Those who hate You, O Hashem, I hate them; and I quarrel with those who rise up against You! With the utmost hatred, I hate them; they have become enemies unto me."
>
> One must hate the enemies of Hashem and contest them with all one's might, until they become his enemies as well. Only then will he be free of them and their company!

✣ A Flowing River

The nature of a river, noted the Dubno Maggid, is that it flows rapidly, dragging along with it whatever might happen to stand in its path, such as large stones, sediment, refuse, and the like.

There are many occasions when this can cause damage, such as when the river spews a stone or rubbish onto a riverbank, an area that is commonly used by hikers and passersby. Yet the river itself rectifies the damage, as it washes up on shore a short while later, dragging all of the sediment that it emitted a far distance away.

Such is the nature of a river.

However, continued the Maggid, if the river changes course, the damage will be permanent, as it will no longer be able to retrieve that which it has strewn upon the riverbank.

So, too, said the Maggid, is the case when it comes to money. Money is a precious commodity in the eyes of its owner, but pursuit of money and the desire to amass it can severely damage his character traits and even disrupt his Torah study and *mitzvah* performance.

However, just as money has the power to damage, so too, does it have the power to accrue benefit. For a man can perform many *mitzvos* with his money, such as donating charity, acts of kindness, supporting Torah learning, and funding the construction of synagogues.

Now, this is the case with one who always has sufficient money — then, just as he harmed his personality by pursuing money, so too, can he rectify it by utilizing his wealth in the performance of *mitzvos*. However, it often occurs that the course of his life changes and a man loses his wealth before he has a chance to mend the damage...

๔ *The Dispute*

In a certain city lived two wealthy individuals between whom a dispute had erupted. The quarrel and how it had initially developed became the talk of the city with its residents taking sides as well, until the city had been divided into two opposing camps.

Much to everyone's grief, the disagreement carried on, until a wise man proposed a plan that he felt would restore harmony between the two factions: One of the wealthy men had a son who excelled in both his Torah scholarship and fear of Heaven. The other had a daughter who possessed sterling character traits. Let a match be arranged between them, suggested the wise man, and peace shall reign once again...

There are two opposing forces that do battle within man, explained the Dubno Maggid. On one hand, man possesses a soul, a "portion from G-d above" (*Iyov* 31:2), whose only desire is to fulfill the Torah and *mitzvos*. On the other hand, man's body seeks constant physical gratification.

This is why, concluded the Maggid, Hashem gave man *mitzvos* and good deeds to perform, for they create harmony between the body and the soul.

⇜ The Debtors

A wealthy individual announced that anyone in his city in need of a loan should come to him, and he would receive the entire sum that he needed.

Upon hearing of the wealthy man's offer, scores of people arrived at his home. The wealthy man sat at his table, his notepad opened in front of him. He gave each person the sum of money that he needed, and subsequently jotted down the amount in his notepad.

Some time later, the wealthy man realized that of all the people he had lent money to, not one had paid him back.

It happened to be, that one of the people who had borrowed money truly did not have the means of repaying the debt. He therefore decided to approach the wealthy man and explain exactly why he was late in returning his money. He hoped that the rich man would be kindhearted and understand his predicament.

Upon hearing the man's explanation as to why he was unable to repay the loan, the wealthy man responded, "I certainly excuse you for not having repaid me, as I see that you are speaking the truth. I have but one request to make of you: Please go throughout the city and tell the rest of my debtors to pay me back."

We are all beholden to Hashem, said R' Nachman of Breslov, for the abundance of kindliness that He bestows upon us at each and every moment. But due to our small stature and limited intellect, we are incapable of repaying that debt. What we can do, though, is speak to others and inspire them regarding matters of Heavenly fear, reminding them that they, too, are indebted to Hashem.

❧ The Skilled Tailor

When a skilled tailor mends a garment, his stitches are undetectable. He does this in order to conceal the repair he made and in order that the garment appear brand new. Yet for all the tailor's efforts, the garment no longer possesses its former value, and is certainly not worth more than it was previously.

> So is the case, remarked the Dubno Maggid, with an individual who has sinned and since repented. While he has been forgiven for his misdeed and not a trace remains of his sin, he nevertheless, would have been far better off had he never sinned in the first place.

❧ Remarkable Wisdom

On the verse (*Vayikra* 19:3) "Every man: Your mother and father shall you revere and My Sabbaths shall you observe," the Gemara in *Maseches Yevamos* (5b) expounds, "You are all required to honor Me."

This teaches us that if an individual's parent(s) commands him to violate one of the Torah's precepts, he is forbidden to listen. Why? Because they, too, are obligated to honor Hashem.

To what can this be compared?

Three close friends lived in a certain city. Together they decided that each one of them would travel to a different land and study a particular wisdom of that land. They agreed that upon concluding their studies, they would reunite and demonstrate what they had learned.

They did exactly that. Each one traveled to a distant land and pursued a different field of study.

After several years, the designated time arrived and the three friends came to the appointed meeting place. They were ecstatic to see each other once again, and once the initial joy had passed, they began to show off what they had learned.

"In the land that I was in," said one of the friends, "I met an expert craftsman who taught me how to fashion powerful binoculars that enable one to see extremely far distances…"

"I," said the second friend, "met a remarkable coachmen who taught me how to construct a wagon capable of traveling at great speeds. It can travel the lengthy distance of several *parsaos* in the blink of an eye!"

"And I," said the third friend, "met an elderly doctor who taught me how to concoct an amazing medication capable of healing every type of illness!"

As they were admiring each other's wisdom, the first friend displayed the binoculars he had made.

The friends took turns gazing through the powerful binoculars. Amazingly, they were able to see the capital city, which was a very long distance away. Looking inside the city, they observed a great commotion taking place. People were running through the streets in a panic, expressions of anguish and suffering etched upon their faces.

Adjusting the binoculars slightly, the friends were able to discern the reason behind the commotion: The king's daughter had taken ill, and the doctors had given up hope of finding a remedy. A proclamation therefore went out calling upon anyone capable of lending assistance. In addition, whoever succeeded in curing the king's daughter would receive an enormous sum of money as a reward.

"It is a pity that I am not in the capital right now," said the friend who had been taught the art of healing. "Had I been there, I would have presented the king's daughter with a remedy that would cure her instantly. However, I am too far away…"

"That is not a problem in the least," remarked the second friend. "Why, the coach that I built could get you to the capital in a matter of minutes."

The three friends boarded the remarkable coach, and, indeed, they arrived in the capital in the blink of an eye. They stopped at the palace gates and immediately presented the king's daughter with the amazing remedy.

Lo and behold, upon tasting the medicine, her condition improved considerably. Before long, she underwent a total recovery!

At that point, however, the friends began to argue as to which one of them was entitled to the hefty reward that the king had offered.

"If not for my binoculars," said the first friend, "you would never have known that the king's daughter was sick."

"So what?" answered the second friend. "If not for my coach, it would have taken you a month to get to the capital city."

"You are both correct," said the third friend. "But what good would it have done you to know that the king's daughter was sick? And once you would have gotten to the capital — what would you have done then? Truthfully, it was only my medication that made all the difference!"

The king listened to their claims and after consulting with his sagacious advisors, turned to the men and exclaimed, "It is certainly true that if we are to judge on basis of what transpired in the past, it would be rather difficult to determine which one of you deserves the reward. But if we take the future into account...Let us see," continued the king, "From now on, we will have absolutely no use for your wondrous binoculars. The same thing applies to the spectacular coach. We may very well require more of this unique medicine, however. Therefore, the reward shall be granted to the provider of the medicine!"

> From this parable we can gain a very profound insight, explained the Dubno Maggid. There are three partners in the creation of a human being: Hashem, a father, and a mother. Yet when we desire to know which one of the three a man must obey and fear the most, we must realize that once a

child is born, his parents have fulfilled their part of the partnership. Yet we are forever dependent on Hashem, as He continuously to provides us with life!

This is the meaning of *Chazal's* words, concluded the Dubno Maggid: "You are all required to honor Me!"

Part 3

Proper Speech

✑ Who Is Going to Pay?

While hearing words of *lashon hara* (derogatory speech) may afford pleasure), one must, nevertheless, attempt with all one's might to refrain from listening to it and from lending it credence.

This can be compared, said the Chofetz Chaim, to a charlatan who donned elegant clothing and went out into the city square.

There was a newcomer in the city that day; he was visiting the city for the first time and did not know anyone. He wandered around, gazing wondrously at the streets crowded with people and at the stores stocked with plenty.

Suddenly, the charlatan approached him.

"*Shalom*, to you, my good Jew," said the charlatan. "I can see that you are a visitor here. Perhaps you are in need of something? This is your lucky day, for it just so happens that I have some time on my hands and am willing to show you around the city."

The visitor was overjoyed and grateful for the man's kindness.

The charlatan led the visitor through the city streets, giving him an extensive tour. When they had finished, he told the visitor, "Since you are my guest for the day, I would like to invite you to a lavish feast, fitting for such an esteemed guest as yourself. It will be my treat."

They entered an elegant restaurant and ordered every imaginable delicacy, both food and drink. "Eat, my friend, eat," said the charlatan. "Perhaps you would care for some fruit compote and cookies as well?"

As their meal came to a close, the charlatan slipped out of the restaurant and ran away.

The guest's claims and protests were of no use — he was forced to cover the enormous expense of the meal that both he and his "friend" the charlatan had incurred.

He suddenly arrived at the stark realization that this imposter was not a friend at all, but a bitter enemy.

So is the case, said the Chofetz Chaim, when it comes to *lashon hara*. A man happens to meet his friend one day, and this friend proceeds to speak *lashon hara*. While it may be pleasurable to hear the malicious speech at the time, and he may be grateful to his friend for holding him in high regard and for letting him in on these "precious" secrets, when the time arrives for him to stand in judgment before the Heavenly Tribune, he will be forced to pay for the fleeting pleasure that he derived.

Only then will he discover just how costly that pleasure truly was, and how the person who related the *lashon hara* to him was not his friend at all…

●§ *The Machine in Control of All the Others*

Chazal state that the word "*metzora*" is a combination of the words "*motzi shem ra*" (uttering malicious speech that is false) (*Arachin* 15b).

A *metzorah* is a person who has been afflicted with *tzara'as* (a condition commonly, but inaccurately, translated as leprosy) as a result of violating the grave sin of speaking *lashon hara*.

A metzora who has been declared impure, said the Chofetz Chaim, must approach the Kohen in order to be purified. For a metzora does not leave his state of impurity unless the Kohen declares that he is pure. This comes to teach us the following: Since he was afflicted as a result of sinning with his faculty of speech, i.e., he spoke *lashon hara*, he can only be purified through the speech of the Kohen, who declares that he is pure.

To what can this be compared?

To a youth whose relative worked in a large factory. One day, the youth went to visit his relative. When he arrived at the factory, he looked around and saw a gigantic hall filled with various machines.

"How many machines are in here?" inquired the boy.

"There are exactly two hundred and forty-eight machines!" responded his relative. "Look, this machine spins the threads, this one cuts them, and yet another machine rolls them…"

Suddenly the boy noticed an enormous machine in the corner of the hall. It was enclosed and displayed warning signs forbidding anyone from approaching.

"What does that large machine in the corner do?" the boy continued to ask.

"This machine," replied the relative, "controls all of the other machines in the factory. It is therefore the most important machine of all and requires special attention. For if it would cease to operate, the entire factory would shut down!"

> The same thing applies to man, concluded the Chofetz Chaim. Man has two hundred and forty-eight limbs, but the most important one of them all is the tongue. The tongue ensures the continual operation of all the other limbs, as the verse states, "Death and life are in the power of the tongue" (*Mishlei* 18:21).
>
> If man utilizes his tongue properly and studies Torah, it will have a positive effect on all of his limbs. If he lacks the sense, however, to use his tongue for beneficial purposes and, instead, speaks *lashon hara* — it will have a negative influence on his entire body!

✌§ It Is Better to Speak About Oxen

On one occasion, the Chofetz Chaim was traveling in a stagecoach with a group of animal dealers. Throughout the journey the men spoke about matters pertaining to oxen and horses, while the Chofetz Chaim sat in the corner silently, engrossed in his thoughts.

The conversation took a turn for the worse, however, as one of the men began to deride and degrade a particular dealer.

"Gentleman," remarked the Chofetz Chaim, "until now you have been conversing rather pleasantly about oxen and horses. Why must you now speak about human beings? Such a conversation involves *lashon hara*!"

Not recognizing the Chofetz Chaim, the merchants belittled his words. The Chofetz Chaim, however, did not pay any attention to their insults.

After they had concluded deriding him, the men resumed speaking maliciously about the merchant. Seeing that his words had not had a positive effect, the Chofetz Chaim asked the coachman to stop the coach. And there, in the middle of the road, the Chofetz Chaim descended from the stagecoach.

"It is better to get off in the middle of the road," exclaimed the Chofetz Chaim, "than to hear words of *lashon hara*!"

✑§ The Hour of Payment

The Chofetz Chaim was traveling with his son-in-law, R' Tzvi Levinson, in order to raise money for the Yeshivah in Radin.

At one point during their trip, they met with one of the wealthy men of Moscow, an affluent individual who supported Torah institutions and performed many acts of kindness. He received his esteemed guests with great honor.

The three of them sat and discussed the yeshivah as well as its needs, and the wealthy man listened carefully to their every request.

In the middle of their conversation, R' Tzvi excused himself and went into a nearby room in order to draft an urgent telegram. The Chofetz Chaim turned to the wealthy man and exclaimed, "Do you see? In the next room people are presently sitting and drafting telegrams, thinking about each and every word. Do you know why? The answer is quite simple," continued the Chofetz Chaim, "because when they conclude their telegram they will be required to pay for each and every word!"

✌§ Reliable Advice

Guarding one's tongue from improper speech is a difficult task, and it requires constant and consistent effort. Many people wonder, "Is there truly an individual who can prove successful in the face of such a daunting challenge?"

The *sefer Sha'arei HaLashon* provides us with an amazing parable to illustrate this idea:

There was a city whose inhabitants were stricken by a terrible plague. The finest physicians were contacted, yet none were able to provide the city's ailing residents with a remedy.

Eventually, the population grew despondent and came to terms with their bitter fate.

One day, an expert doctor whose name was known far and wide arrived in the city. The people, however, had given up all hope, to the extent that they did even turn to the doctor for his advice.

There was one exception, however. In the city lived an individual who paid no heed to the opinions of his neighbors. Rather, he ran to the expert physician in order to seek his counsel.

"Why are you rushing to see this doctor after the remainder of the population has despaired from finding a cure?" he was asked.

"You fools," replied the man. "My life is hanging in the balance — do you think it has even occurred to me to consider the public's opinion at such a critical moment?"

If this is the case when it comes to healing the body, how much more so does it apply to healing the soul. David *HaMelech* advised us, "Which man desires life...? Guard your tongue from evil, and your lips from speaking deceit!" (*Tehillim* 34:13,14)

Even if there are those who have already despaired of guarding their tongues, a man must take his own welfare to heart. He must hasten to the physician and accept his advice — for his life hangs in the balance.

Part 4

The War Against the Yetzer Hara

⤳ The Exchange

A certain country had appointed a new king, and a day was set for the festive inaugural ceremony in his honor. The king was to be crowned in the presence of many distinguished kings and ministers, as well as all the noblemen of the land.

In honor of the occasion, the ministers decided to fashion an extraordinary crown for the king, the likes of which had never before been seen.

After investigating the matter, they discovered that in a certain city lived an expert goldsmith who was unsurpassed in his craft. It was he and only he who was fit to fashion a crown for the new king.

Two of the ministers took gold and precious gems from the royal treasury and traveled to the goldsmith.

After they had resided in the goldsmith's house for but a few days, he presented them with a royal crown, he himself bearing witness that never before had so perfect a crown been fashioned.

Crown in hand, the ministers set out for home.

Along the way, they passed several towns and villages. In one of the villages, they observed men plowing their fields with a pair of oxen.

"Would you like to see something unbelievable?" asked one minister. "Indeed I would," replied his companion.

They stopped their stagecoach at the edge of the field. "Perhaps you would care to see something extraordinary?" they asked the villagers.

"We certainly would!" they responded.

One of the ministers removed the beautiful crown from his sack and displayed it before the villagers. Needless to say, they were absolutely awestruck. "We've never seen anything so amazing!" they exclaimed.

"The minister turned to the villagers and asked, "Would you be interested in making a trade? Simply hand over your pair of oxen and you can have this crown in return…"

The farmer readily agreed. "Let's trade," he said.

"You fool!" exclaimed the farmer's friend. "With these oxen, you plow your field and ultimately produce bread! Now, this crown may be very beautiful — but what will you do with it? What will you eat?"

The ministers let out a hearty laugh and exclaimed, "You silly villagers! If you sold a small portion of this crown, you could purchase one hundred pair of oxen! If you sold the entire crown, you could purchase a plot of land one thousand times larger than this entire village!"

> Man knows well, said the Chofetz Chaim, that Torah is the most valuable merchandise and more precious than pearls. The *yetzer hara* comes along, however, and attempts to deceive him. "During the time that you study Torah," he claims, "you could engage in business…You could earn a lot of money…"
>
> Mankind, unfortunately, often takes the bait and succumbs, much like the villagers who refused to exchange a pair of oxen for a golden crown laden with jewels.

✌ Who Is in Control of Whom?

An individual was charged with committing a felony against the king and was placed in prison to await trial.

When it came time for him to stand trial, he was removed from his cell by a guard whose task it was to escort him down the hall to the courthouse.

The guard, suspecting that the prisoner might try to escape, took a pair of handcuffs from his pocket. He then placed one of the cuffs around the wrist of the prisoner and the other one around his own wrist. In such a manner, they marched through the city street.

A crowd of spectators gathered along the sides of the street and jeered the prisoner.

Insulted, the prisoner turned to the crowd and said, "You are making a mistake. He is not escorting me; rather, it is I who is escorting him…"

A wise man spoke up from amongst the crowd. "If that is the case," he said, "then unlock the handcuff on your wrist! If you are capable of breaking free from your escort, it is a sign that you are in control of him. But if *he* can break away, then it proves that he is in control of you!"

> The same thing applies to man and his *yetzer hara*, noted R' Yosef Yozel Hurwitz (the famed *Alter* [Elder] of Novaradok). There are instances when the *yetzer hara* binds himself to a person by habituating him to a repeated transgression. If this person would like to know who is truly in control of whom, let him check himself to discern whether he is capable of breaking his "bad habits" or not.
>
> This is precisely what we request in our morning prayers each day: "Let not the *yetzer hara* dominate us."

❧ The Fool and the Scoffer

In a certain city resided an individual who was known for his foolishness. On one occasion, one of the city's scoffers decided to amuse his friends; he told them that later that day, the fool would leap into the swamp located on the outskirts of the city.

How did he accomplish this? He approached the fool and deceptively offered him various types of sweets, thereby earning his trust. He then suggested that they go for a short stroll outside the city.

As they neared the swamp, the scoffer turned to the fool and exclaimed, "I have a great secret which I am prepared to reveal to you, but you must first promise me that you will not disclose it to anyone."

The fool promised.

"Are you familiar with the big swamp?" asked the scoffer.

"I certainly am," responded the fool. "But I heard that it is quite deep and marshy."

"That is not true," responded the scoffer. "And what's more, you should know that a valuable treasure is hidden inside it...

"While there is a thin layer of mud that lies on the surface, if one leaps in, he will bypass the mud and merit discovering an enormous treasure."

When they arrived at the swamp, the fool, believing the scoffer's words, dived directly into the marshy swamp.

"Help me!" screamed the fool. "Get me out of here!"

"Absolutely not," replied the scoffer. "Do you know how much effort I exerted just to get you to jump into the swamp in the first place? First I will call all of my friends, so that they can see you sunken up to your neck and get a hearty laugh. Only afterwards will I take you out..."

> So, too, remarked the Chofetz Chaim, is the way of the *yetzer hara*. First it entices an individual with meaningless temptations, even giving him fancy gifts and the like, which serve to ensnare him. However, once man has been successfully lured — sunk in the swamp — the *yetzer hara* stands there and laughs heartily...

◆§ The Understanding Horse

A merchant was set to take leave of the marketplace; he therefore hired a wagon driver to safely transport him to his home.

Sitting comfortably in the wagon, the merchant turned to the wagon driver and instructed, "Please listen to me for a moment. I have just eaten a hearty meal and have drunk a small amount of wine. There is no doubt that I will doze along the way. I am therefore cautioning you not to fall asleep as well and to keep a careful eye on the horse lest it veer from the path."

The wagon driver was slightly offended. "You have nothing to worry about," he answered. "This isn't the first time that I've driven a wagon."

The horse began to pull the rickety wagon, and it was not long before the merchant was sound asleep.

The wagon driver, who had also had his share to drink before setting out, was finding it a struggle to keep his eyes open. He eventually succumbed, and after a short while he fell into a deep slumber.

Sensing that the reins were unmanned, the horse began to wander about. When it spied a lush, green pasture, it veered from the road, and the wagon toppled over, straight into the muddy swamp.

The merchant emerged from the swamp dripping with mud and began to scream at the wagon driver with all his might, "Didn't I warn you not to fall asleep at the reins? Just look at what you've caused!"

"Why are you angry?" asked the wagon driver. "Initially, I *was* holding the reins, but I let go of them knowing that my horse possesses remarkable understanding and would know the way..."

"A horse with understanding?" laughed the merchant. "A horse is a horse, and if you don't grip the reins tightly, you'll be thrown from the wagon!"

> A man, noted the Chofetz Chaim, is comprised of a body and a soul. The spiritual soul desires to derive pleasure from *mitzvos* and good deeds, but the body seeks physical gratification, constantly in pursuit of material delights and tasty delicacies.
>
> Man's obligation in this world is to allow the soul to lead the way and to continually keep a tight grip on the body's reins. For if man loosens his grip, the body is liable to veer from the proper path completely.

✌ Jumping From a Wagon in Motion

Two brothers were traveling on a long journey. In the midst of their trip they were assailed by a band of thieves who took them captive.

The thieves' intention was to bring their prisoners to the big city; a fair was being held there, and it was certain that someone would be interested in purchasing them as slaves.

The brothers sat in the thieves' speedily moving wagon, their hearts filled with dread and fear — who knew what their fate would be?

Suddenly they realized that they were passing a populated area. One of the brothers leaned over and whispered into the other one's ear, "Let us hurry, my brother, and jump from this moving wagon. This may be our last chance to save ourselves!"

"I am afraid," whispered the other brother, "that we might injure ourselves jumping from a moving wagon. We may even dislocate an arm or leg…"

"Fool that you are," responded the brother. "Being injured jumping from this wagon is still ten times better than the fate that is in store for us — to be sold as slaves and lose our dignity completely!"

> So too, said the Dubno Maggid, in relation to man's war with the *yetzer hara*. There are times that the war is full of pain, toil, and sweat, as the *yetzer hara* binds a man with ropes as strong as those that pull a wagon. In order to break free, one must sever the ropes and leap from the wagon. While he may even sustain an injury during the escape, can the minor bruises that he may incur compare in any way to the eternal suffering that will be endured by the souls of those who delayed leaping?

⋐ The Role of Supporters of Torah in the War Against the Yetzer Hara

The Chofetz Chaim valued an individual who financially supported Torah study, and he drew the following parable with regard to such people: This be compared to a king who had a mighty soldier in his legion, who fiercely and furiously battled the enemy.

Out of his extreme dedication for the king, the soldier even fashioned his own arrows for battle. During one of the wars, he used up the last of the arrows that he had prepared. He therefore turned to the king and asked, "Your Highness, my supply of arrows has been depleted. May I use the arrows fashioned by another soldier?"

"What difference does it make whose arrows you use?" retorted the king. "Just as long as you win the war!"

All of a man's days in this world, said the Chofetz Chaim, are spent waging a war — the war against the *yetzer hara*!

When a father educates his children to walk in the ways of Hashem, they are his arrows that enable him to triumph. A man who does not have children should offer financial support to individuals who spend their days and nights serving Hashem.

When the war is over and the enemy has been defeated, there is no doubt that the victory will also be attributed to those individuals who so generously supported Torah study.

⁓ *The Difference Between a Talmid Chacham and an Am Ha'aretz*

R' Nachman of Tolchin related the following story:

On one occasion, I traveled with an elderly gentile wagon driver who also happened to be a drunkard. Every so often, the driver would remove a bottle of whisky from his sack and take a drink.

At one point during our trip we passed an old dilapidated building that had not been inhabited for quite some time. The driver asked if I would mind if he went inside for a short while, and I told him that I had no objection.

The wagon driver entered the building and did not exit for quite some time, gazing with amazement and longing at the decimated rooms and the walls that were now covered with moss. When he finally returned to the wagon, I asked him, "Please tell me, why did you spend such a long time in that old ruined building?"

The wagon driver let out a long sigh. "This dilapidated building used to be a popular tavern, where I spent many a day as a youth. I went inside in order to awaken some old memories and relive the past…"

> You understand, of course, continued the Rebbe, that this is what *Chazal* meant when they said, "As *talmidei chachamim* grow older, they gain wisdom. But when *amei ha'aretz* (people ignorant in Torah learning) grow older, they gain foolishness" (*Yalkut Shimoni, Iyov*).
>
> *Amei ha'aretz*, explained the Rebbe, squander their youth with silliness, and in their old age are decrepit and dilapidated, having little more than old memories to rehash. *Talmidei chachamim*, on the other hand, spend their youth battling the *yetzer hara* and subduing their desires. When they grow older they are able to take pleasure from their achievements and serve Hashem without any impediments.

⋄§ *Whose Merchandise is Superior?*

A fabric merchant traveled to a big city in order to purchase material from the wholesalers there. He entered the store of a wholesaler and saw fabrics that were truly magnificent to behold.

"Tell me, please," he asked the wholesaler. "Your fabrics are certainly beautiful, but how can I determine if they are of outstanding quality? Will they endure for an extended period of time?"

"That is not very difficult to ascertain," responded the wholesaler. "I'll give you the names of three individuals who had suits sewn from my fabrics. Ask them for their opinions."

The merchant took the wholesaler's advice and spoke with the three men he had mentioned. Indeed, each one lauded the fabrics with praise and told the merchant that they were extremely pleased.

On his way back to the wholesaler, the merchant entered another store that was likewise selling exquisite fabrics. He approached the storeowner and told him all that had happened.

"You are very fortunate to have entered my store," said the store-owner. "You should know that the wholesaler you were dealing with is a well-known crook! Sure, he gave you names of three people who spoke highly of his fabric — but when did they sew their suits? A week ago, or maybe ten days ago! If you had spoken to someone who purchased his fabrics *half a year* ago, then you would have heard the truth! You would hear how the colors faded and how the material shredded. The suits that were sewn from those fabrics were no longer very impressive looking!

"But I, on the other hand," continued the store owner, "will give you names of customers who purchased my fabrics one full year ago and longer! When you hear what they have to say, you will understand just how superior my merchandise truly is."

> The same idea can be applied to the *yetzer hara*, said the Dubno Maggid. It tempts man with the meaningless pleasures of this world, and occasionally man may even succumb and lend an ear to his deceitful words. Yet after the moment of indulgence, what is left of these trivial pleasures? Nothing at all! The advice of the *yetzer hatov*, however, is to occupy oneself with Torah and *mitzvos*. This is advice that endures forever and its reward is eternal!

❧ Wasting Time

On many occasions, said the Chofetz Chaim, the *yetzer hara* causes man to waste his time by presenting him with a variety of seemingly "valid" excuses and interesting him in various causes — just to keep him from engaging in Torah study. This can be compared to a merchant who traveled to a fair in order to purchase merchandise. The fair was being held in a distant land, and the merchant would therefore be forced to leave his home for an extended period of time.

"Do not be upset," said the merchant to his family. "While I will, indeed, be away for quite some time, and I will certainly miss you, the time will pass, and with Hashem's help, I will return home. You have my word that I will not tarry for a moment longer than is necessary."

The merchant packed his belongings and set out for the fair.

After a lengthy journey, the merchant finally arrived at his destination. Without wasting a moment, he immediately began to occupy himself with his business.

At one of the booths, he met an old friend whom he had not seen in a very long time. After exchanging pleasantries and expressing great joy over having encountered one another, the friend suggested that they travel together to a quiet place. There they could spend a day or two rehashing old memories and sharing past experiences.

"I simply cannot take you up on your offer," responded the merchant. "For did I part with my family in order to engage in trivial conversations? Did I travel so far for the sake of a good time? Immediately upon concluding my business, I will quickly return home!"

> So it is, said the Chofetz Chaim, with man and his *yetzer hara*. Man comes to this world for the sole purpose of performing *mitzvos* and good deeds, in accordance with the will of Hashem. Yet the *yetzer hara* stealthily appears on the scene and attempts to lure man into wasting his precious time with matters of little consequence.
>
> Therefore, concluded the Chofetz Chaim, it is incumbent upon every man to tell his *yetzer hara* precisely what the merchant told his friend: "Did I come to this world in order to engage in silliness? Do not attempt to beguile me into wasting my precious time!"

☙ *A Sworn Enemy*

A young orphan became heir to a vast inheritance. Not knowing what to do with such an enormous sum of money, he turned to a relative of his and asked for advice. The relative, however, was a dissolute thief. He spoke to the boy deceitfully, convincing him that he would manage the money for him and conduct business with it. The profits, he claimed, would be split between them.

The young boy was elated with his relative's "generous" offer and naively transferred the entire inheritance into his hands.

The relative engaged in business and was very successful. None of the money found its way into the orphan's hands, however, as his relative claimed to have squandered it all.

In great distress, the young boy turned to the *rav* of the city and told him what had transpired.

A wise man, the *rav* immediately understood that the relative had behaved in a corrupt manner. He therefore told the young boy, "In all honesty, there is little I can do to help you. For no matter how I advise you, your relative will simply come and contradict my words. Yet there is one thing I can tell you with the utmost certainty: Your relative is a charlatan and a crook! You must veer as far away from him as you can!"

There are many times, said the Dubno Maggid, that the *yetzer hara* pretends that he is an individual's dear friend. He claims to be acting in his best interest, to the extent that if the person were to seek council from Torah Sages, the *yetzer hara* would don a guise as this person's confidant and counter their advice.

There is one thing that we must be aware of and never forget: The *yetzer hara* is our sworn enemy and constantly seeks our harm! The rest is self-understood.

◄§ Why Work So Hard?

The *yetzer hara* seeks to provide man with many justifications for neglecting the *mitzvos*. Man must therefore know how to successfully respond to its claims.

The Chofetz Chaim told an amazing parable in relation to this idea:

This can be compared to a certain Jew who was running through the city square, huffing and puffing as he went.

Along the way, he encountered his friend. "Why are you in such a rush?" the friend inquired.

"Please forgive me," responded the man, "but I don't have any time to talk at the moment. I am rushing to find a means of earning a living. I have a wife and children, and our house is bare of even the most basic necessities…"

"*That* is why you are running?" asked his friend in surprise. "You aren't going to become as rich as Rothschild anyway — you're better off simply relaxing at home."

"I'm surprised at you," said the man. "Just because I won't become as rich as Rothschild, should I sit idly by in my house and do nothing? Why, if I listen to you, there will not even be bread in my home!"

Very often, concluded the Chofetz Chaim, the *yetzer hara* comes to a man and asks, "Why are you working so hard in order to fulfill a *mitzvah*?" Man must therefore respond, "If I listen to your advice, there will be absolutely nothing waiting for me in the World to Come!"

⤟ Proceed According to the Map

A group of soldiers trekked their way through the depths of the forest. At their helm was their commander who held in his hand a map which he had received from the commander-in-chief of the armed forces. He had been given orders to guide the brigade according to the map.

Had the commander obeyed his orders and led them according to the map, the soldiers would have arrived at the army base, where the general, in all his pomp and glory, was waiting for them. There they would have been served food and drink, and given a place to rest their weary feet. Yet the commander chose to disobey his orders and he led the soldiers in the opposite direction.

It goes without saying that traveling in the opposite direction would take them far away from their intended destination!

When the brigade realized that their commander had betrayed his directive, they, in turn, decided to rebel against him. Overpowering him, the soldiers handcuffed the commander, and the most outstanding soldier among them took charge. He directed the soldiers according to the map and did not deviate even one iota, leading them directly to the camp.

Upon greeting the general, they apologized for their delay and informed him of all that had transpired. The general understood and excused the brigade. The defiant commander, on the other hand, was sent directly to prison.

> So, too, said the Dubno Maggid, is man in relation to his *yetzer hara*. Every single individual is regarded as a soldier of Hashem, and he is required to live his life according to the dictates that Hashem has set forth in His holy Torah. There are times, however, when a man falls to temptation and follows his *yetzer hara*, which then leads him astray.
>
> It is at that moment that man must come to his senses, subdue his *yetzer hara*, and quickly return to the upright path!

✑ The Milk That Spoiled

> A man must dedicate every second of his life to the service of Hashem and not succumb to the advice of the yetzer hara, which seeks to lead him into the well of destruction.
>
> The Chofetz Chaim drew the following parable to illustrate this point:

A pauper once decided to travel to a distant land and try his luck at business.

He traveled to faraway Africa, where, due to the stifling heat, there was barely any vegetation, leaving the livestock with little to eat. As a result, milk was quite scare and therefore extremely expensive. The pauper decided that there was money to be made selling milk, and in a short time saw much success in his endeavors and grew very wealthy. Despite the abundance of wealth that he amassed after some time, he chose to remain in Africa and continue his business.

After several years, he received a letter from his wife, requesting him to return home.

"I should definitely purchase additional milk with the money that I've earned," thought the man to himself. "In this way, I will be able to sell the milk upon returning home and earn a hefty profit." And that is precisely what he did.

Before boarding the ship, the man was approached by a diamond merchant, who wished to interest him in purchasing several diamonds for his family.

"Diamonds," he responded, "I can buy anywhere. I am better off purchasing a little more milk…"

After much persistence on the part of the diamond merchant, the man finally agreed to spend his remaining money on a few diamonds.

Upon returning home, the man was horrified to discover that, to his great misfortune, all the milk in his possession had soured and was now worthless.

"For *this* I suffered in your absence all these years?" wailed his wife in bitter anguish.

The man just stood there in utter humiliation, overwhelmed by grief and embarrassment. All of the wealth he had toiled for so many years to earn had been lost in one night.

Suddenly, he remembered the few diamonds that he had purchased prior to boarding the ship. He went and sold the diamonds, and the money he earned afforded both him and his family a grand lifestyle for years to come.

How great was his anguish, however, over not having purchased more diamonds.

Man, concluded the Chofetz Chaim, descends to this world in order to engage in the performance of *mitzvos*. Most of his days, however, are squandered trying to amass material wealth, which is absolutely worthless in the World to Come.

When he stands before the Heavenly Tribunal, they will say, "Enumerate the deeds that you have performed!" Yet he will simply stand there, shamefaced and not knowing what to say… Suddenly, he will recall the pittance of money he gave to *tzedakah*, the *mitzvah* of visiting the sick that he performed, and so on and so forth. It will be these deeds that will procure him a reward in the World to Come.

But how great will his anguish be over not having relegated all of his time to amassing *mitzvos* and performing good deeds!

◆§ Soldiers

A simple man once approached the Chofetz Chaim and asked, "Rebbe, why must there be both Chassidim and *Misnagdim* (lit. "Opponents," referring to Jews of Lithuanian descent who opposed the Chassidic movement)? Even the Chassidim are divided into many groups: there are those whose Divine service is mainly focused on prayer, other groups who make Torah study their main focus, and yet other groups who primarily serve Hashem with joy. Why must there be so many different factions amongst the Jewish people?"

"Instead of asking me," responded the Chofetz Chaim, "go and ask the Russian Tzar! Inquire as to why he needs so many types of soldiers. Comprising his military are soldiers who fight on horseback, others who man the cannons; sailors; and infantrymen!

"The reason," continued the Chofetz Chaim, "is that each type of soldier serves the Tzar in his own unique fashion come wartime. A foot soldier is unable to fight on horseback; a soldier who mans the cannon is capable of doing battle over great distances; even the soldiers who sound the trumpets have an important job, for their trumpet blasts strengthen the hearts of the soldiers in the battlefields.

"This is why," concluded the Chofetz Chaim, "the Jewish nation is divided into various groups as well. Each group contributes in its own unique way, and together we will triumph in the war against the *yetzer hara!*"

❧ Irrefutable Evidence

A man was making his way home after a lengthy journey. But as he traveled along the curved road, a thief suddenly assailed him and attempted to take his life. The man pleaded with the thief to spare him and take his money instead.

A spark of mercy flickered in the heart of the cruel thief, and he conceded to the man's request, allowing him to live. Instead, he took his bundle of money and placed it inside his horse's saddle.

"I have a request to make of you," said the man to the thief. "The money that you took from me was not my own. Would you therefore be so kind as to shoot one of your bullets into my hat? That way, I will have irrefutable evidence that the money was stolen from me and not lost as a result of my mishandling it."

The thief agreed to the man's request. He loaded his rifle and fired a bullet into the man's hat. The bullet pierced the hat, leaving a noticeable hole.

"Could you please make several holes in my coat as well?" the man continued.

The thief agreed and shot at the man's coat.

After firing several shots, the rifle was left without any more bullets. When the man saw this, he pounced upon the thief, overpowered him, and reclaimed his bundle of money!

> This is precisely the way, remarked R' Nachman of Breslov, that man must wage war against the *yetzer hara,* which seeks to seize everything a man possesses and leave him empty-handed. Man must therefore devise various strategies with which to overpower his *yetzer hara.*

It is incumbent upon each and every individual to strengthen himself in the service of his Creator, even during trying times, he must not yield to his *yetzer hara* which attempts to make him sin at every moment.

The Chofetz Chaim related a parable in relation to this concept:

A man encountered his friend who worked as a laborer in a factory; the friend's face was decidedly gloomy.

"What's the matter with you?" the man asked.

"Difficult times have befallen me," said the factory worker. "It has been several weeks now that I have been out of work, and I have not a *perutah* in my pocket."

"In that case," responded the man, "come and work for me for the next several months, until you find a steady job. I will pay you in full for your work."

"I'm afraid that I won't be able to accept your generous offer," responded the friend. "You see, in a few weeks from now, the factory where I worked will resume operations, and the manager will restore me to my post. But if he discovers that I have found another place to work, he will not rehire me. Accepting a temporary job with you will result in my forfeiting long-term employment!"

There are instances, said the Chofetz Chaim, when due to a man's wicked deeds, Hashem hides His face, as it were, from that individual for a period of time, and sends suffering and misfortune his way, in order to purge him of his transgressions. The *yetzer hara* immediately steps in and attempts to entice him to sin. But man must be aware that the difficult situation in which he presently finds himself is but a temporary predicament. His merits will ultimately be recalled, and he will receive his reward for the good deeds that he has performed.

Man is engaged in a constant war against his archrival, the *yetzer hara*. How can man emerge victorious? The Chofetz Chaim imparted the answer to us by means of the following parable:

Two kings had been waging a fierce war for many years, with each one taking turns gaining the upper hand.

One day, the kings decided to put an end to their war. The two met and resolved to wage one battle that would last a total of four days. Whoever would emerge triumphant from this final clash would be proclaimed the victor, and the loser would submit entirely to the will of the conqueror.

The kings began preparing for the deciding battle, and their finest generals taught the soldiers new war tactics and strategies.

When the war commenced, it was clear that both armies were powerful, proficient, and of equal strength. Indeed, on the first day of the fighting, one of the armies proved triumphant, and on the second day, the other was victorious. Towards evening of the third day, one of the generals gathered the heads of his troops and exclaimed, "Men! Tomorrow is the final and decisive day of this war, and we must emerge victorious at any cost. However, as the sides are evenly matched, we must utilize a brilliant plan. Our spies," he continued, "have reported that the enemy's artillery is located in a specific storage room. It occurred to me to send an elite team of soldiers to steal the artillery from the enemy's camp. Without any weapons, the enemy is sure to be defeated."

Everyone agreed, and they implemented the plan. A squad of fierce soldiers secretly entered the enemy camp and stole their weapons.

The next day, there was a loud trumpet blast and the war was on. But when one of the armies rushed to arm themselves, they were shocked to discover that their artillery room was empty. Left with no other choice, they surrendered.

So it is with man's war against the *yetzer hara*, explained the Chofetz Chaim. The *yetzer hara* battles a man all the days of his life. There are occasions when the *yetzer hara* emerges victorious and other times when man proves triumphant. It is at that point that the *yetzer hara* devises the shrewd strategy to steal man's only artillery — i.e., the holy Torah, in the merit of which he is capable of defeating the *yetzer hara*.

We must therefore take caution, concluded the Chofetz Chaim, that the *yetzer hara* not steal our lone weapon. For even if the *yetzer hara* has recently prevailed, man must not despair. Rather, he must gird himself to study the holy Torah, and only then will he triumph!

✍§ The Rabbi and the Wagon Driver

The children of a rabbi and a wagon driver were to be married. As the in-laws lived quite a distance from one another, they agreed to hold the wedding in a city that was midway between their two respective towns.

On the day of the wedding, the rabbi thought to himself, "If I arrive at the wedding dressed in my elegant rabbinical attire — my long silk overcoat and my *shtreimel* — I will embarrass my *mechutan* (in-law), who will be dressed as a simple wagon driver."

The rabbi therefore removed his elegant garb and donned the plain clothing customarily worn by wagon drivers. On his feet he wore boots, and on his head, an ordinary cap.

Unbeknownst to the rabbi, his *mechutan* had a similar train of thought. "My *mechutan* is a rabbi and will wear fine clothing to the wedding," he said to himself. "Should I then be dressed like a simple wagon driver? How unbecoming that would be!"

He therefore hurried and donned a striking silk overcoat and a regal *shtreimel*.

When the two of them arrived at the wedding, everyone thought that the wagon driver was a rabbi and the rabbi a wagon driver.

The same thing can be applied to the *galus* in which we languish, said the Dubno Maggid. We have seen our exile give birth to a "generation of reversals." The gentiles observed the deeds of the Jewish people and realized that they are upright and proper; they therefore try their utmost to model and emulate our fine character traits. However, much to our dismay and shame, the Jewish people, in turn, have learned from the ideals of the gentiles, imitating their ways.

◆§ *Distraction*

Throughout man's entire life, his *yetzer hara* lies in ambush and attempts to steer him away from the path of the Torah. Man must utilize every strategy at his disposal in order to defeat him.

The Chofetz Chaim stated:

This can be compared to a pair of countries who had been at war for many years. One day, the king of one of the countries proclaimed that whoever could resolve their longstanding dispute and restore harmony between them would be handsomely rewarded; he would merit spending an hour inside the king's Treasury, with free rein to take whatever his heart desired.

Some time afterwards, a wise man approached the king and proposed a brilliant plan to end the feud. The king followed his advice, and indeed, peace was restored between the two countries. As promised, a day was arranged for the wise man to come to the palace in order to collect his reward.

As the day drew nearer, the king became concerned. Over the duration of an hour, it was likely that the man would claim many of his most treasured items. Distressed, the king sought the council of his advisors.

"Your Highness," said one of the advisors, "it has become known to me that this man is extremely fond of music. Therefore, I suggest that you place the kingdom's finest orchestra inside the royal treasury. When the man enters to claim his reward, the musicians will begin to play; he will be mesmerized by the melodious tunes which will take his mind away from the royal treasures."

The king was very pleased with the profound advice, and he set forth in carrying it out.

When the man arrived at the palace, the massive doors to the treasury room were opened before him. He requested permission to enter and it was granted. However, as soon he stepped into the treasury he was frozen in place, enraptured by the harmonious resonance of the sweetest sounding music imaginable…

The man stood there for a moment, but immediately reminded himself why he was there in the first place. He collected his thoughts and scrambled for the inner chamber of the treasury.

He began searching through the treasures, but was once again distracted by the music.

He resolved to listen to the hypnotic melodies for only a short moment. But one moment turned into two, and two into three.

"Don't forget why you've come here!" he scolded himself. But the music was just so pleasant to listen to, until finally…

"Your time is up!" announced the officer of the treasury. "The hour has passed."

"But," murmured the man dejectedly, "I haven't taken anything yet…"

"Nothing that you say now will do you any good," said the officer. "The time has passed!" And so the man returned home, heartbroken and embittered over the golden opportunity that he had let slip away by allowing his thoughts to be distracted.

> Man, said the Chofetz Chaim, received an extraordinary gift from Hashem. Throughout his lifetime on this world, he is permitted to amass *mitzvos* and good deeds.
>
> But along comes the wicked advisor — the *yetzer hara* — which entices man with various pastimes that draw his heart away from the Torah and the performance of *mitzvos*.
>
> When the time eventually arrives for man to stand trial before the Heavenly Tribunal, he will sorrowfully recall how he

wasted his precious time listening to meaningless "melodies." By then, however, it will be far too late…

It is incumbent upon every individual, concluded the Chofetz Chaim, to constantly remind himself — every day and every hour — of his purpose in coming to this world. He must not allow the *yetzer hara* to distract him from studying the Torah and fulfilling its *mitzvos!*

≈§ *In the Opposite Direction*

Two young men learned together in the same yeshivah. They were both intellectually gifted and diligent, and each progressed steadily in his Torah studies. When they grew older, however, they went their separate ways: One of them continued to pursue his Torah studies in a different yeshivah, while the other one deviated from the path of Torah study. He studied medicine and eventually became a world-renowned physician.

The first man accepted a position as *rav* of a small town, and earned a meager livelihood that was barely enough to support him and his family. The physician, on the other hand, grew increasingly famous and wealthy.

One day, the two happened to be in the same city and chanced to meet.

Not having seen each other for so many years, they were overjoyed to meet again and took the opportunity to rehash many past experiences.

The physician turned to the *rav* and said, "My dear friend, look at the prominence I've achieved. I earn a tremendous amount of money and I live a life of comfort and serenity. Yet you make little and live a life of dire poverty. Would you not have been better off choosing the medical profession as I did?"

"I will tell you a true story," responded the *rav*. "When it came time for me to return home this afternoon, I asked the wagon driver how much the trip would cost. He told me that the fare to travel to my destination was two rubles.

"At that moment," continued the *rav*, "a man happened to pass by and overheard our conversation. He told me that a magnificent coach harnessed to strapping steeds was parked on the outskirts of the city. If I so desired, he said, I could travel home in it. The ride would be comfortable and quick, and it would cost only a few *perutos*.

"I left the wagon driver," said the *rav*, "and hurried to the outskirts of the city. Indeed, there was a beautiful coach standing there, but it was soon brought to my attention that it was not traveling to my destination; rather, it was going in the diametrically opposite direction.

"Had I boarded the coach without first ascertaining its destination, I would have indeed traveled in comfort, but I would not have arrived home as planned.

"That is the difference between you and me," concluded the *rav*. "You may enjoy a life of luxury and comfort, but you are traveling in precisely the opposite direction from that which you should be traveling. In this direction, you will never reach your destination."

> In this world, remarked the Chofetz Chaim, every man must occupy himself with studying Torah and performing good deeds, which he will ultimately be able to take with him to the World to Come. However, if man chooses to pursue fleeting pleasures and all of the luxuries that this world has to offer, he may travel in comfort — but it will be in the opposite direction!

ᴥᔓ *Like Traveling in the Desert*

> There are instances when an individual violates one of the Torah's prohibitions, noted the Chofetz Chaim, and the *yetzer hara* quickly rears its head and tries to lead him astray. It tells him, "You've already committed a grave sin anyway; it will matter little if you commit another one..."

The Chofetz Chaim compared this to:

A man who was walking in the desert. Surrounding him was sand and utter desolation for as far as the eye could see. The scorching sun beat down upon his head, and he had very little food and water remaining. He continued to walk this way for quite a distance…

Some time later, he opened his sack to see what remained of his food and drink. Gazing down into his opened sack, he saw that there was not enough left for him to survive.

What did he do?

He took a moment to ponder the situation and thought to himself, "Since I don't have a sufficient amount of food and drink anyway, I may as well throw away whatever I *do* have left; after all, my predicament is hopeless…"

This man is a fool!

> Such is the case with man and his *yetzer hara*, concluded the Chofetz Chaim. Man must not permit the *yetzer hara* to lure his heart toward sin. But even if he does fall to temptation, he must remember that "a *tzaddik* falls seven [times], but rises [each time] (*Mishlei* 24:16)."

✍ Years of Life

A farmer succeeded in selling a small amount of vegetables in the market, in exchange for which he received several copper coins. In good spirits, he set out for the tavern with his coins jingling inside his pocket.

"Bartender!" shouted the farmer. "Give me an excellent drink and please be quick about it!"

The farmer was served and he gulped down glass after glass. As his stomach expanded, his pockets grew emptier and emptier…

After drinking to his heart's content and having spent all of his money, the farmer left the tavern. He walked along, staggering and dizzy, and in a throaty voice, hummed a tune commonly sung by drunkards.

> Man is exactly like this farmer, said the Chofetz Chaim. In his youth, he is sure that he has many years of life remaining. He therefore tells himself that right now he will seize the opportunity to enjoy the pleasures that life has to offer. However, he tells himself that in a number of years, when he grows slightly older, will occupy his time with Torah study. After all, there is plenty of time for everything…
>
> He must know, however, that this is the devious advice of the *yetzer hara*. Life passes quickly and a man continues to age. Suddenly, there are not quite as many years left as there were in the past; "if not now — when?" (*Avos* 1:14). As *Chazal* impart to us in (ibid. 2:5), "And do not say, 'When I am free I will study,' for perhaps you will not become free."

✑ﻬ Different Types of Prisoners

A prison contains sections which are both different and strange, just as the sentences that are being served vary from prisoner to prisoner.

An individual who committed an offense of lesser severity serves a shorter sentence and, from time to time, is even allowed to return home for a limited visit. At home, he feasts to his heart's content and spends time with his family, eventually returning to prison.

There is another prisoner, however, who is guilty of a crime of greater severity. He is not granted leave very often, only once every several months. Nevertheless, he is afforded visitation rights in which his family is permitted to visit him in prison and bring him the delicacies he so relishes.

Then there are the criminals whose crimes are so severe that they are sentenced to be confined to a cramped cell and are not allowed to leave under any circumstances. Their relatives are not permitted to visit them either, and they must suffice on meager bread and fetid water that the prison provides for them.

The same thing applies to man's war against the *yetzer hara*. When all of a man's deeds are upright, except for some minor transgression that he may have committed, the impurity that he has imbibed is not powerful enough to keep him prisoner and prevent him from fulfilling *mitzvos* with holiness and purity.

Yet if he committed transgressions more frequently or of greater severity, the impurity restrains him with powerful cables and does not permit him to taste the wonderful flavor of *mitzvos*. From time to time he will be able to savor their sweetness; on a holiday, for example, when he is able to ascend from his lowly state and experience an awareness of holiness.

But those who are "sinners" in the truest sense of the word and have committed multiple transgressions are similar to the prisoner who is locked away in his cell and never merits seeing the light of the sun. Such individuals never experience the sweetness of Torah and *mitzvos*; rather, the taste of their decayed and vile transgressions is all that they have.

◄§ When the Requested Fabric Is Not in Stock

A man walked into a fabric store to purchase a bolt of blue silk. The storeowner — a rather shrewd businessman — knew that he did not have that fabric in stock. He therefore hurried to the shelf and pulled out black fabric that closely resembled silk.

"This fabric," said the storeowner, "is far superior to silk for it is a stronger material. The two fabrics feel exactly the same, and many people actually prefer this one over genuine silk." The storeowner continued his sales pitch, "What's more," he added, "the color black is better for you, as blue has been out of style for some time now. Besides, what is the difference between a darker blue and a lighter shade of black anyway?"

The customer's head was spinning after the storeowner's presentation, but when he managed to collect himself, he replied with the utmost seriousness, "I requested blue silk fabric! If you have it in stock, fine. But if not, I will be on my way!"

> There are times, said R' Yosef Yozel Hurwitz (the *Alter* [Elder] of Novaradok), when the *yetzer hara* attempts to lead an individual astray by telling him, "True, you are certainly required to perform such and such a *mitzvah*, but perhaps you could perform a different one instead?"
>
> We must fulfill that which Hashem has commanded us, and only that!

✎ Scaling the Mountain

When an individual scales a mountain, noted the Dubno Maggid, he must take each and every step with the utmost caution, and must carefully examine every potential foothold, for the slightest blunder could send him plummeting down.

This is certainly the case, added the Maggid, when he is ascending the mountain inside a wagon that is bearing a heavy load. Even when he pauses for a moment's rest, heavy stones must be placed behind the wagon's wheels, to prevent it from rolling backwards.

> The same thing applies, concluded the Maggid, to man's war against the *yetzer hara*. When a man ascends the mountain of Divine service, he must make sure that the path he has chosen is one of holiness and purity. For even the slightest misstep can send man tumbling downwards.
>
> A man must therefore constantly know and remember not to rely on his own futile strength in the battle against the *yetzer hara*. Rather, he must continuously beseech Hashem for His mercy, that He aid and assist him in this great and perpetual war.

✑ A Pot of Broth

There was an innkeeper who was accustomed to cooking meals for all of her guests. Inevitably she ended up preparing food for all the laborers of the town as well, who flocked to her dining room in order to feast to their hearts' content. She served food that was simple yet satiating, and most importantly, reasonably priced.

One day, the innkeeper prepared a large pot of broth. As mealtime drew nearer, she went to check on the food to discern whether or not it was ready to be served. As she made her way towards the pot, a foul odor filled her nostrils.

She quickly ascertained that the ingredients she had used to prepare the broth must have been slightly spoiled, and this was the explanation behind the stench. She was now confronted with a dilemma: Mealtime was rapidly approaching — what would she serve her guests?

What could she do?

She took fragrant spices and sprinkled them generously into the steamy pot; it was not long before the smell of the spices overpowered the stench.

She served the broth to the laborers, and they ate heartily.

"This broth is superb!" exclaimed one of the laborers. "It truly smells like *Gan Eden*!"

Sitting next to him was a patron with a sensitive palate who said, "You are mistaken." "The food is completely spoiled; the smell is coming from spices that hide the foul stench…"

> The *yetzer hara*, remarked the Dubno Maggid, tries to entice man to sin. The sin, however, emits a putrid odor, and the soul immediately perceives the deception and attempts to flee. But the *yetzer hara* clothes the wicked deed in a guise of temptation and appeal in order to conceal the foul stench.
>
> The more putrid the odor, the more spices the *yetzer hara* deceitfully adds…
>
> A person must arrive at the realization that the "food" is spoiled and that he must push it away with both hands!

ᦜ The Three Conditions

The *yetzer hara*, said the Vilna Gaon, will successfully steer a person from the proper path only if he finds a breach in that person's spiritual makeup through which he can enter.

This breach is formed, added the Gaon, when a person serves Hashem and performs *mitzvos* but is not wholehearted in his devotion. It is then that the *yetzer hara* has the ability to infiltrate the breach with ease. However, if a person is firm in his devotions, then the *yetzer hara* is powerless against him!

The Dubno Maggid compared this to a merchant who loaded his wagon with merchandise and set out for the big city. There he intended to go from door to door peddling his merchandise.

However, when the other merchants in the city heard that a competitor had invaded their territory and could potentially impede their business, they had him summoned to a *din Torah* before the *rav* of the city.

After listening carefully as both sides staked their claims, the *rav* presented them with a decision: The merchant, said the *rav*, had the right to sell his merchandise, under three conditions: 1) He would not enter a potential customer's home unless his door was wide open. 2) He would not tell anyone how praiseworthy his merchandise was unless he was asked. 3) Upon leaving a customer's home, he would not exit through the door which he had previously entered. Rather, he would be required to exit through the closest door available.

> So, too, concluded the Dubno Maggid, in relation to the *yetzer hara*: 1) The *yetzer hara* only enters when there is already an opening. 2) He can only praise his "merchandise" to one who is interested in hearing about it. But when it comes to someone who is totally engrossed in Torah, the *yetzer hara* is not permitted to utter a word. 3) If the *yetzer hara* has already entered, it is still possible to repent immediately and kick him out through the closest available door!

~§ The Cause of His Weakness

When a person returns home after a long journey with his knees shaking from fatigue and weakness, he is quite certain that the cause of his weakness lies in the pangs of hunger that gripped him during his trip, for it has been quite a while since he has last had something to eat. His family members, therefore, waste little time and serve him something to eat.

After eating his fill but still feeling weak, the person assumes that this weakness can be attributed to the fact that he did not drink a sufficient amount of water during his journey.

If his weakness and fatigue persist after he has had his share to drink, he begins to suspect that perhaps he has contracted an illness of sorts.

> When an individual craves a particular item, said the Dubno Maggid, be it money or the like, and he still feels the craving burning inside of him even after he has managed to earn a significant amount, it is an indication that the money is not the reason for his craving. Rather, it is due to another cause entirely — the *yetzer hara* — which kindles the flame of desire within him!

~§ The Cleverness of the Polish Thief

> The tactics of the *yetzer hara*, noted R' Yechezkel of Kozhmir, resemble those of a certain Polish thief…

Poland of yesteryear was a country that was severely poverty-stricken. The difficult conditions, however, bred sharp and sophisticated minds…

One day, a storeowner was sitting in his store. Beneath the counter top in front of him was a drawer containing the money earned by selling his merchandise.

Outside the store, a thief was pacing back and forth, devising countless strategies for how he would steal the money from the drawer and empty it into his pocket. There was one problem, however — the storeowner. As long as he remained sitting in his chair by the counter, there was no way for the thief to get to the drawer...

So what did he do? He approached a young boy in the street and offered him two *perutos* if he would agree to enter the store and swipe a sugar cube from the countertop. The young lad willingly agreed.

The boy entered the store, grabbed the piece of sugar and ran for his life. Seeing what happened, the storeowner leaped from his seat and set out after him. At that point, the thief furtively entered the store and emptied the drawer full of coins into his pocket...

> So it is with the *yetzer hara*, concluded the Rebbe. It distracts man with pettiness, and once having grabbed his attention, seeks to make him stumble in a matter of enormity.

◄§ Stolen Merchandise

There was a man who wished to grow wealthy quickly and effortlessly. He decided that it would be worth his while to sell stolen merchandise, figuring that he would be able to earn large profits selling items that he purchased from thieves, who very often sold their merchandise for far less than the item's actual value.

The man filled his pockets with cash and waited in an area that was generally frequented by thieves.

Soon, he caught sight of a large cloud of dust that was formed by a brazen band of thieves who were steadily approaching. They were driving wagons that were loaded with merchandise — goods they had stolen from a group of wagons that had passed them along the way. The man, however, was not given the opportunity to make them an offer. For when the thieves caught a glimpse of him waiting at the crossroads, they immediately pounced upon him and stole everything in his possession. By the time they had gone on their way, the man was left with no more than a thin garment to cover himself.

"I am to blame for my misfortune," cried the man bitterly. "For if I would not have stood in a place frequented by thieves, I would not be bereft of all my possessions. Woe is me ..."

> There are times, noted the Dubno Maggid, when man stands in a place that is frequented by none other than the *yetzer hara*. Let that man not be the least bit surprised when he stumbles and sins!

⋑ Our Days Are Like a Passing Shadow

In a certain city lived a wealthy man who sold jewelry and precious gems. Despite the fact that he was a first- rate connoisseur when it came to jewelry, his business acumen was severely lacking. He therefore formed a partnership with an individual who possessed a shrewd mind and was well versed in the ins and outs of the business world. They agreed that it would be the wealthy man's job to purchase the merchandise, while the partner would manage the store in exchange for one-tenth of the profits.

Shortly thereafter, the partner's wife approached her husband with a complaint: "You are partners with the wealthiest man in the city," she said. "If so, why is his wife adorned with expensive jewelry and I am not?"

"You should know, my wife," responded her husband, "that I am a partner only in the sense that I sell the wealthy man's merchandise. Consequently, my earnings are but one-tenth of his, and I am therefore unable to provide you with the jewelry that the rich men of the land give their wives."

His wife turned a deaf ear to his explanations. She simply refused to believe that her husband received only one-tenth of the earnings.

When the partner arrived in the jewelry store the next day, he asked the wealthy man to calculate how much profit each of them was entitled to.

The wealthy man was rather surprised by the request. "Why do you want to know?" he asked. "Are you interested in finding out how much you have?"

"No," replied the partner. "I am interested in having my wife see how much I don't have…"

> Man, said the Dubno Maggid, believes that he will live for-ever. The *yetzer hara* therefore seizes the opportunity and entices him to sin, whispering to him, "Don't worry; old age is still a long way off, and you will have plenty of time to re-pent for the sins that you've committed…"
>
> A person must be well aware that the days of his life in this world are like a passing shadow (see *Tehillim* 144:4) and that each day is a gift from Hashem.
>
> Man must constantly make an accounting of his years — not in order to know how many he has left, but to know how many he no longer has left!

✑ The Pauper and the Prankster

A pauper arrived in a big city with his bundle slung over his shoulder.

As he walked along, he encountered an individual who derived great pleasure in ridiculing others.

"How are you doing?" he asked the pauper.

"How am I doing?" responded the pauper with a sigh. "Why, it's been several days since I've last had something to eat — and you ask me how I'm doing?"

"In that case," said the prankster, "accompany me to my home, where I will treat you to hearty and scrumptious meals. You will be given a room with a comfortable bed to rest on as well. You will be my guest!"

The unfortunate pauper naively took the bait, and the prankster brought him to the city's most luxurious and expensive inn.

The pauper stayed in the inn and, needless to say, thoroughly enjoyed himself. The room was pleasant and spacious, the bed was clean, and three times a day he was served meals that were fit for a king. He ate well and even had leftovers.

When he was ready to leave the inn, he gathered together his few meager belongings and prepared to step outside…

"Not so fast," said the innkeeper, as he grabbed the pauper by his shirt. "Where are you rushing off to? You haven't paid your bill yet…"

The pauper immediately understood that he had been the butt of the prankster's cruel joke. But as he did not have the money to pay the innkeeper, he was left with no other choice than to leave his belongings behind as collateral. Humiliated, he left the inn and walked out into the street.

It did not take long before he met the prankster once again. This time, however, the prankster was disguised and looked completely different. Not recognizing him, the pauper began relating his tale of misfortune.

"Listen to me," he responded after hearing the pauper's story. "It is certainly true that you were deceived by a cruel prankster. However, my advice to you is as follows: Since your belongings are in the hands of the innkeeper anyway, return to the inn and eat there for a few more days…"

> The way of the *yetzer hara*, said the Dubno Maggid, is to approach an individual in his youth and tempt him to enjoy the delights of this world. When man grows older, however, and realizes that he has erred and will be required to "pay" for all of his actions, the *yetzer hara* approaches him once again and claims, "Since you will be required to pay for all of your actions anyway, you may as well seize the opportunity to indulge in a few more of this world's petty pleasures…"
>
> We must realize that it is the *yetzer hara* which is providing us with this wicked counsel!

◌ঃ *A Personal Escort*

There are certain instances when an individual walks in the company of an escort. While at times this may be a mark of distinction, at other times it is a sign of degradation. For example, when the ruler of the city invites an important guest to his home, he dispatches his servant in order to extend him a personal invitation and to accompany him along the way. Such an escort is a mark of distinction. On the other hand, when a judge sends a bodyguard to a debtor who refuses to pay, or to an individual who has been charged with a misdemeanor, with instructions to escort him to prison, this is an example of an escort being a sign of shame.

How can one tell the difference between them?

The difference is very simple! When the escort is sent in order to accrue the guest honor, he leads the way, walking in front of the guest and guiding him towards the ruler's home. But when the escort marches behind an individual, it is in order to keep an eye on him, lest he attempt to flee…

> This accurately describes the ways of the *yetzer hara*, noted the Dubno Maggid. It initially accords man much honor and walks before him in order to lead him onto the path of sin. Once man has already sinned, however, it treads behind him, making sure that he does not escape his clutches.
>
> This, concluded the Maggid, is what we pray for each and every day: "And remove spiritual impediment from before us and behind us" (*Ma'ariv* prayer).

◌ঃ *A Tiny Nail*

An individual wished to purchase a home, but the owner absolutely refused to sell.

"I will give you an extraordinary amount of money," offered the man. But the owner simply would not hear of it.

The man persisted, nonetheless. "Sell me just one room," he said, "and I will pay you handsomely." However, even that offer was rejected.

"I'll raise my bid," said the man, "if you will sell me an area in your house where I will be able to hammer just one nail…"

Now that offer the owner could not refuse, and in exchange for a huge sum of money, he sold the man the right to hammer one nail into his house.

From that day on, however, the owner no longer had any privacy. The man was constantly entering the house seeking to hang various items on the nail. He would then return in order to remove whatever he had hung. There were even occasions when he arrived in the middle of the night in order to reinforce the nail with loud hammering.

The owner was ultimately compelled to sell the entire house to the bothersome individual…

> The way of the *yetzer hara*, exclaimed R' Yisrael Ba'al Shem Tov, is to acquire a seemingly insignificant foothold in a person. Once it has what it wants, however, it rapidly assumes complete control.
>
> One must not succumb and grant it even an area to hammer a tiny nail!

◈ The Dishonest Servant

In a certain city lived a charlatan who worked as a servant for three wealthy men. He would buy fruits and vegetables for them in the marketplace, but being the thief that he was, he would claim that the produce cost far more then it actually did. He would then pocket the surplus money, and his wealthy employers — who had never set foot into the marketplace and did not know how much fresh produce actually cost — were totally oblivious to his thievery.

One day, the three wealthy men met to engage in some friendly chatter. They decided to take a stroll through the marketplace, but as they were unfamiliar with the paths that ran through it, they asked the servant to accompany them. Each one wished to take his tour at a different time, however, as one desired to go in the morning, another in the afternoon, and yet another toward evening.

The crooked servant feared that his scheme would be uncovered. In the morning, therefore, he approached the first man and exclaimed slyly, "I am absolutely shocked how someone of your stature could saunter through the fruit market. Why, it's filled with shopkeepers and merchants who ride on donkeys and camels. In addition, the large crowds and the noise are most difficult to bear. It would not be fitting for someone as esteemed as yourself to wander through such a place!"

The wealthy man heeded the words of his servant and remained at home.

In the afternoon, the servant approached the second man and attempted to convince him, as well, that it was beneath his dignity to walk through the marketplace. The wealthy man could not be swayed, however, and remained firm in his resolve to be led through the marketplace. Left with no other option, the servant accompanied his employer, but when they arrived at the marketplace, he managed to distract him by telling him delightful business tales. Enjoying his servant's stories, the wealthy man paid no attention whatsoever to the price of the fruits. He did not even hear the shouts of the merchants, as they bellowed out the cheap prices of their merchandise.

When evening had fallen, the servant arrived at the house of the third wealthy man and tried to dissuade him from visiting the marketplace. He, too, insisted on going and the servant's attempts to distract him with various stories floundered as well. Making his way through the market, the wealthy man took careful notice of the prices and realized that the servant had been stealing from them.

Understanding that he would soon be searching for a new job, the servant made one last attempt at deceiving his employer, claiming that the produce in the marketplace was of poor quality and nearly spoiled. He, however, always purchased fruit of the highest quality, which was far more expensive. But the wealthy man was no fool, and he immediately grasped the fraudulence of the servant. He fired him on the spot and warned him never to return.

So it is with the *yetzer hara,* said the *Ben Ish Chai,* R' Yosef Chaim of Baghdad. The *yetzer hara* deceives mankind and offers them wicked counsel. It fears greatly, however, lest people go to hear words of *mussar* (ethical reproach), and therefore tries to convince them not to attend the *mussar* sermons that are delivered in shul. After all, it contends, it is very crowded in shul, difficult to find a seat, and rather warm inside. There are fools who are persuaded by his words, remaining at home or simply meandering from one place to the next.

Then there those who realize that even though it may be crowded in shul, it is still worthwhile to hear a few words of *mussar.* The *yetzer hara* employs various strategies in order to distract such a person: On one occasion, it will cause him to think about issues pertaining to his family, and on a different occasion, it will divert his attention by getting him to look at and think about others. This person may hear the words of *mussar* that are being spoken, but he will be unable to comprehend a word, as his thoughts have been diverted from the topic at hand.

The wise man, however, refuses to be lured by the nonsensical gibberish of the *yetzer hara* and listens to the words of *mussar* from start to finish. Of course, the *yetzer hara* refuses to relent, and attempts to convince him that such lofty words of *mussar* do not pertain to him; such ideas are meant for pious *tzaddikim* who have ascended to very exalted levels of spirituality...

But the wise man will not be fooled and immediately comprehends the source of this wicked counsel. He therefore wastes no time and expels the *yetzer hara,* warning him never to return.

Part 5

Divine Service

The Emperor's Visit

It is incumbent upon man, stated the Chofetz Chaim, to examine his behavior each and every day. He must ask himself if his deeds are refined and pleasant, and if they are not, he must know which areas stand to be improved and how he must go about doing so.

He compared `this to an emperor who informed the commander of his armed forces that he would be coming to visit his troops on a particular day.

The soldiers and their officers were seized with excitement, and they all prepared enthusiastically for the monumental visit. The camp was cleaned, the uniforms were pressed, and the rifles were polished. When the great day arrived, the soldiers stood at attention in orderly rows, suitably prepared to greet the emperor. At the forefront stood the commander, who was both tense and excited. In such a fashion, they stood and awaited the emperor's arrival.

An hour passed, but the emperor had not arrived. Realizing that the emporer was running late, the commander instructed one of the soldiers to man his post and immediately alert him upon spotting the emperor.

The soldier stood at his post and the commander went to rest for a short while…

All of a sudden, the emperor appeared at the gates of the camp without any prior notice. Much to his shock, he discovered a simple private stationed at the head of the troops.

"Where is the commander of the army?" thundered the emperor.

Pale and trembling, the commander rushed out of his room and stood before the emperor shamefaced and utterly mortified.

Infuriated, the emperor stripped the commander of his badges and flung them into the air.

"From this day on," said the emperor, "you are no longer fit to be an officer in the army!"

> The same thing applies to us, remarked the Chofetz Chaim. We all await the arrival of *Mashiach*, and we must greet him amidst repentance and good deeds. While he may delay in coming, we must not abandon our posts. For *Mashiach* will arrive suddenly and unexpectedly, and how will it appear to him if we have deserted our stations?

✌ Lessons to Learn from an Infant and a Thief

R' Zushia of Anipoli was a regular visitor to the holy court of the Maggid of Mezheritch, where his great teacher illuminated his path of Divine service.

On one occasion, the Maggid turned to R' Zushia and said the following: "There are three lessons that you must learn from an infant and seven that you must learn from a thief. By doing so, you will establish a very fine path in Divine service for yourself."

These are the three lessons to be learned from an infant:

- An infant is always happy.
- An infant does not waste a moment; rather, he is busy at all times.
- When an infant requests something from his father — it makes no difference how insignificant the item may be — he cries for it.

These are the seven lessons that you must learn from a thief:

- A thief works at night.
- If a thief does not succeed in attaining that which he has sought, he does not relent; rather, he simply tries again the following night.

- A thief cares deeply about his friends and is willing to give up his life for them.
- A thief will risk his life for an item of little worth, even if it is not certain that he will be successful in stealing it.
- A thief sells his stolen goods in the morning, as he does not want others to know that he is a thief.
- A thief will not admit his guilt; even when he is tortured he continues to claim, "I do not know."
- A thief is happy with his profession and would not trade it for another.

ᴥ§ Good Intention is Good Enough

Chazal state (*Tosefta Pe'ah, Perek* 1) that if a person intends to perform a good deed but is unable to do so, Hashem considers it as if he actually performed it, and he is rewarded accordingly. The Chofetz Chaim drew an amazing parable in relation to this concept:

Reuven was a very wealthy man who possessed exemplary fear of Heaven and excelled in the *mitzvah* of *tzedakah*. He had a son who was an extraordinary Torah scholar and who possessed sterling character traits. One day, a match was proposed between Reuven's son and the daughter of Shimon, a wealthy Torah scholar in his own right. The two sides approved and the match was finalized.

The *mechutanim* (in-laws) agreed that in approximately one month's time, they would each contribute three thousand rubles towards the wedding expenses. It was an enormous sum of money, but befitting the children of two such wealthy individuals.

When a month had passed, Reuven sent a message to Shimon that it was time to pay the money. Shimon, who was rather busy with his work, inquired as to whether Reuven would be willing to push off the pay date for another month. Reuven agreed.

After the month had passed, Reuven once again sent a message to Shimon that the allotted time had arrived. As before, Shimon responded that he was presently unable to pay. He wished to know if Reuven would be willing to allow him an additional month to pay the agreed sum.

This time, Reuven would not accede to Shimon's request, and he called off the match. He then made a match for his son with the daughter of Levi, a very wealthy individual. This time, everything proceeded according to plan.

As the day of the great wedding drew nearer, Reuven sat with his servant in order to prepare an invitation list.

"What about Shimon?" asked the servant. "Shall he be invited to the wedding?"

"Absolutely not!" responded Reuven. "There is no need whatsoever to invite him."

"But wasn't he nearly your *mechutan*?" asked the servant.

"So what?" answered Shimon. "If I were to invite every person who was nearly my *mechutan*, I'd be inviting the entire city — for who does not seek to be my *mechutan*?"

> While this might be the response of all men, said the Chofetz Chaim, it is not the way of Hashem, the King of the World. For anyone who intends to fulfill a *mitzvah* — even if he is ultimately prevented from doing so — is considered to be a "*mechutan*."

◆§ The Way of Merchants

The way of merchants, noted the Chofetz Chaim, is to laud their merchandise in order that customers will be quick to make a purchase at an inflated price. Even if the merchandise is by no means noteworthy, they nevertheless shower it with praise, until even the most hesitant of consumers readily takes out his wallet and completes the transaction.

Would it ever occur to a merchant to degrade his merchandise? He would immediately earn the scornful eye of his peers, who would consider him to be a complete buffoon. For how could any merchant sell goods that he himself claims are of poor quality? Even if he *would* manage to find someone foolish enough to buy them, how much would the costumer be willing to pay for them?

> So, too, said the Chofetz Chaim, in relation to the *mitzvos* that Hashem gave us. The *mitzvos* are similar to excellent merchandise, as one is destined to receive a huge reward for having performed them. It goes without saying, then, that man must treat this merchandise with the proper respect. Each and every individual is required to put forth his best effort in order to fulfill the *mitzvos* as meticulously as possible. For the more precision one displays in the performance of *mitzvos*, the more reward he is destined to receive.
>
> However, those who make light of *mitzvah* performance, fulfilling *mitzvos* simply in order to "meet their requirements" and without any intent or meticulousness, will be held in disdain.
>
> Much to their shame, the reward they receive in the future will reflect their minimal efforts.

➳ Who Was the Guest?

A Jew earned a living managing a small inn that stood on the crossroads leading to the big city. Every so often, a lone traveler or caravan would lodge at the inn; there they would eat to their heart's content, rest from the arduous journey, and then continue on their way.

On one occasion, the Jew was a victim of slander and stood falsely accused of committing a crime against the state. Awaiting his trial, he was informed by reliable sources that if he were found guilty, he would spend the rest of his life in prison.

His loved ones advised him to travel to the capital where the emperor resided. There he would try his utmost to gain an audience with the emperor and present his claims before him. The emperor, said his friends, is a man of truth and will certainly see that justice is served.

"But who will enable me to even approach the palace to begin with?" asked the innkeeper. "Why, the emperor's guards have the palace surrounded."

"You must try, nonetheless," responded his friends.

The emperor had a custom every so often of donning simple farmer's clothing and walking among the populace. In this way, he would get a sense of the mood and would know what the masses were thinking.

On one such occasion, the Emperor arrived at the Jew's inn. There he received food and drink and slept on the floor like an ordinary person.

Some time later, the innkeeper was informed of whom his guest had been. Upon hearing that the emperor had lodged in his inn, the innkeeper took his head in his hands and screamed, "Woe is me! The emperor was in my house, and I could have beseeched him to save my life…"

> Every individual can draw close to Hashem, the King of All Kings, in this world, said the Chofetz Chaim, for here He is accessible. One must seize the moment and draw as close to Hashem as he possibly can, for he will not have the opportunity to do so in the World to Come.

·§ "You Shall be Wholehearted with Hashem, Your God"

R' Yisrael Salanter offered the following parable to illustrate this injunction:

There was a king who sent one of his dukes to perform a task in a foreign land.

"I am making one condition with you," said the king to the duke. "When you arrive in the land, under no circumstances are you to enter into any type of bet with any of the officers there." The duke agreed to the strange stipulation and went on his way.

Upon arriving at his destination, the duke met with the officers of the land and engaged them in conversation. "Your Highness, the Duke," exclaimed one of the officers. "a rumor has spread that you are a hunchback — could such a thing be true?"

"That rumor is an absolute lie!" responded the duke. "I am not a hunchback, nor have I ever been a hunchback!"

"Let us wager one hundred thousand *dinar* that you really are a hunchback," said the officer. "Remove your shirt, and we will all see if the rumor is accurate or not!"

The duke suddenly recalled the king's admonition, but immediately thought to himself, "This is a sure bet, as I am by no means a hunchback — why should I not agree to the wager?"

The duke therefore removed his shirt, and all those who were present indeed saw that he was not a hunchback. Having won the bet, the duke was handed one hundred thousand *dinar*.

Upon returning to the palace, the duke approached the king and related to him all that had occurred in the foreign country. He then mentioned the wager he had won.

"Woe is me!" screamed the king, clutching his head in both hands. "What have you done? You may have won one hundred thousand dinar, but I have lost *five hundred thousand* dinar, as I bet the officers of that land that they would not be able to bait you into removing your shirt!"

> Man, concluded R' Salanter, must perform the Torah's *mitzvos* with wholeheartedness and without innovative rationalizations that make him feel justified in shirking his obligations. It is incumbent upon each Jew to simply follow the Torah's instructions and no more! "You shall be wholehearted with Hashem, your God"! (*Devarim* 18:13).

A n individual was heavily in debt to all his friends and acquaintances. On one occasion, he sorrowfully poured out his heart to a close friend.

"What shall I do?" he asked. "My creditors are pressuring me and demanding that I repay them."

"I will give you a piece of advice," answered the friend. "When the creditors approach you, begin to sing and dance, pretending to have lost your mind. When the creditors see your sorry state, they will realize that it was brought upon by your difficult predicament. They will then leave you alone…"

The man was elated with the clever advice and did as his friend had instructed. Whenever a creditor approached him, he would feign insanity and they would let him be.

One day, it came time to repay the friend who had advised him, as he, too, had loaned the man a significant sum of money. However when his friend approached him for the money, he began to sing and dance as he had done with the other creditors.

"You fool!" exclaimed the friend. "Was I not the one who advised you on how to escape your creditors? Do you now attempt to use that same advice against me?"

> So, too, with man, said the Dubno Maggid. Hashem bestowed kindness upon man by granting him the ability to forget, as this enables a person to forget his suffering. Yet man forgets Hashem instead…

The Reward of Previous Generations

F or many years, a man worked in a rich storeowner's textile shop. Throughout the years, he measured fabrics, cut them, arranged the stock, and cleaned the premises.

One day, the worker passed away, and the storeowner hired the man's son as a replacement. The son followed in his father's footsteps and worked with integrity and loyalty.

Some time later, the son died as well, and his son, the grandson of the original laborer, filled his position.

Approximately a week later, the worker entered the storeowner's office holding a list. "I have just made a calculation and figured out that my father and grandfather worked in your store for a total of forty-six years. That being the case, I am entitled to one thousand rubles, which is due compensation for forty-six years of labor!"

"It is certainly true," laughed the storeowner, "that they worked in my store for forty-six years, but do you think that they worked for free? How do you think they supported themselves and their families for so many years?"

> There are times, remarked the Chofetz Chaim, when we sigh over our state of exile. We note how we have languished in this exile for hundreds of years. We mention how even our righteous ancestors groaned beneath the heavy yoke of the exile, and that when the time comes, we will be redeemed in their merit.
>
> Yet we forget that our ancestors, pious individuals of the highest caliber, have already received their reward and continue to receive an inestimable abundance of reward in the World of Truth. We must not claim the reward for their *mitzvos*; rather, we ourselves, must repent wholeheartedly. Only then will Hashem's mercy be evoked, ultimately leading to our glorious redemption.

⋙ The Treasure

A wealthy man was set to embark on a lengthy journey to a distant land. He therefore packed many belongings, as well as food for the way, piling everything into his magnificent stagecoach.

Prior to his journey, he summoned his loyal servant and exclaimed, "I am leaving my home for an extended period of time, and I am appointing you to faithfully watch over it. I have but one request: that you take extraordinary care of my private office, as its contents are very dear to me. Please take extra-special care of it!" The servant agreed, and the wealthy man boarded his stagecoach and set off.

When the clouds of dust that the stagecoach had generated had settled, the servant entered the house and thought, "I am extremely curious as to why my master was so adamant that I guard his private office; an item of great value must be hidden inside."

The servant entered the wealthy man's office and a huge wooden chest sitting in the corner immediately caught his eye.

The servant opened the chest and beheld a most fabulous treasure consisting of silver and gold vessels, precious gems, and pearls. But much to his bewilderment, the entire treasure was covered with mud.

"How odd," the servant thought to himself. "On one hand, my master cautioned me to take special care of his precious treasure, yet on the other hand, he himself is so careless with it that he allows it to become filthy with mud."

> So it is with man, said the Chofetz Chaim. When the time will come for man to stand in judgment before the Heavenly Tribunal, the innermost sanctums of his heart are examined: Were the thoughts in his heart pure, and did he serve Hashem with fear and honesty? For the heart is the most precious treasure contained within man's body, and if it is revealed that his heart is covered with filth and mud, it is due to the mundane thoughts that fill it.
>
> How terrible will his humiliation and shame be at that moment.
>
> Therefore, concluded the Chofetz Chaim, we beseech Hashem each and every day, "And unify our hearts to love and fear Your Name" — Master of the World, please make our hearts contain only love and fear for you and not any alien thoughts!

✌§ A Loan and Repayment

A wealthy man ambled through the city square and suddenly encountered a poor relative of his. The poor man wasted no time and began to plead his case before his rich relative.

"Please save me!" he begged. "I desperately need a loan of one thousand rubles!"

"One thousand rubles?" asked the wealthy man in amazement. "Why do you need such an enormous sum of money?"

"An extraordinary financial opportunity has come my way," responded the poor man, "and it is a golden opportunity that will not come again. However, it requires an investment of one thousand rubles, which I do not have. Truthfully, I do not even have *ten* rubles in my pocket…"

"If so," responded the wealthy man, "I will loan you the entire amount."

The poor man thanked his rich relative profusely and accompanied him to his home. There he received a hefty bundle of money containing a total of one thousand rubles.

He took the money and placed it inside his cupboard. However, the money just sat there, and the poor man did not invest even one ruble.

When it came time to repay the loan, the poor man returned the untouched bundle of money to his rich relative.

When the wealthy man realized that the money had not been used, he grew irate and even began to shout at the poor man. "Are you not ashamed?" he hollered. "You borrowed a huge sum of money from me claiming that you were going to invest it in a worthwhile business, and all you did was let it sit in your closet? Do you have any idea what I could have accomplished with the one thousand rubles during that time?"

> Hashem, said the Chofetz Chaim, endowed man with a precious soul and years of life during which he could engage in the study of Torah and the performance of *mitzvos*. Yet very

often, man does not take advantage of the valuable treasure that is in his possession; rather, he neglects it and opts to squander his days with meaningless activities.

When the time comes to repay the loan, concluded the Chofetz Chaim, and man is required to return the precious treasure to its rightful owner — will its owner not be infuriated seeing that it has remained untouched?

◆§ *The Collector*

In a certain city resided a wealthy merchant whose hobby was to purchase and collect books. He spent an inordinate sum of money building up his collection, never hesitating to spend a bit extra if necessary. When he was presented with a book that he truly coveted, he would purchase it immediately. He bought old books as well as new ones and stored them in a massive library that he had built in one of the halls of his magnificent home.

Once, the man heard that a prominent book collector, living in a distant land, wished to sell his entire collection.

The wealthy man hastened to summon his trustworthy servant. He ordered him to travel immediately to the faraway land and purchase whatever was available. However, he warned the servant not to purchase defective books; rather, he was to examine each book carefully in order to ascertain if it was in mint condition or not.

Understanding his assignment, the servant went on his way without the slightest hesitation.

When he arrived at his destination, he immediately made his way to the book collector's home and requested to view his enormous collection.

The man led the servant into the house where he stored his books. The servant took one look and was speechless — never in his life had he seen so many books…

However, it did not take long for him to notice that the books were in complete disarray and not stored in any particular order. Some of them were even scattered across the floor.

He began to examine the books and quickly realized that the majority of them were damaged. This one was missing pages; this one was damp. Another book was missing its binding, while a different one had printing defects, and so on and so forth.

He ultimately piled a number of books that he found to be in perfect condition and requested to purchase them.

The owner of the books was shocked by the small number of books that the servant had chosen. "That's all you are going to buy?" he asked. "I honestly thought that you had come to purchase the majority of my collection."

"Indeed, I would have," responded the servant. "But what could I have done, as most of your books are damaged and in poor condition. It appears that you did not take very good care of them, for I saw many books lying on the floor and others that were stored quite improperly and neglected…"

> Like the foresaken and neglected collection, said the Chofetz Chaim, so, too, is our fulfillment of Torah and *mitzvos*. An individual is required to perform the *mitzvos* with meticulousness, accompanied by unsullied thoughts and a pure heart. But when man comes before the Heavenly Tribunal and his good deeds are examined, it is immediately revealed that the overwhelming majority of his deeds are flawed — this period of learning was interrupted by an inappropriate thought, and this *mitzvah* was accompanied by feelings of arrogance, and so on and so forth…
>
> At that time, he is filled with embarrassment and shame, and attempts to explain that he was very busy and preoccupied with other endeavors. However, he will immediately be shown how much time he wasted with meaningless conversations and frivolousness.
>
> Upon seeing this, he will be silenced and have nothing to answer!
>
> If a person truly understood in this world what will happen to him at the end of days, would he continue to act as he does? He would undoubtedly improve his ways immediately!

❧ The Safe

A rich man suffered from acute insomnia. Night after night, he lay awake in bed, as worries gnawed at his heart and did not permit him to relax.

What worried him so?

The rich man was a merchant who sold diamonds and other precious gems. Naturally, he stored a massive amount of gems and cash in his home.

"Indeed," thought the rich man to himself, "my money and gems are hidden inside a large and sturdy safe; but what will be if a thief enters my home and terrorizes me into opening the safe? What will I do then?"

This thought disturbed him greatly, and he tossed and turned, unable to sleep.

One night, the rich man leaped from his bed in a state of joy, thinking that he had resolved his problem.

He hired an expert safe maker, who constructed a wall within the safe. Behind the wall, the rich man hid most of his wealth, leaving only a small amount of cash and inexpensive gems in the actual safe.

"If a thief will come now, G-d forbid," thought the thief, "he will find only a pittance of money, and the rest will be safely hidden away."

From then on, the rich man slept soundly.

> When it comes to one's Divine service, said R' Chaim Elazar of Munkatch, a person must act similarly. For if an individual serves his Creator visibly and publicly, he is likely to grow haughty or incur an "evil eye." The majority of a person's Divine service should therefore be performed privately, and only a minute amount should be revealed to the public.

I n a certain city lived the owner of a fabric mill who had successfully developed a new type of fabric. It was an extraordinary
fabric, soft to the touch and appealing to the eye.

The fabric proved very popular, and hordes of people gathered
outside his mill to purchase it. It became so popular, in fact, that he
was simply unable to manufacture enough of the fabric to meet the
overwhelming demand.

While there were many individuals who actually preferred their
old clothes, which were still in excellent condition, they nevertheless, purchased the new fabric and had clothing sewn from it, as
they wanted to keep up with the styles.

One who observed a group of people wearing clothing made
from the new fabric, would have no way of knowing which of them
truly enjoys wearing the clothing and which of them is wearing
those clothes just to be fashionable.

However, there is one way to discern a weaver's true motives. If
the person meets the inventor and makes an effort to thank him for
his innovative achievement, even telling him how pleased they are
with the fabric, it is an indication that the person is truly pleased.

But then there are those who greet the inventor with a sour face
and treat him rather poorly. Given the opportunity, they will even
go so far as to chide him over the fact that he caused them to
spend a great deal of money. Such individuals are wearing the
fabric only to appear trendy.

One can distinguish between the Divine service of various individuals, said the Dubno Maggid, in the very same manner. There
are those who perform the *mitzvos* out of Heavenly fear and love
for the Creator. Then there are those who perform the *mitzvos* by
rote, simply for the sake of discharging an obligation. The only way
to discern between them is by observing the manner in which they
carry out the *mitzvos*. One who fulfills them with joy and excitement and tries to be as meticulous as possible, falls under the
category of one who truly loves Hashem. But if not…

The Harvester's Wage

An individual purchased a portion of a field, intending to build a large house on it. At the time, the field had been planted with wheat; in order to prepare the site for construction, the buyer hired a worker to harvest the wheat.

The next morning, the worker arrived at the field and began harvesting. As the day drew to a close, the owner of the field saw that the worker had managed to harvest one quarter of the wheat in the field.

"Listen to me," said the owner to the worker. "It can take several additional days to finish harvesting the wheat, and I do not intend to delay construction for that long. I will therefore begin building the house tomorrow and will declare the remainder of the wheat ownerless. Whoever would like to take it will be free to do so."

"If you are declaring the wheat ownerless," said the worker, "then I will gladly take possession of it. Give me one more day, and I will harvest as much wheat as I can."

The next day, the worker labored with tremendous vigor, and by the time evening had fallen, he had managed to finish harvesting the entire field!

"I have a question for you," said the owner to the worker. "On the first day, you were able to harvest only a quarter of the wheat, but today you amazingly harvested three-quarters. How did today differ from yesterday?"

"The answer is as follows," replied the worker. "The first day, I worked in order to receive a set wage; I therefore did not overexert myself. Yet today, I labored with the knowledge that I would be receiving the actual wheat in exchange, and whatever I would not harvest, I would lose."

R' Shlomo Kluger quotes, "the *pasuk* "Praiseworthy is the man who fears Hashem, who greatly desires His commandments" (*Tehillim* 112:1). *Chazal* (*Avodah Zarah* 19a) expound, "His commandments — and not the reward [that is earned through fulfilling] His commandments!" One who fears Hashem understands and values the importance of the *mitzvah* itself, and does not desire to fulfill it for the sake of receiving a reward. However, one who lacks understanding and fulfills *mitzvos* only to receive a reward will occasionally put forth a half-hearted effort.

◂§ Tell Me Who Your Friends Are

A rich villager had an only daughter. When she had come of age, he decided to travel to the big city in order to find her a suitable *chassan* (groom).

When he arrived in the city, he made his way to one of its outstanding yeshivos and approached the *rosh yeshivah*. He asked the *rosh yeshivah* to point out his most exemplary student. He guaranteed to fully support the young couple and even provide them with an attractive apartment.

Hearing the villager's words, the *rosh yeshivah* recommended a young man who he claimed was the finest of all the students. A young man of his caliber is seldom seen, he added.

The match was made and the couple were soon married. Following the wedding, they went to live in the father-in-law's village.

Problems began to arise shortly thereafter, however, as the son-in-law became quite enamored with the village's wide-open areas, and its lush green fields. He delighted in watching the stream that flowed on the outskirts of the village, and taking in the breathtaking view of its towering mountain range.

He made new friends as well: One of them was a gooseherd, the other, a water-carrier. Together they squandered many precious hours...

Noticing his son-in-law's behavior, the father-in-law asked to speak with him. "My son-in-law, it appears as though an error has been made. I requested a diligent Torah scholar for a son-in-law, and I have been given a young man who wastes his time like one of the senseless villagers."

The young man was startled by the offensive comparison. "Please forgive me, my father-in- law," he replied. "But can I really be compared to one of the villagers? The gooseherd cannot even recognize a Hebrew letter, and while the water-carrier may be able to recognize a letter — that's all he can do. Yet I am literally bursting with knowledge of the Talmud and its commentaries…

"Even if I will forget a large portion of my learning," added the son-in-law, "I will still know far more than anyone in this village."

"But is that what I sought for my daughter," responded the father-in-law angrily, "— someone who would be the most learned individual out of a group of unlearned simpletons? I requested a *talmid chacham*, the most exemplary scholar in comparison to all the other yeshivah students!"

> So it is with man, explained the Dubno Maggid. The soul, which stems from a lofty source, descends to this world and enters man. But man soon begins to associate with unlearned individuals and learns from their foolish ways. He consoles himself, however, rationalizing that even though he has indeed fallen to such a lowly state, he is, nevertheless, superior to his friends.
>
> He is making a grave error! For Hashem expects him to be outstanding in comparison to those who are of an equally high stature and not to laud himself with meaningless praises!

⪧ The Cost of Lodging

At times, an individual invests a tremendous amount of time and energy into his material pursuits, forgetting that man's yearly sustenance is already determined and that all his effort is in vain!

This can be compared to a pair of neighbors who lived in a small village; one was a stingy miser, the other, a kind-hearted, merciful Jew.

On one occasion, a visitor arrived in the village and sought a place to spend the night. He knocked on the first door he came to — much to his misfortune, it was the door of the miser.

"Please forgive me," said the visitor. "I am passing through the village and am searching for a place to rest my weary feet — perhaps I could lodge in your house?"

"Lodge in my house?" shouted the miser. "Nothing is free in my home! If you wish to lodge here, you must first perform various chores around the house — only then will I permit you to spend the night."

With no other choice, the visitor agreed, and the miser told him what to do. "This item needs fixing," he instructed. "Scrub over here… these vessels could certainly use a good shine and polish…"

When the visitor completed his arduous labor, he approached the miser and inquired as to where he could rest his head.

"Come with me," he answered, "and I will take you to my neighbor's house. He is very hospitable and will certainly allow you to lodge with him."

The miser's scheme having been revealed, the visitor began to lament bitterly, "Woe is me!" he cried. "I could have come to this house initially and requested to spend the night. All of my toil was in vain!"

⋙ The Match

An ignorant villager won a lottery and became exceedingly wealthy. His newfound wealth did not affect his lifestyle and behavior, however, and he remained the boorish commoner that he always was. Yet it did affect his self-image, as he now considered himself to be an esteemed and venerable rabbi.

When his daughter reached marriageable age, the villager asked the matchmaker to find him a groom who was befitting someone of his "distinguished" stature.

"To tell you the truth," whispered the villager to the matchmaker, "I would very much like my daughter to marry the *Rav*'s son."

"The *Rav's* son?" asked the shocked matchmaker. "Who would possibly present the *Rav* with such a match?"

"Why, you, of course," replied the villager. "In return, I will give you gold coins, more than you have never seen."

When the matchmaker heard the villager's offer, he agreed to present his daughter to the *Rav*.

At first, the *Rav* totally refused to consider the matchmaker's offer. But the matchmaker — true to his profession — would not relent. He proposed the match again and again, stopping at nothing, until the *Rav* finally acquiesced and the match was made.

Never has there been seen a happier father-in-law than the villager on the day of his daughter's wedding. Dressed in regal rabbinical attire, he proudly escorted the *Rav's* son to the wedding canopy.

His joy was to be short -lived, however. For it was soon discovered that the *Rav* was humiliated over the match and refused to so much as even speak with the villager...

In a state of distress, the villager turned to the matchmaker for an explanation. "Would anyone believe," wondered the villager, "that a pair of in-laws would not speak to each other at all?"

The matchmaker brought up the matter with the *Rav*, who explained in no uncertain terms, "This villager thinks that he is a very prominent individual who was fitting to receive such a match; he is therefore bewildered as to why I refuse to associate with him and why I am embarrassed over the matter. But if he would realize that he is from the lowliest of the villagers and that his conversations revolve only around growing potatoes, he would understand why it is not befitting the *Rav* of the city to become his in-law. If he realized his true stature," concluded the *Rav*, "he would not be bewildered in the least!"

> There are times, noted the Dubno Maggid, when an individual performs *mitzvos* with indifference and a lack of enthusiasm. Let him not wonder why he feels so distant from Hashem; rather, he should examine his deeds and beseech Hashem to "Create a pure heart for me, O God, and a steadfast spirit renew within me" (*Tehillim* 51:12).

◆§ *"Do Not Answer a Fool According to His Foolishness" (Mishlei 26:4)*

There was a certain individual who was renowned for his hospitality, which was of the highest caliber. He provided every guest with a place to rest as well as three generous, delectable meals each day. His righteous wife cooked a wide array of delicacies and served all of the food on elegant dishes, which only served to enhance the guest's feeling of contentment.

On one occasion, an individual with a stomach malady visited the man's home. He sat at the table and ate with the other guests, partaking of whatever food was served. It was not long before he began feeling ill and had to be taken to the hospital.

When his host came to visit him in the hospital, the guest berated him harshly, calling him a wicked man who inflicted harm upon others.

The host listened to the barrage of insults and replied, "Why don't you go and ask the other guests if they think as you do? They will tell you that you are ill and prohibited from eating the foods that you ate. The truth is that I did not prepare the food for sick individuals such as yourself. Therefore, *you* are to blame for your condition!"

The wicked, remarked the Dubno Maggid, assert that there are too many *mitzvos*! An individual is severely punished for violating any one of the six hundred and thirteen *mitzvos* that Hashem gave us. With so many *mitzvos*, it is inconceivable that man will not stumble and incur a harsh sentence!

The answer to their obviously invalid claim, said the Maggid, is as follows: For the righteous, *mitzvah* performance is an opportunity to climb the ladder of achievement and self-improvement — for which the reward is eternal. The wicked, on the other hand, stumble over the very same *mitzvos*, as *Chazal* state in *Yoma* (72b), "If he merits — it will be for him an elixir of life. If he does not merit — it will be an elixir of death." Similarly, the verse states: "The righteous will walk in them and sinners will stumble over them" (*Hoshea* 14:10).

✒ *A Valise Filled with Diamonds*

A wealthy diamond merchant once sent his trustworthy servant to reclaim a valise filled with rare and precious gems that he had deposited with a friend.

The diamond dealer stood gazing from the window of his home, anxiously awaiting his servant's return. When he caught a glimpse of his servant — who seemed to be having a difficult time drawing a breath, huffing and puffing as he struggled to carry what appeared to be an extraordinarily heavy load — he was horrified.

"Woe is me!" screamed the diamond dealer as he held his head in his hands. "A terrible tragedy has occurred! For it appears as if thieves have stolen my precious gems from the valise and left heavy rocks in their place; after all, someone who is carrying diamonds should not have to struggle to such a great extent…"

> The verse states, said the Dubno Maggid, "So that you cannot carry it, because the place (*HaMakom*)…is far from you" (*Devarim* 14:24). It is possible to understand the verse in the following manner: "So that you cannot carry it" — If a Jew is groaning and sighing beneath the yoke of Hashem's *mitzvos*, it is a sign — "Because *HaMakom* [*HaMakom*, which literally means "place," is also used as a reference to Hashem and His Omnipresence] is far from you." In other words, such an individual is clearly distant from Hashem, his Father in Heaven. For Hashem's *mitzvos* are pure, and they should evoke neither sigh nor groan.

✑ *The Contract*

An individual decided to build a lovely new house for himself. He therefore hired a well-known contractor to construct it for him.

The man met with the contractor and gave him a detailed description of how he wanted his house to be built: "I would like my home to consist of five bedrooms," he said. "In addition, please build a large living room, a spacious kitchen, and two storage rooms."

They eventually arrived at an agreement and signed a contract requiring the contractor to build a house with a specific number of rooms, doors, lintels, and locks. Each and every detail was agreed to and signed upon.

The contactor commenced his work. He picked up the contract and read that he was required to install twenty windows. He therefore prepared twenty windows and placed them in the storage room. Next, he prepared the necessary number of doors and placed them in the storage room as well. He followed the same pattern for each and every one of the building materials. However he did not build the house itself…

When he had finished preparing all of the materials, he turned to his employer and said, "Here are all the components of the house, just as we agreed upon in the contract. At this point you have all the essential materials to construct your home, if you'd like. As for me, please compensate me accordingly."

"Absolutely not!" roared the man. "While these may be the necessary building materials, if you take a good look at our contract, you will see that you were obligated to build me a house and not only supply the materials."

> The first and foremost obligation of a Jew, said the Dubno Maggid, is to serve Hashem, as *HaKadosh Baruch Hu* said to Moshe Rabbeinu, "When you take the people out of Egypt, you will serve G-d" (*Shemos* 3:12)! The Torah then provides us with all the necessary details as to how we are to go about serving Him.

When a person performs the *mitzvos* but lacks the proper intentions, he is similar to the contractor who prepared all of the materials but failed to construct the house at all.

✌§ The Honor of Sages

In a certain city lived a wise man renowned for his extraordinary sagaciousness. He sat at home and studied his many books, disseminating profound counsel to all those who sought it.

In those days, there was a charlatan who would travel from village to village and from city to city claiming to be the famous sage. Individuals who did not recognize the wise man and were unfamiliar with his appearance actually believed him, and he was therefore accorded an abundance of honor wherever he went.

When the sage heard about his impersonator, he was absolutely elated. "I am overjoyed," he explained, "that my name is held in such high regard that anyone who makes use of it merits receiving such great honor…"

> The nations of the world, said the Dubno Maggid, worship idols of wood and stone. They do so, however, because they believe that their god is the true G-d. This results in the Name of Hashem being exalted and honored in the world either way.
>
> This is as the verse states, "From the rising of the sun to its setting, Hashem's Name is praised" (Tehillim 113:3)!

✌§ A Time to Serve Hashem

A king had four sons whom he loved with all his heart. The sons, unfortunately, were in poor health and became ill quite frequently.

Seeing this, the king invited an illustrious physician to reside in the palace and constantly look after his sons' well-being. When the physician deemed it necessary, he would give the sons various medications, in this way preventing them from becoming ill.

On one occasion, the sons refused to take the bitter medicines. It was not long before they all grew seriously ill.

The king was furious with the physician.

"Your Highness," asked the physician in surprise, "why are you angry with me? You should be angry at your sons for refusing to drink the medicine I prescribed them!"

"That is certainly true," replied the king. "However, when I look at you, my anguish is intensified. For had there not been an expert physician in the palace, I would have given up hope and come to terms with my sons' condition. However, now that I have a physician whose skills are unmatched, I am terribly distressed that we are in such a predicament."

> All week long, noted the Dubno Maggid, man is busy trying to earn a livelihood. Hashem has therefore given him Shabbos and the Festivals in order for man to serve Him in a state of serenity and peace of mind. However, if man does not utilize these days for their intended purpose, Hashem says about him, "My soul detests your New Moons and your appointed times..." (*Yeshayahu* 1:14).

৺ Serving Hashem With Joy

A person who is traveling to a *simchah* (festive occasion), such as a wedding or the like, sets off happily and is sad when he must return. On the other hand, an individual who is forced to travel somewhere against his will — to a court hearing, for example — is not very happy to be going, but is elated upon returning.

It is apparently impossible for an individual to be joyful about both the commencement and return of his journey!

> This is not so, said the Dubno Maggid. For a person who is serving Hashem is just as happy to go and fulfill a *mitzvah*, as

he is to complete it. This is as we recite in the morning prayers for Shabbos, "Glad as they go forth and exultant as they return." Why? Because "They do with awe their Creator's will"!

❧ Two Brothers

A story is related about a wealthy individual who had two sons living in a distant city. One of the sons was a successful businessman who had grown fabulously wealthy; the other, a destitute pauper. It had been many years since the two brothers had last seen their father, and their reasons for this varied according to their respective situations: Due to his business dealings which were extremely time-consuming, the first brother was simply unable to spare the time to visit his father. The second brother, on the other hand, endured day-to-day hardships that did not allow him to leave home.

One day, the wealthy brother decided that enough time had passed since he had seen his father. He therefore resolved to take a short leave of his business and visit him. He approached his brother and suggested that he accompany him on his lengthy journey.

Upon hearing his brother's words, the poor brother thought to himself, "This is a golden opportunity for me. As a rule, I hesitate to go around the city collecting charity, for this would be an embarrassment to my distinguished brother. However, now that we will be taking leave of our city, I will be able to go from door-to-door in order to raise money."

The brothers set out on their long journey, each one with a different motive in mind. The first brother wished to see his father, while the second wanted to collect alms in places where he would not be recognized.

At the same time, their elderly father was sitting in his home and thinking, "I have two sons in a distant city who do not have the free time necessary to pay me a visit. I yearn to see them, but what can I do?" He immediately decided, "I will travel to them instead!"

And so he did.

Traveling on the road, the brothers met up with their father. However, while the wealthy brother was overjoyed to encounter his beloved father, the poor son lamented his lost opportunity.

> A *tzaddik's* sole intention when he eats, said the Dubno Maggid, is to sustain his body in order to serve Hashem. A *rasha*, however, eats in order to satisfy his cravings.
>
> If a person wishes to discover which category he belongs to, it is not very difficult to ascertain: Let him simply observe his reaction if he becomes satiated before having finished his portion. A *tzaddik* feels great joy over having fulfilled his purpose in eating; a *rasha*, on the other hand, suffers terribly…

✍ The Innkeeper's Compensation

An officer traveled at the head of a large caravan in order to perform an important task that the king had assigned him. The sun set in the middle of their trip, and spotting an inn alongside the road, they headed directly towards it.

The innkeeper was delighted to merit the honor to host the king's officer. He therefore tried his utmost to make his esteemed guests' stay a pleasant one. In their honor, he arranged a table replete with various delicacies, and when they had eaten their fill, he prepared comfortable beds that would provide them with a good night's sleep.

Upon rising in the morning, the officer asked the innkeeper how much he owed him for their stay, and the innkeeper requested a substantial sum of money.

The officer paid the full amount and thanked the innkeeper. He then took his place at the head of the caravan and continued his journey, quickly forgetting all about the inn and the innkeeper.

Several days later, he arrived at another inn, and this time as well, was showered with exceptional hospitality as the innkeeper went well beyond the call of duty. Wanting to please his guests, the innkeeper served them delicious food and beverages, and provided them with comfortable sleeping arrangements as well.

The next day, the officer approached the innkeeper and requested to pay for his stay. The innkeeper, however, would not hear of it.

"Absolutely not!" he said to the officer. "It is both a pleasure and an honor that a great individual such as yourself would choose to lodge at my inn! The honor you have accorded me will be my full compensation!"

Upon hearing the innkeeper's heartfelt words, the officer was filled with tremendous affection for the simple man. He therefore commanded one of his servants to go and bring a particularly heavy chest from one of the wagons. Opening the chest, he removed magnificent jewelry and gems and presented them to the innkeeper.

"Here you go, my dear sir," said the officer. "This is a small portion of the reward that you shall receive for the loyalty that you have shown me. In addition, if you ever need anything from the king, do not hesitate to turn to me!"

The officer went on his way, but never forgot the innkeeper and his kindliness.

There are two types of servants of Hashem, said the Dubno Maggid. The first one serves Hashem in order to receive a reward. Hashem certainly looks upon his Divine service favorably, but he ultimately receives only his due reward.

This is not the case, however, with one who serves Hashem with joy over having merited to serve the King of All Kings. His reward is many times greater and brings Hashem much gratification.

This is what *Chazal* have stated in *Avos* (1:3): "Be not as servants who serve the master for the sake of receiving [even a token] of reward, but rather, be like servants who serve the master not for the sake of receiving a reward"!

≈§ Manning the Store

It is self-understood that, if an individual asks his storekeeper friend to leave the premises for a short while in order to do him a favor, the individual who needs the favor will remain to man the store in his absence. After all, the storeowner left his store because of him!

> The same thing applies, said the Dubno Maggid, to the suffering that a *tzaddik* endures. When a *tzaddik* serves Hashem with pristine faith, there are times that Hashem causes him to suffer in order to atone for the sins of his generation. When that happens, however, he is assured that Hashem will stand by him and take care that the suffering does not blemish his perfected Divine service in any way. After all, he is not being afflicted on his own account.

≈§ The Servant and the Merchant

The difference, said the Dubno Maggid, between one who serves Hashem with fear and one who serves Hashem with love is the difference between a servant and a merchant. A servant who works for an important individual stands in the outer chamber throughout the day and waits to be summoned by his master. The merchant, on the other hand, appears before the master periodically and offers to display his merchandise. If the master happens to be busy at the time, he asks the merchant to wait in the outer chamber until he concludes his business and will have a moment to deal with him.

Both the servant and the merchant are waiting, but there is a monumental difference between them. The servant is forced to wait lest his master summon him, but in truth, he would prefer not to be called at all. The merchant, however, desires desperately that the master beckon for him and entreat him to enter his royal chamber.

So, too, with servants of Hashem, explained the Dubno Maggid. One who serves Hashem out of fear of punishment fulfills the *mitzvos* begrudgingly, as if he is being forced to do so; in truth, he would prefer peace and quiet and to be free of his obligation. However, one who serves Hashem out of love constantly and enthusiastically seeks additional opportunities to perform *mitzvos*!

◆§ *A Lesson in Etiquette and Proper Behavior*

One of the prominent wealthy men of the city hired a personal tutor in order to teach his son etiquette and to instruct him how to act in a manner befitting the son of one of the richest and most highly regarded individuals of the land.

On one occasion, the son of a pauper, unruly and dressed in tattered clothing, came to the house as the tutor was delivering a lesson on table manners.

The pauper asked if he could listen to the lesson and was told that he could.

"The first rule," instructed the tutor, "is as follows: Upon being invited to an individual's home for a meal, it is proper etiquette to initially reject the offer. Only after being asked a second time should one concede to the request.

"The second rule," he continued, "is as follows: Upon arriving at the meal, never sit at the head of the table; rather, choose an unassuming and inconspicuous seat.

"And third," he concluded: "When the food is served, do not rush to grab your portion before everyone else. Rather, allow those at the head of the table and the other participants to take their portions first."

After the lesson, the son of the wealthy man turned to the son of the pauper and asked, "Did you actually benefit from hearing the lesson? It seems to me that you wasted your time, for when was the last time that princes and barons invited *you* to a meal?"

In *Tehillim* (147:19-20), said the Dubno Maggid, it states, "He relates His Word to Jacob, His statutes and judgments to Israel. He did not do so for any other nation; such judgments — they know them not..." How we must thank Hashem for giving us the Torah of truth and its upright laws and ordinances! Other nations, however, were not given the Torah. For what purpose would they study its statutes?

✿§ Extending a Greeting

A businessman's dealings forced him to travel to a distant land. He spent quite some time there, but in his heart he constantly yearned to be reunited with the family that he missed so dearly.

Whenever he encountered a fellow traveler, he immediately asked him if he had perhaps passed through his hometown and had brought with him greetings from his family.

One day, a pauper visited the land in hopes of collecting alms. When the businessman spotted him, he recognized him at once — this pauper was from his hometown! Elated, he ran over to him and asked him for an extensive report about his family's well-being. The pauper, however, was not very accommodating and brushed him aside. "I have come here to collect money, and I have no time for meaningless conversations..."

"How much money do you intend to collect?" asked the businessman.

"I wish to collect three *zehuvim*!" was his reply.

"If so," said the businessman, "I will give you three *zehuvim* on condition that you sit and talk with me."

The pauper happily agreed and sat with the businessman in his home. But as they began to speak, the pauper dozed off and drifted into a deep slumber.

Furious, the businessman shook the pauper until he woke up. He then exclaimed harshly, "Did I pay you three *zehuvim* for you to fall sleep in my house? If you'd like to sleep, return my money and go from door to door collecting alms!"

So, too, said the Dubno Maggid, in relation to man's livelihood. All week long, man is busy trying to earn a livelihood for himself and his family, and he is unable to dedicate a sufficient amount of time to Divine service. Hashem therefore gave man Shabbos, the day of rest, in order that he should be free to serve Him without any distractions.

How disappointing it is when instead of spending the day studying Torah, man squanders the day with sleep and other meaningless activities!

◆§ Uninvited Guests

A wealthy man celebrated a *simchah* (festive occasion) to which he invited many friends and guests to his home. He heaped the tables with a profusion of delicacies, and he even hired a band to play joyous melodies. When the inhabitants of the city heard the sounds of celebration and the music emanating from the house, they wasted little time and made their way towards the man's home. Upon seeing the tables overflowing with scrumptious food, they were unable to resist and grabbed whatever they could.

The news that the wealthy man was having a *simchah* spread like wildfire, and it was not long before all the beggars of the city had flocked to his home. It came to the point where there was no longer any room left for the invited guests. The wealthy man, therefore, made an announcement requesting all those who were not invited to leave and make room for those who were.

Man, said the Dubno Maggid, was created with many senses and abilities so that he will be able to serve Hashem with perfection and cling to Him and His *mitzvos*. The problem is that man wastes these abilities in his youth pursuing the trivial pleasures of this world. Ultimately, it comes to the point where all of his talents are devoted towards these insignificant pursuits, with none remaining to facilitate his achievement of the true purpose for which he was created.

He is therefore left with no choice but to ask the "uninvited guests" to leave!

✒ According to the Exertion Is the Reward

An amazing parable is cited in the book *Sichos Chullin shel Talmidei Chachamim:*

A king wished to build a magnificent palace for himself, the likes of which had never before been seen. The king's officers therefore hired a world-renowned architect who was known to be an expert in his field.

The architect was brought before the king and, shortly thereafter, presented him an extraordinary blueprint for a palace that would be both enormous and awe-inspiring.

The blueprint found favor in the eyes of the king, and he gave orders to commence construction at once. He had but one request to make of the architect, however: He desired that the palace be completed on the anniversary of his ascension to the throne. He would then stage a gala celebration, during which the new palace would be dedicated.

The builders expended much effort and, indeed, a glorious new palace, whose beauty was unmatched by any other edifice, stood completed one month before the designated time.

In order to paint the palace walls, the king hired four expert painters. Each one was assigned one wall and was instructed to paint it with vibrant and cheerful colors.

Three out of the four painters began working immediately. They mixed colors together and decorated the walls with an array of patterns. One of the painters, however, sat idly by and did not begin painting.

"Why have you not begun working?" asked one of the painters. "If you do not start now, you will be unable to finish in time!"

"Don't worry," responded the painter. "I will have plenty of time to finish."

Nearly one month later, the three painters had produced walls of sheer beauty; a fantastic kaleidoscope of colors blended harmoniously into matching patterns that were amazing to behold. The fourth wall, however, stood embarrassingly empty of any color or magnificence whatsoever.

One day before the king's anniversary, the painter went to the palace and hung large mirrors on the fourth wall that reflected the other three walls. Now the fourth wall appeared to be painted as well, and it looked quite splendid.

When the king entered the palace and beheld its sheer beauty, he was ecstatic. Wishing to show his appreciation for his workers' efforts, the king ordered his servants to bring in three bags filled with gold coins and jewelry.

He then instructed them to hang the bags on the three painted walls.

"Here you go," said the king to the painters. "Your reward is hanging on the wall that you painted."

"But what about my reward?" asked the clever fourth painter.

"Your reward," answered the king, "is reflected in the mirror that you hung on the wall…"

> The lesson that this parable imparts to us is clear — the reward is in proportion to the exertion (*Pirkei Avos* 5:26)!

◆§ The Chief Cupbearer

It is customary for kings to have a plethora of servants at their disposal, befitting men of their royal stature. One king had a large staff of servants, among whom was a chief cupbearer, whose job it was to constantly stand before the king and pour him a quality beverage whenever he so desired.

As he served the king on a regular basis and stood before him continuously, he became quite familiar with the king and did not feel the slightest bit of fear in his presence. Rather, he stood before him like one stands before his friend.

When the king realized this, he commanded the chief cupbearer to serve him while fasting! "You are not to eat or drink anything the entire day," commanded the king. "Only when evening falls and you have been dismissed from your post will you be allowed to eat and drink!"

"What is the explanation for this decree?" asked those closest to the king.

"This officer," explained the king, "has a very easy job, yet earns a vast reward like one of my elite servants.

"However," he continued, "why do the elite servants deserve such a great reward in the first place? The answer is as follows: When they serve me, they stand before me in utter dread and fear; in return, I grant them a substantial reward. But the chief cupbearer feels no fear whatsoever! Why then should he be rewarded so generously? I therefore commanded him to serve me while fasting and in a weak state; if he nevertheless serves me adequately, it shows that he is deserving of his reward!"

So, too, noted the Dubno Maggid, in relation to one's Divine service. When an individual serves Hashem with Heavenly fear, it is an indication that his Divine service is exemplary, making him fitting to receive a great reward. However, one who serves Hashem lackadaisically and performs *mitzvos* by rote without any fear or dread whatsoever — why should he receive a full reward? Hashem therefore commanded the nations of the world to relentlessly oppress the Jews; when the Jews serve Hashem with Heavenly fear despite their hardships, it shows that they are truly deserving of a full reward!

◄§ Therefore He Gave Them Torah and Mitzvos in Abundance

A young man, the son of a wealthy merchant, decided that the time had come for him to enter the business world as well. His father gave him a generous sum of money, and he traveled to the big city, lodging in an inn that was located in the center of town.

He then made his way to the home of a relative who resided in the city. The young man explained how he had journeyed there in order to purchase merchandise with hopes of reselling it. He therefore asked his relative to assist him, as he was completely unfamiliar with the city.

The relative hastened to inform the many merchants that he knew that a rich young man had arrived in the city and wished to purchase merchandise.

The merchants wasted little time; they made their way to the inn and knocked on the young man's door. When he opened the door, he was presented with a grand display of goods from which he bought whatever he could.

When the young man realized that he had only enough money remaining to cover his traveling expenses, he decided that it was time to return home. He therefore went to bid his relative farewell. "Did you have a pleasant stay in the city?" asked the relative.

"Truthfully," answered the young man, "I did not have so much as a free second to enjoy myself. From the day that I arrived here until now, I have been engaged in business with the merchants and peddlers. I did not have any time to see the city."

"You should know, my dear relative," he replied, "that it was I who caused you to be as busy as you were. I did so, however, because of my concern for you and your money. I know you quite well," continued the relative, "and I am well aware that had you begun to stroll about the city streets, it would not be long before you had spent all your money on meaningless items and souvenirs. I therefore made sure that the merchants would not allow you to rest for even a moment...This way, you were able to conduct business, which was your intention in the first place."

> Hashem, said the Dubno Maggid, sent man to this world in order for him to learn Torah and perform *mitzvos*. The *yetzer hara*, however, tries day after day to lead him astray and distract him. It attempts to entice man into wasting his time with deceitful vanities and trivialities.
>
> This is the reason why Hashem gave man such an abundance of *mitzvos*; before he has completed the performance of one *mitzvah*, it is already time to perform another.
>
> This is as *Chazal* have stated in *Makkos* (3:16), "R' Chananiah ben Akashia says: The Holy One, Blessed is He, wished to confer merit upon Israel; therefore He gave them Torah and *mitzvos* in abundance, as it is said (*Yeshayahu* 42:21): 'Hashem desired, for the sake of its [Israel's] righteousness, that the Torah be made great and glorious.'"

᥍§ Make an Accounting

In a certain city lived a prominent wholesaler who would routinely purchase vast amounts of various items for thousands of *zehuvim*. He was not a proficient mathematician, however, and was therefore oblivious as to whether he was earning a profit or incurring a loss.

One day, he got word that a friend of his — a successful merchant like himself — had lost all of his wealth and was now a destitute pauper who was forced to flee from his creditors.

The merchant let out a deep sigh. "Woe is me," he said. "I deal in the exact same area of business as my friend did, and if he underwent such a devastating collapse, who knows what will be with me..."

> It is human nature, said the Dubno Maggid, for a person to judge himself favorably and to turn a blind eye to any faults that he might hate. It appears to him that all of his deeds are pleasant and flawless.

However, when he looks at the righteous of the land, he begins to grasp his own meager stature.

✑ Concentrating on One's Work

Workers who repair and seal cracks in building facades normally lower themselves down from the roof by way of a rope which is securely fastened around their bodies. Despite the fact that they are suspended in midair, they nevertheless go about their labor fearlessly, not concerned in the slightest that they might fall. Rather, they place their trust in the strong rope that is fixed firmly around them and they concentrate fully on the work at hand.

> This should also be the way of a servant of Hashem, said the Dubno Maggid. He must trust that Hashem will protect him from all harm, which will enable him to devote his full concentration to serving Him. This is implied by the *pasuk* "Trust in Hashem and do good" (*Tehillim* 37:3).

✑ Advancements

When a young child begins to learn the *alef-beis*, we are able to notice significant day-to-day advancements. At first, it is quite difficult for him to even read letters, yet in a short while he is able to read simple syllables. This is not the case, however, when the child grows up and becomes knowledgeable in the Talmud and its commentaries; at that point, the progress is not quite as readily obvious as before.

Someone with a superficial perspective will claim that the young child is advancing at a far quicker pace than the young man — but anyone possessing understanding will discard such a claim.

So, too, in relation to Divine Service, said R' Yisrael Ba'al Shem Tov. There are times when a person does not see how he is growing in his Divine service. He must know, however, that the small amount that he has achieved today is far more valuable than whatever he achieved in his youth.

∽§ The Great Fair

An annual fair took place in a big city, and it drew the participation of merchants from all across the land. The atmosphere was absolutely tumultuous, with merchants buying, selling, trading, and renting all at once.

On more than one occasion a merchant incurred great expenses traveling to the fair, in hopes of reaping great profits.

One day, a man approached a merchant who had traveled to the fair and asked him a question: "Please explain something to me," he said. "You are not certain that you will be able to sell your merchandise. That being the case, why did you spend such an exorbitant amount of money traveling to the fair? You would have been better off simply sitting idly by in your home; at least you would have saved yourself a significant sum of money."

"From your words," replied the merchant, "it is clear that you do not know the first thing about business. It is true that I spent a lot of money in order to come here, but with Hashem's help, I will be able to earn profits that far exceed my traveling expenses. This is the way business works…However, if I would have stayed home, true, I would have saved myself the traveling costs, but I could not have hoped to earn even the slightest amount of profit."

This world, said R' Yaakov Yosef of Ostraha, is compared to a fair. Every man has material needs and must therefore eat and sleep in order to have strength to serve Hashem. However, he hopes to fulfill many *mitzvos* as well, in order that his profits will exceed his expenditure. But an individual who spends all of his time in pursuit of materialism will not reap any profits whatsoever, and what will he bring back "home"?

~§ Hashem Wants a Man's Heart

A king sent his son to a distant land so that he would receive tutelage from its elders and wise men. After several years of study, the son returned to the palace replete with worldly wisdom.

The king wished to test his son's newfound knowledge. He therefore presented him with an enormously heavy rock and instructed him to carry it up to the roof of the palace. There was one condition, however: he was to carry it all on his own, without receiving the slightest assistance.

"But father," wondered the son, "even ten men would not have the strength necessary to lift such a huge rock! How, then, can I be expected to carry this rock to the roof all by myself?"

"Is this why I sent you away to study wisdom?" asked the father. "After all that you have learned, do you still not know how to lift this rock?"

The son was not ashamed to admit that he had absolutely no idea.

"It's actually very simple," said the king. "All you have to do is take a hammer and smash the rock into little pieces..."

> Hashem, said R' Nachman of Breslov, wants man to serve Him wholeheartedly, with holiness and purity. The problem is that our hearts are made of stone...Man has but one choice: He must take a hammer — i.e., the Torah and good deeds — and smash his stone heart! "Like a hammer that smashes a rock..." (Yirmiyahu 23:29).

~§ Toil and You Will Be Rewarded

A doctor informed a sick individual that the key to restoring his health, lay in perspiring. The man therefore joined a group of construction workers and began to labor alongside them. He dragged stones, lugged heavy pieces of wood, and carried many heavy bundles upon his shoulders. Through the numerous arduous tasks he performed, he managed to work up quite a sweat.

When evening had fallen and the workers lined up before their employer to receive their wages, the ill man stood with them. But while the employer paid all the other workers for their day's labor, he refused to pay the ill man.

"You already received your reward," said the employer, "when you sweated as the doctor instructed you to. You will have to be satisfied with that. The other workers gained nothing from their sweat, and are therefore entitled to their wages..."

> The righteous, said the *Ben Ish Chai,* R' Yosef Chaim of Baghdad, toil in their Torah study and performance of *mitzvos* solely for the sake of Heaven. Their reward is incurred through the toil itself, as it purges them of the pollutants that contaminate their souls, thereby purifying and uplifting their Divine service. This is not the case with those who do not fulfill *mitzvos* for the sake of Heaven. For even though they may be toiling as well, they are not rewarded for it, as it does not serve to purify them.

◆§ A Gift for the King

A man took ten *kavin* (a Biblical measure) of excellent grapes, placed them into an expensive vessel, and presented them to the king as a gift. The vessel, however, was not full and could have held additional grapes. The king thanked the man for his gift and instructed his servants to remunerate him by presenting him with silver that was equal to the value of the grapes that he had brought.

Then there was another individual who brought the king a small but attractive vessel containing only six *kavin* of grapes. The vessel, however, was filled to the brim and could not hold even one more grape.

The king thanked the man for his generosity and, this time, commanded his servants to present him with a gift of one hundred *zehuvim*!

"Your Highness," asked one of his servants, "the first man brought you ten *kavin* of grapes yet only received their market value in return. Yet this man brought you a mere six *kavin* of grapes and, nevertheless, merited receiving a gift of one hundred *zehuvim*!"

"The first man," responded the king, "may very well have brought a sizeable portion of grapes, but he did not show me the proper degree of respect. By not bringing me a full vessel, he demonstrated that in his eyes I am worth no more than ten *kavin* of grapes. The second man, on the other hand, filled the vessel completely, and would have added more grapes if he could have. If he had a larger vessel, he would have undoubtedly filled that one as well. This was an appropriate display of respect and I rewarded him accordingly."

> It is incumbent upon man, said R' Yosef Chaim of Baghdad, to serve Hashem with all his strength and to be as meticulous in his performance of *mitzvos* as he possibly can be. This demonstrates that he is acting for the honor of Hashem, and it is Divine service of this nature that He deems most desirable!

Part 6

This World
and the
World to Come

❧ This World Is Like a Vestibule

Chazal have stated in *Avos* (4:21), "This world is like a vestibule before the World to Come; prepare yourself in the vestibule so that you may enter the banquet hall."

Man must prepare himself in this world by amassing *mitzvos* and good deeds in order to be worthy of entering the great banquet hall — the World to Come.

The Chofetz Chaim illustrated this concept with a parable:

There was a wealthy man who wished to build himself a lovely new home. He therefore hired an architect in order to plan the construction.

"Listen carefully," said the wealthy man to the architect. "It is of primary importance to me that the living room be large and comfortable, yet I would also like the foyer which leads to the living room to be spacious as well."

The architect measured the plot of land on which the wealthy man wished to build his home. After making various calculations, he said to him, "You should be aware that there is not a sufficient amount of space on which to build both a spacious living room and foyer. So please tell me which you would prefer — a large living room or a large foyer?

"I will give you a piece of advice," added the architect. "Most people are accustomed to building themselves a large living room and a small foyer. I'd suggest you do the same; after all, if you do the opposite, you will be the object of ridicule…"

During our stay in this world, said the Chofetz Chaim, we must be concerned about ensuring ourselves a large portion in the World to Come. How do we go about doing this? Through fulfilling the Torah and its *mitzvos*!

How foolish is the man who spends his entire life worrying about ensuring himself a pleasant and enjoyable life in *this* world. He is similar to the wealthy man who built himself a large foyer and a small living room. In the end, he will be the subject of ridicule!

ᴥᶘ The Dowry

The Chofetz Chaim gave the following parable to illustrate what the days of a man's life are like:

A wealthy man had an only son who was extremely pampered and fastidious. When the son reached marriageable age, the father married him to a girl who was just as spoiled as he was. He gave his son a sizeable dowry and provided all of his meals for him as well.

The son sat comfortably at his father's table and lacked nothing.

After several years, the father said to him, "My dear son, the time has come for you to support your family. There is a fair that is presently being held in the big city; take the dowry that I gave you and invest it in some quality merchandise."

Money in hand, the son traveled to the fair.

Walking from booth to booth, the son caught a glimpse of beautiful shiny vessels that appeared to be fashioned from genuine gold.

"How much do these gold vessels cost?" he asked the peddler.

The peddler quickly realized that he was dealing with a very naïve individual. A dishonest crook, he took full advantage of the opportunity to swindle him. "These vessels are indeed made from pure gold and they are therefore very expensive," he replied. "But since I am in dire need of cash, I will sell them to you for half price." He then quoted a ridiculously exorbitant sum.

Thinking that he had cut a great deal, the son agreed to the price and bought all the vessels at the booth. With the remainder of his money, he purchased forged bills of debt that a different charlatan conned him into buying.

Upon returning home, his father requested to see the merchandise he had bought. When he saw the vessels, he broke out into a fit of rage: "You fool!" he yelled. "Do you mean to tell me that you wasted most of your money on these vessels? These are ordinary wooden vessels that are painted gold!

"Show me what you bought with the rest of the money!" he demanded.

When the son displayed the phony contracts, the father's shouts made the first bout of rage pale in comparison. "What have you done, you good-for-nothing? You bought forged contracts! Not only are they worthless, but the king's guards may even arrest us for purchasing them."

We are the children of Hashem, said the Chofetz Chaim, and each one of us received a dowry from birth, consisting of a set number of years. We are required to utilize these years in order to fulfill the Torah and its *mitzvos*.

But what does man do? He acts like the foolish son and wastes his time on nonsensical things. While these things may appear to be genuine gold, in truth, they are no more than "ordinary wooden vessels." He wastes his precious time in this world on "forged contracts."

Will a father not inevitably rebuke such a son when he comes before him?

◢§ A Home to Return To

A certain peddler was accustomed to roaming from town to town and from city to city. He would purchase merchandise in one place and then travel to another place in order to sell it. In such a manner his days were spent, wandering from one place to the next.

On one occasion, his friends met up with him and noticed that he was wearing a most gloomy countenance. "What's the matter?" they asked him. "Why do you look so depressed?"

"My house was destroyed," he replied, "and I no longer have any place to return to. I will simply be forced to wander the roads…"

"If that is the case," they asked, "then why are you so upset? Didn't you always wander the roads in any case?"

"I certainly did," he responded. "However, I have always had the comfort of knowing that I had a home to return to where I could rest in tranquility if I so desired. But now, I am left with nothing, and I am forced to roam about…"

> This world, said the Chofetz Chaim, is but a vestibule leading to the World to Come. Each and every individual traverses this vestibule, but the righteous await the day when they will complete their "business" and will be able to return to their true home — the World to Come. The wicked, on the other hand, have no home to which they will ultimately return and must simply wander about.

❧ A Place of Honor

Chazal state in Sanhedrin (90a), "All Israel has a share in the World to Come!"

Chazal's statement presents us with an apparent difficulty, noted the Chofetz Chaim. For we are taught in Megillah (28b), "He who studies Torah laws each day, has the assurance that he will be in the World to Come." If all of Israel is guaranteed a portion in the World to Come, how are we to understand Chazal's statement that it is specifically those individuals who learn Torah laws who will be admitted into the World to Come?

The answer, said the Chofetz Chaim, can be explained according to the following parable: There was a wealthy man who arranged a wedding for his son. He sent a messenger to the *rav* of the city, with instructions to extend the *rav* a personal invitation. When he arrived at the wedding, the father went out to greet him and respectfully escorted him to the head table, where he was served the choicest food and beverage.

A pauper who also resided in the city heard about the magnificent wedding that was taking place, and he rushed to the hall as well. He pushed and shoved and managed to make his way into the hall, but when he arrived, no one came out to welcome him, as had been the case with the *rav*, and it goes without saying that he was not invited to sit down. He simply sat in a corner and helped himself to some of the leftover food...

It is true, explained the Chofetz Chaim, "All Israel has a share in the World to Come." But someone who learns Torah laws every day will be considered one of the distinguished guests in the Next World and will be granted a most honorable place indeed, befitting one who has toiled and exerted himself in the study of Torah.

ᴥᔞ The Days of Our Years

The Torah states, "You shall count for yourself seven cycles of sabbatical years, seven years seven times; the years of the seven cycles of sabbatical years shall be for you forty-nine years" (*Vayikra* 25:8).

Why, asked the Dubno Maggid, did the Torah elaborate by enumerating the number of years that comprise the seven cycles of sabbatical years? It would have been sufficient to simply write, "You shall count for yourself seven cycles of sabbatical years."

The Maggid offered a parable to explain:

This can be compared to a poor man who had spent his entire life going from door to door collecting charity. On one occasion, he was boasting to his friends about the large amount of money he had managed to amass.

"Why are you boasting?" asked one of his friends. "All these years, you have gone from one home to another and have grown accustomed to counting each *perutah* you receive. While you may have collected many *perutos*, if you were to exchange them for gold *dinarim*, you would see that there is only a small sum of money in your hand."

> So it is with man, concluded the Maggid. Man believes that he has a long life ahead of him, because he calculates his life span according to months and years; he will spend seventy years in this world, he tells himself, maybe even eighty. Thinking in such a manner leads one to believe that he is actually in control of his life and his home.
>
> But if a person reflects on how many *shemitos* he has to live and, all the more so, how many *yovlos* (cycles of fifty years), he will immediately arrive at the stark realization that he is but a mere sojourner in this world, here but for a limited duration.

৵৳ The Prize

A king's son was once walking along the way, when he reached a fork in the road. Suddenly, a band of thieves attacked him, intent on murdering him. Much to his good fortune, however, a pauper dressed in rags happened to be walking along the road at that very moment. When he saw the thieves, he gathered up his courage and in a display of great strength, vanquished them and saved the king's son.

Upon hearing of the pauper's heroics, the king had him summoned before him. When the pauper arrived, the king thanked him and exclaimed, "As a reward for having saved my son, I hereby permit you to spend an entire day in the royal treasury; you may take anything that your heart desires."

When the gates of the royal treasury were opened for the pauper, he joyously fell upon the massive piles of gold and diamonds, and began to gather all that he could.

When evening settled in and the pauper exited the royal treasury, he had undergone a complete transformation. In one day, he had gone from being a destitute pauper to an extraordinarily wealthy man. The next day, this former pauper went into business, and in a short while he became eminently successful. He had now become one of the wealthiest men in the land, and he completely forgot about his former life of poverty and deprivation.

Every year, the former pauper staged a lavish feast on the day that he had been blessed with the good fortune of entering the royal treasury. He invited all of his friends and relatives to the feast, and it was a custom that lasted for many years.

One year in the middle of the feast, the wealthy man turned to his friends and asked, "Which day of my life do you think was the happiest of all for me?"

"It must be this very day," responded the guests. "This day on which you have made a feast for all of your friends must be the happiest day of your life! After all, on this day your palace is decorated, your servants surround you, and all of the distinguished individuals in the land accord you great honor!"

"You are mistaken," said the wealthy man. "While this day is certainly one of great joy, it is but a remembrance of the day on which I was remade, literally transformed from a lowly beggar in ragged clothing to a man possessing enormous wealth. *That* day was the happiest of my life.

"I spent that entire day," he continued, "inside the royal treasury. I felt neither hunger nor weariness; rather, it was as if my complete being was focused on only one goal — amassing the valuables that lay inside the treasury. The more valuables I amassed, the more joy I reaped. I have yet to experience a happier day than that one."

> So it is with us, said the Chofetz Chaim. Hashem grants a person life as a gift. Throughout his life, man has the ability to amass as many *mitzvos* and good deeds as his heart desires.

An individual who is able to view the world with this perspective is truly the most praiseworthy of men. The only thing that prevents us from gaining such a perspective is our heart which has been dulled by the trivialities of this world…

At the end of days, when Hashem will remove the "foreskin" that prevents our hearts from gaining true understanding, we will finally be able to recognize and rejoice over the great value of life that Hashem has given us. Similarly, we will delight in the limited merit that we have been granted — to study Torah and amass scores of *mitzvos*.

◄§ The Fair

A large fair was being held in a port city, and scores of merchants from all over the world were in attendance. The merchants spent many days readying themselves for the fair, preparing both merchandise as well as contracts. When they arrived, they made their way to different booths and began to engage in business, with this one buying, this one selling, and yet others trading — in the manner that fairs have always been held.

At the conclusion of the fair, a group of merchants set out for home. On the way, they discussed how each one of them had fared. Some had earned vast profits, while others had earned less; there were those who succeeded in selling all of their merchandise, while others were left with most of the goods they had initially brought.

Suddenly, they noticed one of the merchants sitting on the side and not participating in the conversation. "And what about you, *Reb Yid*?" asked the merchants. "Do you have nothing to report about the fair?"

"I really don't," responded the merchant. "I'm returning home with all of the merchandise that I brought with me — I did not attempt to sell a single item."

"You silly Jew!" jeered the merchants. "Why, you expended so much effort in packing up and transporting merchandise to sell at the fair, and when you got there you didn't even *attempt* to sell anything?"

When the heckling had died down, the merchant gave a detailed explanation as to why he had been idle at the fair. The other merchants understood and left him in peace.

Although the merchants were no longer jeering him and he had many reasons to justify his behavior, he was nevertheless left a destitute pauper...

> This world is compared to a great fair, remarked the Chofetz Chaim, where it is possible to purchase a wide variety of "merchandise," in a variety of quantities. There are those who engage in the study of Torah and the performance of *mitzvos*, and in the World to Come they will be able to exult on account of the goods that they have acquired. Then there are those who come to the "fair" but simply waste their time. Even if they will be able to offer valid excuses as to why they acted as they did, they will nevertheless remain totally devoid of any possessions!

⇜ Two Merchants

A story is related about two merchants from the same city that traveled to the fair. The first saved up a pittance of money over the course of the year and used it to purchase a small amount of merchandise. However, the second borrowed large sums of money from all of his friends and bought a massive quantity of merchandise.

Returning home from the fair, the first merchant decided to lodge at an inn on the crossroads for the night. He therefore tied his donkey to the trough, placed some hay before it, and climbed into his bed.

A short while later, the thunderous sound of galloping horses and rolling coach wheels could be heard approaching to the inn.

The innkeeper woke up the merchant and said, "Get up quickly and take your donkey away from the trough! A distinguished merchant leading a caravan of servants is approaching the inn. Please hurry and leave at once!"

The merchant rose from his bed in order to see who was riding towards the inn. He took one look and realized that it was the merchant from his city who was infamous for being heavily in debt.

He considered it obscene to have to leave on account of this individual, but he nevertheless kept quiet and abided by the will of the innkeeper.

Some time passed, and the merchant's debtors eventually came to collect their money. Unable to pay them, he was hurled into jail.

His friends gathered together and discussed how they could help him out of his bitter predicament. They decided to go from door to door and request donations, hoping that individuals would be generous enough to contribute to the cause.

Making their way around the city, they arrived at the house of the first merchant. Their story jogged his memory and he instantly recalled all that had transpired with the merchant previously. He then thanked Hashem that he himself had been content with what he had and that he had not coveted wealth and material goods.

> Man, said the Dubno Maggid, is the most exalted of all the world's creatures, and he therefore feels pride in his lofty status. However, when the time comes for him to stand in judgment before the Heavenly Tribunal, he will be required to give an accounting of all his deeds and demonstrate how he utilized that elevated standing…

◆§ Owner of the Tavern

A father wished to provide his son with an ample source of livelihood. He decided to buy him a tavern, as well as large barrels of wine and beer, which he placed in the tavern's cellar.

"My dear son," said the father. "You are permitted to allow anyone who wishes to drink in your tavern. I have but one warning for you: You may have first-rate wine in your possession, but you are not to sip even the slightest amount.

"Believe me," continued the father, "I am speaking in your best interests — leave the drinking to the drunkards of the town!"

> So it is with this world, said the Dubno Maggid. Hashem created the delights and pleasures of this world, and it is all intended to benefit the Jewish Nation. Hashem, however, imparts wise counsel to us: "Do not waste your time with meaningless pleasures... 'You shall be to me a kingdom of ministers and a holy nation!'" (*Shemos* 19:6)

ᴥᲛ King for a Year

R' David HaNaggid drew a beautiful parable which is printed in the *sefer Midrash David*:

The inhabitants of a certain land had a custom: Every year they would go out to the main road which led to their country, and when they spotted a stranger approaching, they would crown him as their king. This newly appointed king would then decide all the matters of the land.

At the year's end, they would remove him from his throne and expel him from the country. Stripped of his royalty, he would leave just as he had come. The people would then go out to the main road once again and find themselves a brand new king. This scenario repeated itself year after year.

On one occasion, a pauper happened to be treading the main road. While he lacked money, he possessed great wisdom and an amazing breadth of knowledge. Suddenly, he saw a massive parade, joyful and exuberant, heading his way. Before he even had a moment to grasp the cause behind the excitement, he was adorned in regal garments and a royal crown was placed upon his head. He was brought directly to the royal palace in the capital city, where he was inaugurated for the coming year with an elaborate ceremony.

Thinking about the strange events that had taken place, the king summoned one of his ministers, who offered him a detailed explanation of the land's custom.

"Amazing," thought the king. "It seems that after a year, I will once again be a destitute pauper. How interesting..."

What did he do? Over the course of the year, the king dispatched to his old home as much money, jewelry, merchandise, and items of great worth, as he was able to.

When the year drew to a close, the people entered his room and brought him his old pauper's clothing. They then expelled him from the country with a warning never to return.

The man returned home where the massive treasure which he had so exerted himself to amass was awaiting him. From that treasure the man was able to support himself and his family, providing them with a life of wealth and luxury for years to come.

> Man, said R' David *HaNaggid*, comes to this world for but a limited length of time. There are times when he is totally immersed in the pleasures and trivialities of this world and does not pay heed to the time that is quickly passing. Eventually, his years pass by and he arrives in the World to Come emptyhanded, having nothing to show for his stay in this world.
>
> This is not the case, however, with the wise man who possesses a great deal of foresight. In this world, he toils in order to send ahead a treasure of *mitzvos* and good deeds, which will stand in his merit on the day of accounting.
>
> Praiseworthy is he and praiseworthy is his portion!

✎§ *Army Personnel*

The soldiers and personnel in the king's army are fully provided for by the king's treasury. Without any exceptions, each one of them receives matching uniforms, eats the same simple food, and sleeps on the army's mattresses.

The way to discern between the soldiers is by viewing them after they have been dismissed from their military service and they return home. The wealthier among them remove their army uniforms and don the fine garments that are waiting for them. They help themselves to scrumptious food, and the bedding and blankets in their homes are fashioned from fabrics of the highest quality that are pleasant to the touch.

The poor soldiers, on the other hand, are depressed upon concluding their military careers. For in the army they were provided with both clothing and food, while in their homes they must make do with no more than shabby clothing adorned by one patch on top of another. There is not much food to speak of either, with little more to eat than stale bread and water. The comfortable sleeping conditions that they were accustomed to in the king's service seem like a distant dream when compared to the tattered straw mattresses that lies upon the cold floor at home.

> In this world, said the Dubno Maggid, we are all mixed together and it is difficult to differentiate between one individual and another. In the future, however, when each and every individual will stand trial before the Heavenly Tribunal, the great distinction between a lofty *tzaddik* and an *am ha'aretz* will be revealed to all. For the *tzaddik*, the gates of *Gan Eden* will be opened wide, and an eternal reward will be waiting for him on account of the good deeds and *mitzvos* that he was wise enough to fulfill in this world. But for a person who chose not to study Torah and to instead remain an *am ha'aretz*, may Hashem have mercy…

Part 7

Humility

"You Shall Remember that You Were a Slave in the Land of Egypt"

The requirement to recall "that you were a slave in Egypt" enables an individual to avoid feelings of haughtiness. To what can this be compared? The *Sha'agas Aryeh,* R' Aryeh Leib of Metz, drew the following parable:

There was a king who set out on a hunting trip. As he was exploring the fields in the hope of finding game, he happened upon a shepherd who was sitting next to his flock of sheep and playing a flute.

The king was enchanted by the pleasant tunes that were emanating from the flute, and he found himself unable to move from his place. After a certain amount of time, the shepherd concluded his melody. The king approached the shepherd and engaged him in conversation, only to discover that he boasted a razor-sharp intellect and possessed great wisdom as well.

The king was amazed by the shepherd's profundity of thought, and he invited him to reside in his palace. The shepherd agreed and went with the king.

From then on, the shepherd lived in the royal palace, and the king sought his counsel regarding all matters. In time, the shepherd rose to become one of the king's highest-ranking ministers.

The other ministers were filled with envy towards this newly appointed minister who was so beloved by the king. They decided to slander him, informing the king that his trusted minister had stolen from the royal treasury.

The king summoned the shepherd for an interrogation, but he managed to convince all those who were present that he was an honest and upright individual. However, the jealous ministers still managed to persuade the king to conduct a search of the shepherd's quarters, in hopes of finding some evidence of theft.

They all went together to search the shepherd's quarters, but found nothing more than a modestly furnished home, lacking any luxuriousness whatsoever. They went from room to room finding nothing suspicious, until they came to a room that was sealed by both lock and bolt.

"What is inside this room?" asked the king.

The shepherd fell to his knees and began to plead with the king. "Your Highness, I beg of you, do not ask me to show you what lies beyond this door! I am embarrassed by what you will find there."

The shepherd's pleas only served to strengthen the king's suspicions, and he demanded that the door be opened.

When the door was opened, they glanced around the room but saw nothing more than the old clothing of a shepherd and a flute.

The king and his officers were bewildered.

"Your Highness," explained the former shepherd. "from the day that I came to your palace, I have not grown the least bit haughty or conceited over the prominence that I have achieved. This is due to my daily visits to this room, when I sit here and play my flute, recalling my days as a simple shepherd."

> So, too, with a Jew, concluded R' Aryeh Leib. Remembering "that you were a slave in Egypt" will prevent a Jew from becoming arrogant. For whenever he feels himself swelling with pride, he will recall his days as a lowly slave in Egypt and the haughtiness will thus be banished from his heart.

⊷§ The True Owner of the House

A man arrived in a big city and began to meander about its streets. Along the way, he came to a street of the most magnificent homes he had ever seen. One of the homes particularly impressed him with its beauty, and he therefore decided to enter and get a glimpse of its interior.

The man knocked on the heavy oak door. When it was opened, he was greeted by the sight of a genuine palace. Expensive rugs lined the floor, crystal chandeliers hung from the ceiling, and elegant furniture adorned each room.

The servant received him dressed in a lavish white uniform with gold buttons.

"Who is the owner of this beautiful home?" inquired the visitor.

The servant arrogantly stuck out his chest and responded, "It is my house! Look around — everything that you see is mine! I am the owner of this house!"

The door suddenly swung open and in walked the true homeowner. He had overheard his servant's lies and was decidedly livid.

Humiliated, the servant hurried from the room.

> When a person is haughty, said the Dubno Maggid, it is an indication that he has forgotten that Hashem is the true Master of the world!

✑§ Where Is the Fault?

A wealthy man had a beautiful daughter who had come of age. He therefore sought a groom who would befit his lofty standing as well as his daughter's.

Matchmakers from all corners of the land knocked on his door and presented various candidates, mentioning prominent young men who hailed from affluent homes. However, the wealthy man rejected them all, inevitably unearthing a minor flaw of some kind.

One day a matchmaker approached the father and presented a young man who was a Torah scholar and one of the finest yeshivah students in the land. Additionally, he was the son of a wealthy man who had strong ties to the king.

The matchmaker lauded the young man with an excessive amount of praise, spending a long time enumerating to the father all of his positive attributes and intellectual capabilities to the father.

"What shall I do?" thought the wealthy man. "It sounds like a good match, but I have not yet laid eyes on the young man. Maybe he is physically unappealing?

"On the other hand," he thought, "it would be improper to ask the young man and his father to come to me in order that I should be able to see him. For if I am unsatisfied, they will have gone to so much bother for no purpose at all...

"Listen here," said the wealthy man to the matchmaker. "Your offer sounds like a good one, but I would first like to find out if my daughter will find favor in the eyes of the young man. For who knows? — maybe he will find something unseemly with her. I would therefore like you to request from him to come and see her. Then we will be able to make the necessary further arrangements and ultimately wed the young couple..."

> Humility demands, said the Dubno Maggid, that one not seek out the faults in others; rather, let him try to find his own imperfections...

❧ A Watch for a Gift

A rich father wanted to persuade his son to accompany him to the great fair in Leipzig, but the son adamantly refused and would not agree to join him. The father then made his son an offer: If he would be willing to accompany him, he would buy him an expensive watch as a gift. The son agreed and they were on their way.

When they stopped to lodge at an inn, they encountered a poor peddler who offered to sell the father a very expensive watch at half price.

"This watch," said the peddler, "is worth one thousand *zehuvim*! Yet I will sell it to you for only five hundred *zehuvim*."

Despite the attractive offer, the father declined and did not purchase the watch.

"My dear father," said the son. "It appears as if you do not actually intend to buy a watch at all. For if you are willing to reject an offer at half price, what will happen when we arrive at the fair? There the merchants will demand the full cost of the watch, and you will certainly be reluctant to purchase it!"

"No, my dear son," responded the father. "This poor peddler knows absolutely nothing about watches, and he was under the impression that the ordinary watch which he was selling was worth one thousand *zehuvim*! He may have wanted to sell it to me for five hundred *zehuvim*, but it was not worth even that much. Just wait and see; when we arrive at the fair, we will make our way to an expert watchmaker. He will sell us a watch of outstanding quality for one hundred *zehuvim*, and even if he wants to earn a hefty profit, it will not be more than one hundred and fifty *zehuvim*..."

> *Chazal*, noted the Dubno Maggid, teach us in *Avos* (2:6), "An unlearned person cannot be scrupulously pious." This is due to the fact that an unlearned individual has no comprehension of the true value of Divine service. He therefore believes that his service of Hashem has already reached the level of Moshe Rabbeinu's — and if he is truly humble, the level of the later prophets.
>
> This is not the case with a Torah scholar who recognizes his own lowliness and is fully aware of the spiritual level that he has attained.

✑ The King's Sons

A king had two sons; one was extremely haughty, constantly gloating and full of conceit. The other was exceptionally humble, modest, and congenial.

One day, the king decided to send his sons to different lands in order to see if they would be able to annex them to his kingdom.

The arrogant son arrived at the land to which his father had sent him, and he began to stride about.

When the people of the land saw the king's conceited son and ascertained what type of person he was, they immediately grasped his intentions and drove him out of their country in disgrace.

On the other hand, when the second son arrived in the land to which he was sent, he quickly won the heart of its inhabitants with his pleasant demeanor, and it was not long before they asked him to rule over them.

> A haughty individual, said R' Yisrael Ba'al Shem Tov, is quickly recognized for what he is and is able to rule for only a short while. But a person who possesses the quality of humility — even if he may not be noticed immediately — is soon noted for his pleasant nature, and is willingly accepted as a ruler.

⮜ੳ Perfect Character Traits

In a certain city resided a wise Torah scholar who also happened to be quite wealthy. Despite all of his positive traits, he was, unfortunately, exceedingly arrogant.

This flaw in his personality distressed his close friends. "It is such a pity," they told him. "If you were humble, you would be a perfect individual!"

The man heeded his friends' advice and adapted the traits of humble individuals.

Shortly thereafter, a particular individual taunted him.

"Who do think you are insulting?" asked the wise man. "You should know that I possess every positive quality that it is possible for a human being to possess. Furthermore, I am extraordinarily humble, and there is no one who even approaches me in this area…"

> Any person who knows that he is humble, said R' Yisrael Ba'al Shem Tov, is comparable to the arrogant wise man.

❧ At the Mountain Peak

An individual took a lengthy journey in his wagon, and the bumpy ride caused him to doze off. As he slumbered, the wagon ascended a mountain; some time later, he suddenly awoke.

"Where are we?" he asked his driver.

"We are presently at the peak of a very high mountain," he answered.

"At the peak of a mountain?" asked the man in surprise. "You must be mistaken, for we were traveling on a level plane!"

But when the man realized that the wagon had begun to descend the slope, he understood that they had indeed been traveling on top of a mountain.

This parable demonstrates, said R' Yisrael Ba'al Shem Tov, that when an individual is not mindful of the path he is treading in life, he may believe that he is both humble and modest. In reality, however, he is scaling the mountain of arrogance without even realizing it. When he "awakens," however, and examines his deeds, he discovers — much to his surprise — that he was actually on a "mountain peak"...

❧ Who Is Great and Who Is Small

A group of merchants were on a ship with their merchandise. They sailed over oceans and rivers, as their voyage grew ever lengthier. One day, a dispute erupted between one of the wealthiest merchants on the boat and a merchant who was rather poor. Despite his poverty, he did not hesitate to respond to his wealthy opponent; quite the contrary, he gave him a thorough tongue-lashing.

"You have some nerve!" said the wealthy merchant. "How dare you answer back to me? Why, I am ten times greater and more distinguished than you are!"

"What gives you that idea?" responded the other merchant. "Is it because you have much more merchandise sitting in the belly of the ship than I do? If that is what makes you think that you are greater than me, you are sorely mistaken. For there are menacing pirates sailing these seas, and they could potentially seize control over the ship and steal all of the merchandise they find. In that case," continued the merchant, "while we are at sea, we are equals; when we return home — then we will see who is great and who is small…"

All the days of a man's life in this world, said the Dubno Maggid, are spent in great peril. He is like that ship in the heart of the sea, as the *yetzer hara* lies in ambush, waiting for a ripe opportunity to cause man to stumble.

Only when man reaches the World of Truth will it be revealed who is small and who is truly great.

Part 8

Tzedakah/ Charity

◈ The Yetzer Hara of the Rich and the Poor

A married man who studied in the Chofetz Chaim's yeshivah in Radin, an extremely diligent scholar, suffered from dire poverty. Every so often, he would turn to the Chofetz Chaim and complain about his predicament: "*Rebbi*," he would say, "if Hashem would shower me with wealth, I would give generously to *tzedakah*!" Shortly thereafter the man started a small business and was blessed with success. In a short time, he actually became an extraordinarily wealthy individual. Unfortunately, he forgot all about the promise that he had made to the Chofetz Chaim, and not only did he not give *tzedakah*, but he became a full-fledged miser as well.

Several years later, the Chofetz Chaim happened to visit the wealthy man's city, and his former student came out to welcome him.

"*Rebbi*," said the wealthy man, "I have been stricken with the trait of miserliness. It is as if my hand is sealed shut with both lock and bolt, and I am unable to give any *tzedakah* at all. What should I do?"

"I will tell you a parable," replied the Chofetz Chaim.

"A farmer from a village approached a storeowner and asked to purchase a ruble's worth of flour.

"'Go ahead and fill your sack with flour,' said the storeowner to the villager.

"When the farmer heard that he could take the flour on his own, he quickly rushed and got a large sack, which he then filled with flour. When the sack was filled to capacity, he went over to the storeowner and handed him a ruble.

"'My friend,' exclaimed the storeowner in surprise. 'You have filled up such an enormous sack with flour and yet you pay only me one ruble?'

"'That is correct,' responded the farmer. 'I requested a ruble's worth of flour, and you told me to fill up my sack.'

"'True,' replied the storeowner. 'But when I saw the huge sack that you brought, I figured that you had changed your mind and wished to buy a larger quantity of flour. As you placed more flour in your sack, the weights on the scale grew heavier and heavier...'

"What did you expect?" concluded the Chofetz Chaim. "Did you really think that you could amass hordes of wealth, and your *yetzer hara* — which persuades you to close your hand to the needy — would remain exactly as it was when you were poor?"

◈ *The Wealthy Miser*

Deriding the negative trait of miserliness, the Chofetz Chaim drew an amazing parable:

In a certain city resided a very wealthy man. Just as great as his wealth, however, was his propensity towards stinginess. On one occasion, he thought, "I eat a serving of meat every day. Who says that I have to eat the entire serving? From this day on, I will eat only half of it and save myself hundreds of rubles every year..." And so he did.

Approximately one year later, the miser once again pondered his financial situation. "Perhaps I should reduce the amount of bread I consume daily. This will save me many rubles." As before, he implemented his idea and limited the amount of bread he ate.

Shortly thereafter, the miser began feeling ill and had to be taken to the hospital. The doctor examined him and concluded that the miser appeared to be stricken with weakness and a shortage of blood.

"Your remedy," said the doctor, "is to eat a full serving of meat each and every day. In addition, you must eat your fill of bread and then some...

"I will also prescribe a powerful medicine for you," continued the doctor, "that will be effective in restoring your strength. I must inform you, however, that this medicine is very expensive, but your condition being the way it is, you have no other choice than to take it.

"If I may ask," continued the doctor. "What brought on your weakness?"

The miser told the doctor all that had transpired.

The doctor laughed and said, "How much money did you really save in the end? Now you will have to spend many times more than that before you regain your strength."

There are times, noted the Chofetz Chaim, that an individual hardens his heart and refuses to give *tzedakah* to a poor person. Not only that, but he even evades the *gabba'ei tzedakah* (the ones in charge of collecting funds for the needy) who visit his home.

Let this man take an accounting of his soul and he will discover just how great a loss he incurs by behaving in such a manner. He will undoubtedly have more money by being benevolent.

⇜ "Hashem Stands at the Right of the Destitute"

An embittered pauper related his tale of woe to the Chofetz Chaim. In an attempt to console him, the Chofetz Chaim told the following parable:

In a certain city lived two wealthy merchants named Reuven and Shimon. On one occasion they were falsely accused of having committed a felony against the government by counterfeiting money. They were therefore incarcerated in prison — to languish there until the day of their trial.

Their families tried their utmost to save them, hiring the finest lawyers in the land and even going so far as to bribe the king's officials in order to sweeten their verdict. These efforts cost the families an extraordinary sum of money and nearly depleted their assets. By the time their endeavors had concluded, Reuven was left with twenty thousand rubles, and Shimon with only two thousand.

When the day of the hearing arrived, their defense attorneys stood before the judges. Reuven was represented by one of the most superb legal minds in the land, while Shimon was represented by one of the king's ministers!

Seated on the defense bench, Shimon leaned over and whispered to Reuven, "Your situation is certainly better than mine! Since you have ten times as much money as I do, you will be able to resume your business activities and maybe even get rich again…"

"You are mistaken," responded Reuven in an undertone. "Although you have less money than I do, you nevertheless have a better chance of being exonerated, as the king's minister is vying in your favor. Now, I may have more money than you — but who will be able to ensure that I will be found innocent?"

> "So it is with you," said the Chofetz Chaim to the poor man. "You may not have any money, but Hashem in all His glory is standing at your right side, as the verse states: 'For He stands at the right of the destitute, to save [him] from the condemners of the soul' (*Tehillim* 109:31). Is there anything greater than that?
>
> "Think about it for a moment," concluded the Chofetz Chaim. "What would you rather have, the money of the rich or Hashem standing at your right side?"

⛵ To Save Someone from Drowning

Streaming through the center of a certain town was a deep river that was spanned by a rickety bridge. One day, a group of about thirty men were crossing the bridge. When they were at the halfway point, the bridge gave way and collapsed, sending the men plummeting into the river below.

Two bystanders immediately dove into the water and began swimming towards the men in order to rescue them. Another bystander gazed at what was transpiring, and called at the men who had jumped into the water, "You fools!" he shouted. "Why are the two of you jumping into the water? Can't you see that their group consists of about thirty men? In any event, you won't be able to save all of them. You would therefore have been better off simply remaining on the riverbank."

It goes without saying that this man was speaking nonsensically. For even if the two men had succeeded in saving only one person from drowning, it would have been well worth their efforts!

> The same thing applies to giving *tzedakah*, remarked the Chofetz Chaim. There are instances when a man is approached to give *tzedakah* and he thinks to himself, "How much of a benefit will truly be accrued by my giving a pittance to *tzedakah*? There are so many poor people anyway..." He must know that he is acting in a manner similar to the shouting bystander.
>
> For, in fact, the truth is as *Chazal* have stated (see *Menachos* 110a), "[It does not matter] whether one does more or whether one does less, provided his mind is directed towards [the service of] Heaven."

❧ The Crooked Partner

Reuven and Shimon were partners in a thriving business. They had come to an agreement that they could each take whatever they needed from the business fund in order to provide for themselves and their families, while the remaining money would be split evenly between them.

Their luck eventually took a turn for the worse, and the business was no longer generating as much profit as it did originally. The two partners met and tried to devise a plan that would enable them to conserve their depleting funds. They decided that each of them would curtail the amount of money they had been spending on their domestic needs and would no longer buy the large quantities of food and drink to which they had grown accustomed. From now on, they would purchase only that which was absolutely necessary to sustain themselves.

Reuven, who was an honest fellow, abided by the agreement and bought only that which was essential to his family's health and well-being. Shimon, on the other hand, betrayed his friend's trust and continued to spend exorbitantly, indulging as if the business was as prosperous as it had been in the past.

Some time later, the two partners returned and took note of the fact that business had not improved. Once again, they tried to come up with a plan. But as they read through their financial records, Reuven came to the startling realization that he had been duped. While he and his family had been coping on near-starvation rations, Shimon and his family were indulging on delicacies that were fit for a king.

"You deceptive thief that you are!" screamed Reuven with all his might. "My family and I are starving for bread, and you go ahead and steal from the business fund? You've destroyed our business with your very own hands!"

> There is a type of partnership that exists between man and Hashem, said the Chofetz Chaim. Hashem provides man with all his needs, supporting and sustaining him constantly. Man's responsibility is to set aside *tzedakah* from his money. When hard times befall man and it is difficult for him to earn a livelihood, he must, nevertheless, maintain his end of the partnership by spending less on his domestic needs and continuing to give *tzedakah*.
>
> However, there are individuals who act like the crooked partner. While they continue to spend without restraint when it comes to their household necessities, they neglect the obligations of their partnership with Hashem, by not giving the requisite *tzedakah*.
>
> Let him not be the least bit surprised if he is held accountable for his behavior.

⧫§ The Treasurer

In a certain city resided a distinguished officer who enjoyed a close relationship with the king. The king loved the officer very much and appointed him the highest-ranking officer in his kingdom. The officer's esteem continued to escalate, until he was entrusted with the responsibility of supplying the king's army with their provisions of food.

Every month, the officer would receive a considerable stipend from the kingdom's coffers, which he would use to buy food for the army units that were stationed throughout the kingdom.

Some time later, the officer began to abuse his post. What did he do? Instead of purchasing provisions with the money he was alloted, he would spend only half of the money and then pocket the other half.

The soldiers, whose rations of food had been severely reduced, were literally starving. Yet none of them had the gall to broach the matter to the king — for who could be so audacious as to accuse his beloved officer?

The scenario persisted until, one day, the king paid his troops a visit. In one of the camps, he asked the soldiers if they were satisfied with the quality and quantity of food that they were receiving.

At that point, one soldier gathered up his courage and related to the king that they had been receiving reduced rations of food for quite some time.

The subsequent investigation quickly revealed the officer's guilt, and he was brought before the king, shamefaced and humiliated.

Infuriated, the king approached the officer, stripped him of his rank, and ordered that he be imprisoned until the ensuing trial would be held.

The king then turned to the soldier who had divulged the truth and asked, "Are you prepared to fill his position?"

"Absolutely, Your Great Highness!" replied the soldier happily.

The soldier proved to be an able replacement, carrying out his task with integrity. In a short while, matters reverted back to the way they had been initially.

When the day of the deposed officer's hearing arrived, he was taken from his cell, and brought to the king. He stood before him, embarrassed and disgraced.

"Did you truly think," thundered the king, "that the money you received from the kingdom's money supply was to be spent on yourself? Certainly not! You were to buy food for the soldiers; you served only as a treasurer!

"You have betrayed my trust!"

Hashem, exclaimed the Chofetz Chaim, gives man wealth in order for him to fulfill the *mitzvah* of *tzedakah* and come to the aid of the unfortunate. Man must realize that he is but is merely a treasurer who is required to make use of the money to perform acts of kindliness, as this was the reason he received the funds to begin with.

But if man chooses not to give *tzedakah* and pockets the money instead — he has betrayed his trust.

As a result, he is stripped of his rank, and the money is given to another who will act more sensibly when using the money that was placed in his care.

⋑§ The Sewing Machine

In a certain town lived a poor tailor who barely managed to earn a livelihood. On more than one occasion, hunger prevailed in his dilapidated home.

One day, the tailor was informed that he had become heir to a massive inheritance, and overnight, he was literally transformed into as wealthy an individual as Korach.

From that day on, the tailor drastically altered his lifestyle. He exchanged his meager hut for a magnificent mansion, and in place of his ragged clothing, he would stride about clad in fine silk garments.

In the center of his lavish living room, he placed a breakfront with glass doors in which he displayed the old pair of scissors and various sewing machines he had used in the not-so-distant past.

On one occasion, a newfound friend — one of the wealthiest men in the city — paid him a visit. The tailor gave him a guided tour of his magnificent home.

When they came to the living room, the guest gazed in amazement at the items that were, strangely, being displayed in the breakfront. "What are these items doing in here?" he asked.

"This," responded his host, "is my sewing machine. It is of such outstanding quality, that it has never needed to be repaired! And these are my scissors — they are as sharp as a razor and can cut any garment in an instant!"

"Indeed," retorted the visitor, "the tools that you own are certainly of a most excellent quality, but they do not belong here. If you were actually putting these items to use, then I could understand their value. But to simply display them in a breakfront? You would be better off placing gold and silver vessels inside instead."

> The Dubno Maggid explained Hashem gave man money, and man must know how to put it to proper use. He can use it to help the poor or to support Torah study, for in essence, money is but a "work tool," meant to further man's Divine service. If he utilizes his money in such a manner, he is indeed praiseworthy. However, if he lacks the sense to do so and simply hoards it — of what value is it?

❧ The Informer

A pauper's family had become so dreadfully impoverished that he decided to become an informer. This is what he would do: When he would discover that produce had been smuggled into the country illegally, he would quickly inform the authorities, who would then arrest the perpetrator. Having provided them with a "tip-off," the authorities would reward the pauper with a monetary bonus.

On one occasion, the pauper, as had become his custom, stood on the crossroads and waited for some evidence of wrongdoing. Suddenly, he noticed a caravan of merchants leading wagons that were laden with smuggled goods.

The pauper approached the merchants and requested that they have mercy on him and give him a respectable donation.

A few of the wiser merchants immediately noticed that this pauper was eyeing the merchandise they had with them. They therefore hurried and gave him a generous donation.

Other members of the caravan turned him away, saying, "We don't even know you — why should we give you any money? You say you want a respectable donation? Here's a penny."

"It is beneath my dignity to accept a mere penny," responded the pauper. Seeing his reaction, the merchants sent him away in disgrace.

The pauper went to the ruler of the city and informed on the merchants who had refused to give him charity. About the merchants who were wise enough to give him a donation, he uttered not a word.

The ruler dispatched his police force, who made their way to the inn where the merchants were lodging. They located the merchants and hauled them off to prison in iron chains.

On their way to jail, the merchants spotted the informer.

"Have mercy on us," they cried. "Accept our generous donation, just as long as we do not have to go to prison."

"It is far too late," replied the pauper. "It is not in my power to save you once the matter has been given over to the authorities."

The same thing applies to man's livelihood, explained the Dubno Maggid. Man's sustenance is allotted to him from one Rosh Hashanah to the next with extraordinary exactitude, and it has already been determined precisely how much he will profit and how much loss he will incur.

Therefore, if a wealthy man is wise, when he is asked for tzedakah, he will give the poor person a respectable gift and assist him to the best of his ability — for a man does not become impoverished through giving tzedakah.

However, if he is a fool, and when the poor man approaches him, he turns him away in disgrace, claiming, "Why should I give you any money?" — he is making a grave mistake. For then the pauper will walk away in a state of anguish, shedding tears on account of his pain, and Hashem, Who hears the cries of the unfortunate, will punish the wealthy man. Ultimately, the wealthy man will fall ill, and in his grief, will turn to the pauper he had previously offended, offering him a generous donation and beseeching the pauper to pray on his behalf that he may recover. But at that point, the ruling will have already been given over to Heaven, and the man will require a great deal of Heavenly mercy.

"Praiseworthy is he who contemplates the needy, on the day of disaster, Hashem will deliver him" (*Tehillim* 41:2).

৵§ *Delight in Hashem*

A wealthy man had two sons who lived in a distant city. The first was a rich merchant like his father, while the second was a destitute pauper. It had been many years since the two brothers had last seen their father.

One day, the wealthy son received a letter from his father stating that their youngest brother was getting married. He therefore requested that his sons join them for the wedding.

"However, I have a request to make of you," wrote the father. "Do not be frugal in the slightest; rather, purchase lavish attire in my honor, and come celebrate this joyous wedding with us. You needn't worry — I will cover all of the expenses."

Heeding his father's request, the wealthy son, wife and children all bought beautiful silk clothing, befitting individuals of their stature. When the day of the wedding arrived, he ordered a magnificent coach to transport them to the celebration. Prior to setting out, he sent for his impoverished brother ordering him to rush to his house.

The poor brother arrived wearing clothing that was tattered and torn. He wondered why he had been summoned.

"Ascend the coach quickly," urged the wealthy brother. "There is no time for explanations. We are going to travel to our father in order to participate in the wedding of our youngest brother."

When news of his sons' imminent arrival reached the father's house, he and his household, as well as his *mechutanim* and all of his servants, went out to greet them. Adding to the festive atmosphere was a band of musicians, who marched in front of them, playing pleasant and joyous melodies.

When the coach arrived, the wealthy son and his family — dressed ever so elegantly — descended from the coach, only to be followed by the poor brother who was barefoot and wearing rags.

"Who is this man?" whispered the shocked townspeople.

The more perceptive of the bunch were quick to answer, "Don't you recognize him?" they said. "He is the man's second son."

The wedding was held in grand style, and after seven days of feasting, the wealthy son approached his father to in order to bid him farewell.

"Go in peace," said the father. "May Hashem ensure you a safe journey."

"But father," asked the son audaciously, "what about the expenses that you promised to cover?"

"Look carefully at what it says in the letter that I sent you," responded the father. "I guaranteed to compensate you on condition that you purchased beautiful clothing *in my honor*... Yet you did nothing whatsoever to honor me!" exclaimed the father. "All of the money you spent was solely to enhance your own honor! For if you were truly concerned with my honor, you would have made sure that your brother was dressed appropriately as well. Just look at the humiliation you've caused me by allowing my son to arrive barefoot and shabbily dressed!"

> Chazal, said the Dubno Maggid, have taught us (*Beitzah* 16b) that all the money that an individual spends in order to honor Shabbos and Yom Tov will eventually be returned to him by Hashem, Who guarantees, "Trust in me and I will repay!" A

person should therefore try his utmost to honor and enjoy the Shabbos.

But how can it be that a person could sit in his home, dressed in elegant attire and partaking of scrumptious delights, while his unfortunate brother sits in his home like a mourner, eating nothing more than seeds?

Sadly, this is an indication that the money he spent on his Shabbos delicacies was not for the purpose of delighting in Hashem, but rather, simply to indulge himself!

Hashem does not guarantee to reimburse such expenditures.

The Wise Man and the Simpleton

An affluent individual had two sons; one was wise and intellectually astute, the other was a simpleton. When the father passed away, he left a large inheritance, with instructions that the entire estate be bequeathed to the wise son, who would in turn support his simpleton brother.

Some time later, the wise son complained to his friends that fully supporting his brother had become a significant burden.

Hearing his words, one of the friends offered him sound rebuke. "Such an attitude is unwarranted," he said. "Why, not only did you inherit your rightful share of the estate, but you received your brother's share as well. Your massive wealth, therefore, is also in his merit. That being the case, why are you complaining?"

> There are times, noted the Dubno Maggid, when Hashem grants an individual enormous wealth in order that he should be capable of assisting others. This person must constantly keep this in mind and not complain, Heaven forbid, that the impoverished are a perpetual nuisance and inconvenience.

Part 9

Reward and Punishment

The Young Boy and the Printing Press

As his *sefarim* neared printing, the Chofetz Chaim traveled to the city where the printing press was located.

When he arrived at the printing establishment, the Chofetz Chaim observed a young boy working with great diligence.

"How old are you?" asked the Chofetz Chaim.

"Fifteen years old," was the boy's response.

"Do you earn a decent wage from your work?" he asked.

"The truth is," said the boy, "that I am not earning as much as I need; I make just enough to cover my most basic living expenses. But while my life may presently be difficult," he continued, "in another five or six years, after I have mastered the skill of printing, I will open my very own printing shop. Then I will be able to reap large profits and live like a wealthy man."

The Chofetz Chaim was amazed by the words of this young boy, and upon returning home to Radin, he related them to a crowd that had gathered to hear him speak.

"Do you hear these words?" asked the Chofetz Chaim. "It is worthwhile for an individual to work hard now in order to subsequently live a life of comfort! So too, it is worthwhile for every man to perform mitzvos and good deeds in this world — even if he presently finds it burdensome — in order to receive a great reward in the World to Come!

"Today for their performance and tomorrow for their reward" (*Eruvin* 22a).

"Neither Them Nor Their Reward!"

The Gemara (*Berachos* 8b) relates that R' Elazar had fallen ill. R' Yochanan went to visit him, and upon entering his home, observed that R' Elazar was enduring terrible suffering. R' Yochanan then asked him, "Is this suffering beloved to you?"

"Neither them nor their reward!" responded R' Elazar. "I do not wish to suffer, nor do I covet the reward that is accrued by suffering."

"Give me your hand," said R' Yochanan. R' Elazar placed his hand in R' Yochanan's, and R' Yochanan lifted him to his feet. R' Elazar's suffering came to an end.

When we read the words of this Gemara, said the Chofetz Chaim, we are immediately struck with the following perplexing question: In the same manner that R' Elazar rid himself of his pain, so, too, should every individual be able to simply state, "Neither them nor their reward," and be worthy of having his suffering vanish!

Rather, answered the Chofetz Chaim, the matter can be explained by way of a parable.

This can be compared to a king who built a large prison with high walls and watchtowers in his city. A warden was appointed to oversee the prison and scores of guards were brought in to ensure that security was maintained.

For the next several weeks, not a crime was perpetrated, and the prison remained empty.

The warden feared that if things would continue in this fashion, he would lose his job. He came up with a plan. He ventured out into the street and met a hapless pauper dressed in rags, collecting alms. The warden approached him and asked, "Would you be interested in performing some light labor?"

"What type of labor exactly?" asked the pauper.

"Very light labor," answered the warden. "I will dress you in a prisoner's uniform and place you in prison, where you will be adequately fed and provided for. You will even be given a daily drink of whiskey, as well as some spending money."

The pauper listened to the offer and agreed.

Eventually, the prison grew crowded with criminals. No longer requiring the pauper's services, the warden sent him on his way.

Some time later, the pauper committed an offense and the judges sentenced him to a stint in prison.

"Absolutely not!" said the pauper. "Under no circumstances will I agree to accompany you to jail unless you give me a daily drink of whiskey and spending money."

"You fool!" laughed the officers. "Originally, you had not committed any crime and were innocent of guilt; you were therefore entitled to the benefits that you received. But now you have been found guilty in a court of law and must therefore sit in jail like any other prisoner"

> The suffering which R' Elazar endured, concluded the Chofetz Chaim, was certainly not on account of his sins. Rather, he had accepted it upon himself in order to reap the rewards accrued by one who bears it. He was therefore able to decide that he wanted "Neither them nor their reward." We, on the other hand, are punished as a result of the sins we have committed and are therefore unable to say the same thing.

⋙ The Orchard

A wealthy man had a beautiful orchard filled with fruit trees bearing luscious fruit that emitted a pleasant fragrance discernable from quite a distance. In the center of the orchard, the man built a hut in which he would be able to sit and enjoy the sight of his lovely orchard.

Sitting in his hut one day, he noticed an intruder enter his orchard through an opening in the fence and proceed to pick fruits from one of the trees.

The owner of the orchard observed but did not say a word.

The intruder picked one fruit after another and eventually said to himself, "Why should I overexert myself by picking individual fruits? Let me simply take a branch at a time!"

He then began to remove branches laden with fruit from the magnificent tree, but the wealthy man still remained silent.

A short while later, the intruder grew tired from removing the branches. He therefore paused for a moment, wiped his brow, and said out loud, "Why should I only take branches? I'll uproot the entire tree!"

Upon hearing this, the owner of the orchard could no longer restrain himself. He ran over to the intruder and shouted, "You wicked man! Initially, I figured that you must have been starving and simply wanted to eat a few fruits. I therefore judged you favorably and did not say a word. Even when you tore off a few branches, I nevertheless forgave you. But now you wish to uproot the entire tree? I will never allow this to happen!"

> There are wicked individuals, said the Chofetz Chaim, who do not wish to go in the ways of Hashem. Initially, they sin by transgressing the rabbinical enactments. When their behavior goes uncontested, they begin to "break off branches," and transgress the Torah's prohibitions. Subsequently, when they have grown accustomed to the ways of sin, they attempt to uproot everything.
>
> The Owner of the orchard, however, will not forgive this act.

✑§ Rebels and Their Punishment

There are individuals who question Hashem's ways and ask why the righteous must suffer while the wicked prosper. The Chofetz Chaim drew an extraordinary parable relating to this idea:

There was a distinguished family of the aristocratic class, whose prominent standing in the royal kingdom was unsurpassed. The king was extremely kind to them and enjoyed a close personal relationship with each of the family members. They, in turn, displayed remarkable loyalty and dedication toward the king.

The years passed, and some of the younger members of the family began to resent the king and decided to rebel against him. When the king was informed of this, out of his great love for the family, he sent messengers to appease them and convince them not to rebel against him. The rebels, however, stubbornly refused and persisted in their revolt.

Left with no other choice, the king dispatched a legion of soldiers who defeated the rebels. Having triumphed, the soldiers arrested the rebels and hurled them into prison where they were to await execution as traitors to the throne.

After several days, the prison warden approached the king and exclaimed, "Your Highness, I would like to request permission to tell you something that I witnessed in the jail. It appears to me as if an injustice is taking place."

"What did you see?" asked the king.

"I saw the rebels submitted to extremely brutal conditions. Indeed, they are starving and bitterly cold; is it not sufficient that they have been sentenced to death? Must they suffer so extensively as well?"

"You are correct," answered the king. "I therefore want you to perform a thorough investigation and discern which of the men truly desired to rebel against me and which of them simply followed suit. To those who wished to rebel against me and will be soon put to death, you may give food and drink that is fit for a king. To those who were just swept along, however, you shall give only stale bread and water in small measure — that will be their punishment."

The warden did as he was instructed, and the rebels ate to their heart's content, while their brothers, who had remained faithful to the king, received only stale bread.

Hashem chose our forefathers, said the Chofetz Chaim, from all the other nations to be His treasured people. He gave us the Torah, the Land of Israel, and built the *Beis HaMikdash* for us as well. Despite all of this kindliness, there were those who chose to rebel against Hashem and His Torah. The righteous, on the other hand, remained loyal and refused to defy their Creator.

Those who rebel against Hashem are treated to a life of pleasure and enjoy the myriad delights that this world has to offer. In truth, however, they are receiving all of their reward during their lifetime, for their ultimate sentence is going to be a harsh one. Those who are faithful to Hashem, on the other hand, may experience suffering and distress in this world, but it is only a result of Hashem's mercy, as He wishes to purge them of their sins. They will then be worthy of being transported from darkness into light!

~§ The Garments' Debate

Regarding the question as to why the righteous suffer while the wicked prosper, R' Tzvi Hirsch Eichenstein of Kaminetz related an astounding parable:

A king was accustomed to staging an annual gala celebration on the anniversary of his ascension to the throne.

On the tenth anniversary of his reign, the king planned a celebration that promised to be truly incredible. In honor of the occasion, he had a brand new silk cloak — the likes of which had never been seen — sewn for himself. In addition, he desired that new uniforms be sewn for each and every one of the servants in the palace.

The king hired a world-renowned tailor, who was famous for the magnificent garments he routinely produced. He went about his task with alacrity, as the king had issued him but one warning: "Work quickly," said the king. "For there is much work to do and time is short…"

The tailor first approached a fabric merchant and purchased a large quantity of ordinary wool with which to weave the servants' uniforms. He then bought silk of extraordinary quality that had been imported from China, as well as linen and purple fabrics whose splendid colors were absolutely breathtaking.

Without giving it much thought or planning, the tailor quickly sewed the servants' uniforms, as his main objective was to finish them in as little time as possible.

He then shifted his attention to sewing the king's cloak. This was an altogether different task, one which he approached with fear and trembling. He took measurements once and then took them again, marked the area that he intended to cut, and proceeded to do so ever so cautiously. Next it was time to stitch the garment, which he did with expert craftsmanship, concealing the stitches so as not to mar its beauty. He hemmed the cloak, and concluded by ironing it; it was now ready to be presented to the king.

The cloak began to boast before the woolen uniforms, "Look at how exquisite I am! You, on the other hand, are ordinary and coarse."

The woolen uniforms did not take the insults lying down; rather, they offered a reply. "Why are you acting so arrogantly?" they asked. "Just look at how many times the tailor punctured you with his needle; why, he did so time and time again! Not only that, but upon completing each stage of your sewing, the tailor pressed you with a steaming hot iron."

While their claims were indeed correct, the cloak did not bother to retort to such fools. Rather, he chose to bear their words in silence.

When the anticipated day of the anniversary arrived, the king stood exalted and glorified as he wore his stunning silk cloak, while the palace staff wore their run-of-the-mill woolen uniforms…

Only then did the uniforms realize that they had been mistaken. All of the suffering which the king's cloak had endured was simply in order to transform it into a magnificent cloak!

> So it is in this world, said R' Eichenstein. All of the suffering which the righteous endure is only for the sake of purifying them so that they will be able to be magnificently radiant in the World to Come.

❧ The Depth of Judgment

> At times, noted the Chofetz Chaim, man mistakenly believes that there is such a thing as "minor" sins. In truth, however, each and every deed is taken into account.

This can be likened to a merchant who earned his living buying and selling a broad range of merchandise. However, he fell upon hard times, and lost all his wealth. To make matters worse, he had many creditors to whom he owed money, which varied from large amounts to lesser ones.

The creditors met with one another in hopes of devising a plan that would enable them to recover their money.

"The merchant owes me one thousand rubles," said one of them. "To me he owes *two thousand*," said another. "I am presently owed three hundred rubles," chimed in another creditor. "I," began a fourth creditor, "am owed four rubles..."

"Four rubles?" wondered everyone in amazement. "That is a very paltry sum!"

"Yes, indeed," he answered. "While it may be a small sum of money, it is nevertheless a debt..."

They continued to discuss alternatives that would enable them to recoup their money. They ultimately resolved to go directly to the merchant's home and forcibly confiscate his belongings.

They headed straight for his house, and once there, began confiscating everything that they could. Even the creditor who was owed a mere four rubles joined the fray and snatched the merchant's possessions.

Seeing this raised the other creditors' ire. "What right do you have to take anything?" they said to him. "You are only owed four rubles; that is but an insignificant debt."

"True," he responded, "but it is, nevertheless, a debt! Indeed, if we were sitting together and collecting our loans, I would take no more than I was owed. But now that we are simply grabbing anything that we can, why should I not do the same?"

A person believes, said the Chofetz Chaim, that some sins warrant a minor punishment while others are deserving of a harsher penalty. However, when the awesome day arrives and man must stand in judgment before the Heavenly Tribunal, even his "minor" sins will "demand" retribution.

~§ The Wedding

A wealthy man who owned many lands, fields, and vineyards had an only son whom he was set to marry off in grand style.

He prepared his guest list and saw that it consisted of all the wealthy and distinguished men of the city, officers and barons, his acquaintances and friends, and all of the workers and sharecroppers in his fields.

"What should I do?" thought the wealthy man to himself. "How can I possibly sit the noblemen and barons together with my workers, who are but simple villagers?"

After giving the matter some thought, he decided that he would make a special feast for his workers the day before the wedding. The next day, he would stage the magnificent wedding in the presence of his dignified friends. And so he did.

A day before the wedding, when all of his workers were partaking of the feast that the wealthy man had prepared for them, passersby who happened to catch a glimpse of the festivities were astounded. "What has happened to this wealthy fellow? Why is he according such honor to a group of villagers, farmers by profession? Why, it appears as if that he has forgotten to invite the city's most respectable residents!"

A particularly astute individual happened to be passing by at the time as well. "You fail to understand," he said. "His sole intention is to free himself of his responsibilities to these villagers, as he does not wish to have them at his son's wedding. You can rest assured that to the wedding he will invite only the city's most notable citizens."

In this world, noted the Chofetz Chaim, we witness the righteous suffering and the wicked prospering. This should not perplex us in any way, for it is due only to the fact that Hashem wishes to reward the wicked in this world for the few *mitzvos* they have performed. The righteous, on the other hand, have their complete reward waiting for them in the World to Come, where they will bask in the presence of the *Shechinah*.

An extraordinarily wealthy merchant was the most respected resident of the city in which he lived. There were those, however, who grew envious of his prominence and great wealth, and decided to slander him by spreading a vile rumor that he had forged monetary notes.

Forgery was deemed a grave infraction of the law, and he was therefore sent to prison until the conclusion of his trial.

When the case was brought to court, the merchant's enemies hired false witnesses who testified against him. Found guilty, he was sentenced to torture in the city square and to subsequently be exiled to a desolate country where he would be forced to perform backbreaking labor.

Many of the city's inhabitants came to witness the merchant's afflictions. Shackled in iron chains like a common criminal, the merchant ascended the platform where the officer who was to inflict the tortures already waited.

Amongst the spectators was a fellow merchant — who was likewise a wealthy individual with many influential friends. When he saw that the man being led to the platform was an old acquaintance of his, he quickly rushed to the ruler of the city.

"Your Honor," cried the merchant, "this man is the victim of a vicious libel! I know the accused quite well, and I can vouch for his incomparable honesty and integrity!"

The ruler knew the merchant and thought rather highly of him. He therefore put a halt to the punishment for the time being, until the matter could be further investigated.

The false witnesses were unable to be located as they had fled from the city wasting little time. Nevertheless, enough uncertainties cropped up in their testimony and in the details of the case for the merchant to receive a sweetened sentence. He would not be tortured, nor would he perform oppressive labor; he would however be exiled to a different land. There he could live like a free man, but he would be not be permitted to return to his home.

The wealthy man was elated upon having his shackles removed, and he thanked his fellow merchant profusely for intervening on his behalf; shortly thereafter, he was exiled. One day, the other merchant happened to visit that land and he encountered his exiled friend. But when he saw him, he noticed that his eyes were bloodshot from bitter weeping.

"Why have you been crying?" he asked his friend.

"I cry," responded the merchant, "over not being able to return to my homeland. Indeed, my sentence was lightened, but this exile is most difficult to bear as well. For here I am bereft of my family and I am extremely lonely."

In the future, remarked the Chofetz Chaim, the day will arrive when sinners will be punished on account of their wrongdoings. Once they have been dealt their punishment, they will sit and cry over not having performed more *mitzvos* in this world.

But by then it will be far too late, for in the World of Truth one is unable to amass *mitzvos* and good deeds. They will simply sit there and cry, inconsolable.

◆§ Examining the Fabrics

Hundreds of merchants would come to the great fair, each one with a wagon laden with merchandise. Once there, each one would unload his colorful goods and, in a blaring voice, begin to promote his merchandise and laud it with superlatives.

One day, a merchant arrived at the fair, with a large wagon brimful with bolts of fabric whose striking colors were amazing to behold. Even before the merchant and his assistants had an opportunity to unload the merchandise, a large crowd had gathered around them, recognizing immediately that this was quality fabric that could be purchased at a bargain price.

"Give me one hundred measures from this bolt of silk fabric!" yelled one eager customer. Another customer attempted to push ahead, "I want one hundred and fifty!" he screamed, trying to drown out the other man's voice.

"Please, be patient!" said the merchant. "You must know that I simply do not have the time to sell each customer a specific measure of fabric. Rather, I am selling the fabric *by the bolt*, and each bolt consists of five hundred measures of excellent fabric."

Despite his sudden announcement, the merchant did not have much difficulty selling the bolts. For as soon as he finished speaking, a group of merchants consented to purchase them. Some wanted one bolt, while others bought as many as three or four.

"Forgive me," asked one of the customers, "but how can I know with certainty that there actually is five hundred measures of fabric in each bolt? I am sure that you do not want us to spread out each one and measure for ourselves!"

"You are right about that," answered the merchant. "However, you can do the following: select one bolt of fabric from the pile and measure it. Without a doubt," he added with a smile, "you will choose the bolts which appears the thinnest. If it nonetheless turns out to be five hundred measures, then it is an indication that the others are of equal measure..."

Said the Dubno Maggid, Hashem has six hundred and thirteen *mitzvos* in His treasury, and the reward for adhering to each one is greater than man could ever fathom. Man is guaranteed that he will be compensated sevenfold for any expense he may incur as a result of his *mitzvah* performance.

A man may ask, continued the Maggid, "But are there not instances when one spends heavily on a particular *mitzvah*?" Hashem therefore responds by telling him to select one *mitzvah*; for example, the *mitzvah* of tithing one's produce. "Put Me to the test," says Hashem. "See the reward that man receives for faithfully performing this commandment." As *Chazal* say on the words (*Shabbos* 119a), *"Aser ta'aser"* (You shall surely tithe) — *"Aser bishvil she'tis'asher"* (You shall tithe in order that you become rich). This is in an indication that the same holds true for all of the other *mitzvos* as well.

A horrific fire ravaged a city, destroying all of its homes. The city's inhabitants, overcome with grief, were left penniless.

When word of the tragedy spread, the countryside's populace immediately mobilized, to carrying out the sacred mission of assisting their unfortunate brethren. They loaded wagons with a variety of goods and rushed to the decimated city.

Among those who came to help was a wealthy man and his son who had arrived at the scene of the tragedy carrying a bag filled with scores of gold coins. The wealthy man stood in the scorched city square distributing gold coins to all those who requested.

The wealthy man's son was approached by an individual who pleaded that he be given a significant number of coins. With tears in his eyes, he explained how he had formerly been a wealthy man who had lived in a magnificent home. Now, he cried, he was left without a roof over his head.

The wealthy man turned to hear the man's plea. He instantly recognized him and realized that he was not telling the truth.

Infuriated, the wealthy man exclaimed, "I know who you are and I am well aware that you were a poor man! You are lying to us!"

> In the next world, said the Dubno Maggid, Hashem will bestow a wonderful reward upon all those who feared Him. When those individuals who excelled in their Divine service will line up to receive their eternal reward, how will it look if, standing amongst them, is a man who lived his entire life mired in sin? What place does he have among those who are destined to be rewarded?

❧ The Appraiser

I n a certain city resided a successful businessman whose store stocked a wide assortment of goods. His neighbor was a wicked man who coveted his enormous wealth and was extremely envious of his good fortune. As a result, he constantly devised strategies that would enable him to steal merchandise from his neighbor's store. What did he do? One day, he cunningly persuaded one of the wealthy man's workers, a shrewd and able-bodied young man, to steal his employer's merchandise, telling him that he would pay him cash for it.

The two collaborated with one another and carried out the vile deed. When they saw that they had been successful, they perpetrated their dispicable act again and again...

By chance, the storeowner found out what was taking place.

Pretending to be completely oblivious, he told his worker that he would be taking him to court. When they arrived in court, the storeowner showed the judges a detailed list enumerating all of the merchandise that was missing. The judges immediately ruled that the young worker was responsible to remunerate the storeowner for the cost of the stolen merchandise, as evaluated by expert appraisers.

The storeowner then turned to his sinister neighbor and requested that he serve as the appraiser.

The neighbor "kindly" conceded to the storeowner's request, and in an attempt to find favor in his eyes, appraised the merchandise at a value which was many times more than its actual worth.

At that point, the storeowner demanded that the neighbor repay each and every penny of the theft that he himself had assessed!

The judges listened as the storeowner related the entire story about how the neighbor had influenced his worker, and they required the neighbor to pay the entire sum in gold coins!

In the future, said the Dubno Maggid, Hashem will ask the nations of the world to adjudicate and decide just how great a punishment the Jewish people deserve for sinning against Him. In their wickedness, the gentiles will exacerbate the sentence and decree far more punishment upon the Jews than they are actually liable to receive. Ultimately, however, their plan will backfire and that which they intended to do to the

Jewish people will be leveled against them, as a result of their having scattered the Jewish people amongst the nations and causing them to sin.

◄§ Between Israel and the Nations

An individual chanced to enter a classroom and observed the teacher explaining a Talmudic topic to a pair of youths. The boys' minds were somewhat sidetracked, and they did not comprehend a word their teacher was saying. The teacher rebuked one of the students and punished him severely, while to the second student, he said not a word.

The visitor's curiosity was peaked. He asked the teacher for an explanation as to why he had acted in such a manner. "Excuse me," he asked, "but I am rather curious as to why the first student paid so dear a price for failing to understand the material, yet the second student received no punishment whatsoever. After all, they both studied the same topic, and neither one understood a word!"

"True," responded the teacher, "they were studying the identical topic, but they nevertheless vary greatly in regard to their abilities. While the first student is intellectually gifted and possesses great profundity of thought, the second student has poor acumen and must exert much effort simply to grasp a fraction of his studies. I therefore punished the first student — for with his superior intellect, he could have understood the lesson well, but allowed himself to be distracted. The second student, however, I opted not to punish at all."

The Dubno Maggid noted that Hashem is more exacting when it comes to judging the Jewish people than He is with the other nations. Due to the Jewish people's lofty level, they must far surpass the conduct of the other nations. If they choose, however, to stoop to the level of the nations of the world and to act as they do, they deserve to be punished.

◈§ The Inn

When a visitor arrives in a big city and seeks a place to spend the night, he has a choice of a broad range of inns and other lodgings where he will be able to rest comfortably. If he happens to be dissatisfied with the particular inn he has chosen, he can easily pick himself up and relocate to another inn that will meet his standard of approval.

This is not the case, however, when an individual arrives in a city that is almost entirely populated by gentiles. He must spend many hours searching in the hope of finding a single Jewish home where he will be able to lodge. Indeed, it may be only after considerable exertion, that he will find a Jewish home located on the outskirts of the city, whose owner is delighted to welcome a guest into his home.

Now, if the visitor is dissatisfied with any detail — for example, the bed is not as comfortable as he would like, or the food is not very tasty — would it even occur to him to leave the home?

> When Hashem wished to give the Torah, said the Dubno Maggid, He first offered it to all the nations of the world, but they refused to accept it. Only the Jewish Nation accepted the Torah, as they stated, "We will do and we will obey!" (Shemos 24:7).
>
> In the futurer, the gentiles will also desire a reward. They will therefore attempt to slander the Jewish Nation, claiming that the Jews also did not fulfill the Torah's laws to perfection, and that they should therefore receive their reward instead.
>
> Hashem will therefore respond, "How could I possibly reject this 'inn'?"

◈§ The King's Lodgings

A king had embarked on a lengthy journey with a massive entourage under his command. Heavy snow began falling during the course of the journey, and the horses managed to pull the magnificent coach only with great difficulty. The blizzard grew more furious by the minute, and the men began to fear that they would soon be stranded en route.

From a distance, they suddenly caught a glimpse of lights flickering in the homes of a small village. The horses were pressed further and with their last vestiges of strength, succeeded in dragging the caravan to the village, where the entire entourage descended and headed for the modest inn in the center of the village.

The innkeeper — a rather coarse and unsophisticated fellow who was not accustomed to housing such distinguished guests — excitedly went out of his way to accommodate them. For years to come, he would recount how the king, in all his glory, chose to spend the night under his roof.

"You foolish man," remarked one clever fellow. "Do you think that the king actually *chose* to lodge in your inn? With the snow falling as hard as it was, he was left with no choice other than to stay in your dilapidated inn...

"Now," continued the man, "if the king would arrive in a big city where there are a multitude of palaces and castles, and would still choose to stay in the inn of a simpleton such as you, that would indicate that he truly values the individual who assisted him in his time of distress."

The same concept applies to Hashem and the Jewish Nation, said the Dubno Maggid. In *Zechariah* (2:15) it states, "Many nations will join to Hashem on that day, and they will become a people unto Me; and I will dwell in your midst."

Hashem chose to rest His Name in the midst of the Jewish Nation. Perhaps one will claim that this was not by choice, as it were, and that there was simply no other place for Hashem to rest His Name. The *Navi* therefore states, "Many nations will join to Hashem" — there will be an abundance of nations, but, nevertheless, — "And I will dwell in your midst"!

◄§ The Difference Between One Guest and Another

There are times when a person visits the house of his dear friend who goes out of his way in order to please him: The host instructs his family members to prepare his friend fine delicacies, set the table with fancy dishes, and even care for the horses that are harnessed to his coach. This is all carried out with one purpose in mind — to please his guest, for he is beloved to him.

There are other times, however, when the guest is not a dear friend at all, but rather a cruel and evil man. Here, too, the host will prepare delicious food and set the table elegantly — but his actions will not be motivated by the love that he feels for his guest; quite the contrary...

There is another notable difference between the service the two guests receive: When it comes to the second guest, the host will not instruct his workers to work at a quicker pace in order to accommodate him, nor will he concern himself with the guest's horses; for this man is an uninvited guest, and the host has no other choice than to cater to him.

> In the World to Come, said the Dubno Maggid, Hashem will grant a wonderful reward to those who fear Him, and out of His great love for us, will also concern Himself with all of our trappings!

◄§ The In-Laws

A wealthy man had a daughter with outstanding virtues who had come of age, and he sought a groom who was both a Torah scholar and a person of fine character. After much searching, the father found a young man of exceptional caliber. Since the young man's father lived in a distant city, the wealthy man dispatched his luxurious coach to bring him to his town to finalize the match.

When the father arrived, he met with the wealthy man, and for an undisclosed reason, decided to reject the match.

Noting the father's disapproval, the wealthy man attempted to bribe him. He therefore whispered to him that besides the dowry that he intended to give the couple, he would also give him four hundred gold coins.

Despite the attractive offer, the father remained firm in his resolve and would not agree to the match. Seeing this, the wealthy man turned to the son instead, and the match was quickly made without the father's consent.

After the betrothal, the father of the groom approached the wealthy man and requested the four hundred coins that he had promised him.

"Absolutely not," replied the wealthy man. "It is true that I offered you such a sum, but it was only intended to persuade you to agree to the match. But now that the match has already been signed without your consent, I owe you nothing at all."

The Dubno Maggid explained, Hashem betrothed Himself to the Jewish Nation, as it were. But the primary match was made with their souls that yearn to fulfill the *mitzvos*.

However, continued the Maggid, the soul is in the body's hands, so to speak, and whenever it desires to perform a *mitzvah*, it must request its permission. For the soul needs the legs to want to go to the *beis midrash* as well; it requires the consent of the hands in order to wear *tzitzis* or a pair of *tefillin*, etc.

Therefore if the body is willing and cooperates with the soul, it deserves a measure of reward in this world. But if the body is reluctant to do the soul's bidding then strictly speaking, it does not deserve to derive any pleasure from this world whatsoever. If it does derive benefit, it should be well aware that it is consuming the meager reward that awaits it in the World to Come.

❧ The Son's Punishment

A young boy was his father's only son. On one occasion, he infuriated his father to the point where the father punished him rather harshly. Shortly thereafter, the father thought to himself, "What did I do? Why did I punish my dear son so severely?"

The father, anguished and heartbroken, fainted.

When the son's teacher heard what had transpired, he summoned the child and struck him with his staff.

"But didn't my father already punish me?" cried the young lad.

"Indeed he did," answered the teacher. "Your father, however, punished you for the deed you committed. I, on the other hand, am punishing you for compelling your father to punish you."

> When a man sins, said the Dubno Maggid, he immediately incurs a punishment from his Father in Heaven. But, in truth, the punishment that man receives is itself comparable to a sin, for why did Hashem — Who is compassionate and gracious — have to act contrary to His attributes and experience anguish, so to speak, for having to punish him?

❧ The Adviser

An officer had inherited a large city. He was a quiet and humble person, and he lacked any experience whatsoever in managing the affairs of a city, so he enlisted the aid of a distinguished gentleman who would advise him regarding all governmental matters.

The man sat with the officer and explained to him the proper way to collect taxes as well as how to manage the economy. He was told how to act when it came to matters concerning the public, which areas were worthwhile to develop, and which stood to be improved.

The officer heeded the words of the wise adviser and appointed officials who would ensure that the law was obeyed and that order was upheld.

One day, an individual was arrested and thrown into prison for not having paid the city taxes. It just so happened that this criminal was none other than the adviser's son.

An elderly man turned to the officer and said, "My Master! It is certainly true that the penalty for committing such a crime is imprisonment. Nevertheless, it appears that you should be lenient in this particular case; after all, the prisoner is the adviser's son, and without his father's advice you would never have known how to collect taxes in the first place..."

> Avraham Avinu, said the Dubno Maggid, was the first individual to believe in Hashem and accept upon himself the yoke of His Heavenly Kingdom. From then on, Hashem was referred to as "Master" (*Adon*).
>
> We are the descendants of Avraham Avinu and Hashem therefore deals with us leniently, beyond the letter of law!

◄§ Manager of the Estate

A ruler owned a large estate encompassing many fields and vineyards, which was well stocked with animals and birds. He sought a trustworthy individual who would be capable of bearing the responsibility of managing the estate. The overseer would have to know how grain was harvested, and how provisions were accrued, how wine was pressed from the vineyards, and oil from the olive trees. Furthermore, it was essential for him to possess a keen understanding of how to tend the animals and the birds.

The ruler searched and searched but was unsuccessful. He finally decided to travel the length and breadth of the land in hopes of chancing upon someone who was fit for the job.

Walking along the road, he passed a village, and he decided to stop and rest in the home of one of the villagers. His host was unfailingly gracious and served him a hearty meal. At the conclusion of the meal the regal visitor wished to pay, and his host presented him with an itemized bill: The meat and the wine cost such an amount; and so much for the fresh bread and vegetables...

"Your bill comes out to a total of ten rubles," said the villager, "and believe me when I tell you that it is a cheap price. It is approximately as much as I paid for all the food and ingredients when I purchased them in the market."

The ruler paid his host and went on his way. Shortly thereafter he took up lodging in the house of a different villager. There, too, he was served a filling meal, but when he finished and requested to pay, he was told, "Why should you pay me — everything you ate was homemade! I baked the bread myself, grew the vegetables in my yard, and the chicken you ate came from the coop in the back of the house..."

The ruler was absolutely elated — he had found the man he was looking for! The villager standing before him was the talented individual who would surely be able to manage his estate.

"Nevertheless," he thought, "it would not be fitting for me to withhold payment from this man; I will therefore pay him the amount that I paid the first villager who had purchased the ingredients from the marketplace."

The reward that man accrues for expending effort in conquering his *yetzer hara* is very great, exclaimed the Dubno Maggid. Nevertheless, an individual who has been steeped in piety and purity from the day he was born will not have his reward withheld in the slightest. For should his reward be diminished simply because he did not have to struggle in order to achieve his lofty level?

He will undoubtedly receive a reward that is on par with that of the person who exerted himself in conquering his yetzer hara!

✒ *The Merchant Who Was a Spendthrift*

Chazal (*Shabbos* 32a) state in the name of R' Yannai, "A person should never stand in a dangerous place and rely on the fact that Heaven will perform a miracle for him...for perhaps a miracle will not be performed for him ... And if it is, it will deplete his merits!"

When a miracle is wrought for an individual, it diminishes the merits that he accrued through performing *mitzvos*!

This can be compared to a magnificent inn that stood in the capital city. Its living areas were bedecked with expensive carpets and crystal chandeliers illuminating with a multitude of lights hung from the ceiling. The meals that were served were elaborate feasts that were truly fit for royalty and there was a band that played soothing and melodious tunes on a daily basis. As could be expected, the fees charged at the inn were astronomical, and, as a result, only members of the affluent upper-class were able to enjoy the services and delights that it offered. Needless to say, the guests were rather surprised when they saw one of the simple merchants from the city sitting in the inn and feasting to his heart's delight.

Their shock grew all the more when one of the staff related to them that this was not the first time that the merchant had eaten there. Rather, for the past month, both morning and night, this merchant had been one of the customers at the inn...

"Such a poor man!" remarked one of the guests.

"Poor?" asked his friends in bewilderment. "How could you possibly refer to him as poor? Could a pauper afford the fees accrued by eating at this inn?"

"My intention," answered the wise guest, "was not to say that the merchant is presently poor; he is undoubtedly quite rich. Rather, I meant to say that he will grow poor very quickly by continuing to squander his money on these luxuries!"

So, too, is a man that has a miracle wrought for him, explained the Dubno Maggid. While he may perform *mitzvos* and indeed has amassed an abundance of merit, if he places himself in a dangerous situation and is saved by way of a miracle, in a few short moments, he will have wasted what he toiled so dearly to amass.

❦ His Pride Will Be Exalted with Glory

In *Tehillim* (112: 9,10) it states, "His pride will be exalted with glory. The wicked man will see this and be angered, he will gnash his teeth and melt away; the ambition of the wicked shall perish."

The Dubno Maggid asked, to what can this be compared?

It is similiar to a father whose son had caused him to lose a significant amount of money. The father was furious with his son and pondered how he should be punished. Should he strike him? That he did not wish to do, as he was not accustomed to striking his son. So what did he do? He ran to a renowned tailor and bought an expensive silk fabric. He sewed a beautiful garment from it and quickly rushed to present it to his second son.

In addition, he purchased an expensive felt hat and gave it to yet a different son.

The first son saw the gifts that his father had given to his brothers, and his heart sank.

> In the future, noted the Dubno Maggid, Hashem will seek to punish the wicked of the land. But it is not the way of Hashem — Who is completely good — to afflict an individual. He will therefore exalt the righteous and "the wicked man will see this and be angered, he will gnash his teeth and melt away…"

❦ The Village Doctor

A king's son became seriously ill and was confined to bed. All of the kingdom's prominent physicians were quickly summoned to examine him, and they unanimously decided that the king's son must refrain from eating dairy products, as these were the cause of his failing health.

The king heeded the doctors' advice, and he selected one of them — a doctor renowned for his expertise in the medical field — to live in the palace and make sure that his son adhered to the doctors' restrictions.

The doctor agreed and took up residence in the king's palace.

Initially, the king's son took care to follow the doctor's orders, but he soon began to disregard them and to eat whatever he desired.

The doctor, who was a mild-mannered and polite individual, did not have the audacity to punish the king's son; he therefore turned to the king and requested that he rebuke his son for neglecting his health. The pampered son did not listen to his father, however, and before long he fell ill once again.

When the king saw this, he decided that in order to protect his son, he would have to send him to the village, to the home of a simple doctor. An unsophisticated fellow, the villager was totally insensitive to the reverence that was accorded those who resided in the king's court. The king was well aware that if his son dared eat foods which were detrimental to his health, the village doctor would have no qualms about punishing him in an effective fashion.

> Hashem presented us with expert "doctors" who would protect us from all harm said the Dubno Maggid; they are the *Sanhedrin* (High Court) and the *Kohanim* in the *Beis Ha-Mikdash*, who disseminated halachic rulings in Israel according to the word of Hashem. When we heeded their words, we merited sitting at the table of our Father in Heaven in Jerusalem, in the proximity of the *Beis HaMikdash*, and we lacked nothing whatsoever.
>
> However, continued the Maggid, when we rejected their words, Hashem found no other remedy than to scatter us among the gentiles. The gentiles, who do not recognize the honor due Hashem, overpower us and treat us cruelly until we succumb.

The Partnership

A fire broke out inside a man's home, and it was not long before the entire house was utterly decimated, leaving the man destitute.

His neighbors took pity on him and gave him a small storage room nearby, where he and his family could reside. Dwelling in the storage room, he began to accumulate garbage and refuse and needed a place to dispose of it. He therefore decided to take the pile of garbage and dump it where his house had stood before it was razed to the ground.

The garbage pile grew day by day...

Some time later, the man found favor in the eyes of the ruler of the city and related his sad story to him. Upon hearing the tale of woe, the ruler generously decided to build the man a magnificent home in the place where his former house had stood.

"Clean up the area," said the ruler, "and I will then send you building materials as well as builders who will construct your new home." The man cleared away the mountains of trash; this involved considerable expense, and he was eventually forced to borrow money from his friends to facilitate this overwhelming cleaning task. He contacted the ruler after the area stood spotless, and the ruler promptly made good on his promise.

Shortly thereafter, a magnificent and spacious edifice stood in place of his original home. Adding to its striking appearance was a lovely garden surrounding it.

Some time later, the ruler heard that the man was boasting that he and the ruler had been partners in building the new home.

Infuriated, the ruler had the man summoned to appear before him.

"What's this that I hear?" asked the ruler. "Were we truly partners in the construction of this house?"

"Indeed we were," answered the man. "I will show you exactly how much money I spent in order to have the garbage cleared away from the building site."

"You fool!" responded the ruler. "Who dumped all of that garbage there in the first place, if not you? You dumped it there, and you are therefore the one who must dispose of it!"

There are instances, noted the Dubno Maggid, when man feels as if he deserves an abundance of reward for all of the effort and toil which he invested into ridding himself of his negative character traits and illusory cravings.

But in truth, concluded the Maggid, why is he deserving of a reward if he was the one who incorporated those attributes into his personality in the first place?

⊷§ Compensation or Charity

A poor tailor would wander from village to village and from city to city with his work tools in hand. Wherever he went, he would offer to mend any garments needing minor repairs. One of his trips brought him to the house of a wealthy man, and he inquired whether he possessed a garment that needed mending.

The wealthy man brought the tailor into his room and opened his closet which was literally packed with different types of clothing. He requested that the tailor inspect the clothing himself and find those that needed to be repaired.

The tailor examined the various articles of clothing and saw that they were all in excellent condition, not one in need of any mending whatsoever. He therefore took one of the man's most elegant outfits and undid all of its stitches!

When the wealthy man saw what the tailor had done, he wanted to call the police and have him arrested. But the tailor pleaded with him and said that he would quickly repair whatever he had damaged.

The wealthy man acquiesced and the tailor worked with alacrity to remedy that which he had ruined.

When the tailor had finished, he presented the man with a mended garment that appeared just as it did before it had been unstitched. Seeing that the repair had been completed, the wealthy man removed several coins from his pocket and handed them to the tailor. The reward that the tailor received was not compensation for his labor, obviously; he did not deserve anything at all since he was the one who damaged the garment to begin with. Rather, it was charity in its simplest form, a gift to help a needy man.

> All of the reward which man receives for the good deeds that he performs, said the Dubno Maggid, can be categorized as reward for a *mitzvah*. But if an individual fasts in order to atone for impurities of the heart, then strictly speaking he is not deserving of any reward whatsoever; after all, he is the one responsible for those flaws, and now he is merely rectifying them.
>
> The reward that he inevitably receives for those fasts, however, is outright charity and kindliness from Hashem.

∾§ A Free Gift

A pauper was drifting from city to city and from village to village. Wherever he went, he would knock on the doors of generous individuals and collect donations. He did so for many years.

One day, he met a man who had formerly been quite wealthy but had lost his entire fortune and was now forced to rely on charity in order to sustain himself. The two paupers became acquainted with one another, and began to collect charity together.

On one occasion, they arrived in a city where there resided an extraordinarily wealthy man, an innkeeper by profession who was renowned for his hospitality. The two paupers hurried to his home.

They sat in the wealthy man's house for several hours but were not served a morsel of food or drink.

"Do you think we should ask the innkeeper for some food?" asked the inexperienced pauper to his veteran friend.

"Absolutely not," he replied. "Don't say anything at all. When the wealthy man wishes, he will invite us to the table."

Shortly thereafter, a group of merchants who had come from afar and had been on the road for a long time arrived at the inn. Not having eaten a decent meal in quite some time, the merchants immediately requested food and beverages, and they were quickly accommodated, being served aromatic dishes whose fragrance could be detected from quite a distance away.

"Maybe we should put in a request as well," the pauper suggested once again. "Why are the merchants any different than we are?"

"No, no," replied his friend. "Don't ask for anything; you will shortly see the difference between the merchants and ourselves..."

Surely enough, at the conclusion of the meal, the innkeeper approached the merchants and presented them with a bill for the meal. The merchants, in return, paid with solid gold coins.

After he finished with the merchants' bill, the innkeeper approached the paupers, graciously inviting them to be his guests and dine at his table.

> There are individuals, exclaimed the Dubno Maggid, whose sole desire is to constantly pursue the delights that this world has to offer. All of their days are spent seeking pleasures and luxuries. Let them know that there is a notepad in Heaven which is being inscribed, and the time will come when the Creator will present them with an exact bill for all that they indulged in.
>
> This is not the case with the righteous, who detest the trivialities of this world and are oblivious to its pleasures. Hashem presents everything to them as a free gift.

❧ Penny After Penny

Two paupers were accustomed to sitting together in the city square and collecting charity. One pauper was a very wise and profound individual; the other was a complete buffoon.

The foolish pauper never had more than the one penny that he had most recently collected in his possession, for the moment that he would be given money, he would use it to purchase food and drink.

This was not the case with his sagacious friend, however, who did not squander a single cent. Rather, he collected one penny after another, and when he had amassed many, he would exchange them for a coin of higher value. After he had a respectable amount of these coins in his possession, he would exchange them for one of even greater value and so on, until he had amassed an adequate sum of money with which to sustain himself.

A righteous man, noted the Dubno Maggid, acts wisely. He therefore does not waste a single day, utilizing each one to learn Torah and perform *mitzvos* in the service of Hashem. His *mitzvos* eventually add up, until he possesses an abundance of Torah and good deeds for which the reward is very great.

The wicked, on the other hand, squander their days with meaningless endeavors and foolishness, never possessing anything more than the fleeting pleasure of the moment, which inevitably leaves no more than an empty void in its place.

Ultimately, they are left with nothing at all!

✑ Hospitality to Guests

A wealthy man was renowned for the hospitality he accorded guests. There was not a single pauper, traveler, nor guest of any sort to whom he did not offer sleeping accommodations as well as a hearty meal. In addition, the wealthy man personally served each guest who lodged in his home.

One day a traveler appeared in the wealthy man's home and, after removing his backpack, sat himself down at the wealthy man's table.

"What can I serve you?" asked the wealthy man. "We prepared many delicacies today in honor of the guests."

"I am not hungry nor do I have an appetite," replied the guest. "Would you happen to have some whiskey in the house? I'll down a glass or two, and maybe that will stimulate my appetite."

"Why would I do such a thing?" asked the wealthy man. "The whole purpose of my hospitality is to satiate the hungry — not to hunger the satiated! If a hungry individual comes to me, I will immediately fulfill his request and feed him the finest delicacies. But why should I extend myself to make a satiated person hungry?"

There are times, the Dubno Maggid pointed out, that Hashem rewards an individual for the good deeds that he has performed, and grants him enormous wealth. Such a person must thank Hashem and be content with what he has been given. It would be a terrible thing, however, if his wealth led him to covet money and to pursue additional riches and possessions.

The purpose of reward is to satiate the hungry — not to hunger the satiated!

◄§ The Three Beloved Companions of the King

A king had three loyal companions who were very dear to his heart. One day, nefarious individuals slandered them and claimed that they were plotting to rebel against the king. These men were not loyal at all, they claimed, and the king had misjudged them.

The king summoned his three friends and commanded each one of them to take possession of a dog from the king's kennels and to care for it for three months. After three months had elapsed, they were to return to the palace.

The king then instructed that any funds that were necessary to care for the dogs would be allotted from the royal treasury to the three men.

The first man took the money but did not use any of it to care for the dog. Instead, he fed the dog his own leftover food and used the money to purchase a beautiful gold crown as a gift for the king.

The second man gave the dog just enough food in order for it to remain alive.

The third man, on the other hand, spent all of the money on food for the dog, and the dog grew so fat that it was unrecognizable.

When the three months had passed, the friends came before the king.

The first man presented the king with the beautiful gift that he had purchased. The king was delighted and, in return, gave the man a reward from his treasury that was worth many times more than the crown.

The second man showed the king the weak and emaciated dog; the king sent him home without any reward whatsoever.

When the third man displayed the overweight dog, the king — enraged over the fact that the man had wasted the money by spending it so unwisely — snatched the dog away from him.

> There are three types of individuals in the world, said R' Yisrael Ba'al Shem Tov: The first are the righteous, who do not derive any pleasure whatsoever from materialism and employ all of their powers in the service of Hashem. With the good deeds they perform, they fashion a beautiful crown for their Creator — how great is their reward!
>
> The second group consists of those individuals who derive just enough benefit from the world in order to sustain their bodies, not a drop more or less.
>
> The third group consists of those who waste away all of their days pursuing the delights of this world. In the next world they will be punished for investing all of their powers in order to feed their bodies.

✥ Foot Soldiers and Horsemen

A king has two types of soldiers in his army: foot soldiers and horsemen. Foot soldiers march courageously and fearlessly toward the enemy and station themselves directly opposite them. When they attack, they do battle face to face and make no attempt to flee. Horsemen, on the other hand, can move in whichever direction they see fit, and if they encounter an overpowering enemy, they can escape with ease. With a tug of the reins, the horse will speedily gallop away and take them to a secure area.

Now, if the king is victorious, the horsemen come riding on their steeds and seize a large portion of the booty. The foot soldiers, however, know that all of the booty belongs to the king alone and that he is well aware of who was truly responsible for winning the war.

> Servants of Hashem, said R' Yisrael Ba'al Shem Tov, are compared to foot soldiers who courageously wage war in any situation, all for the sake of Hashem's great Name. Those who pursue the delights of this world, on the other hand, are compared to horsemen riding strapping steeds. When blessing and bounty descend to the world in the merit of the righteous and the battles they fight, the frivolous pleasure-seekers snatch all that they can, while the righteous stand by, knowing full well that the Master of the World has guaranteed their reward!

◄§ "I Have Set Hashem Before Me Always"

A man was standing before the king, awestruck with fear and trembling. While standing there, he was approached by an individual who slapped him soundly across the face.

The man restrained himself and did not respond, thinking to himself, "Either way, it is not to my benefit to react. For if the king had instructed this fellow to slap me — then I have absolutely no say in the matter, for so decreed the king. But if this man slapped me without having been commanded to do so — the king will undoubtedly punish him for his impudence."

So it is with man, said the Maggid, R' Yaakov Yosef of Polonoye. Man must constantly feel as if he is standing before Hashem, the King of Kings, as the verse states, "I have set Hashem before me always" (*Tehillim* 16:8)! If he is able to accustom himself to feel and think in such a manner, he will happily accept whatever befalls him.

Part 10

Torah

~§ The Apprentice

An expert glass blower taught his apprentice the fine art of glass blowing.

One day, the apprentice was working in the glass blower's shop and fashioned a fine-looking glass dish. The glass blower noticed the dish and it pleased him very much. He liked it so much, in fact, that he asked his apprentice to give it to him.

"I will happily give it to you!" answered the apprentice. "However, you must pay me full price for it."

"Insolent one!" shouted his teacher angrily. "It was I who trained you to fashion such dishes. You were sitting in my shop when you made it, using *my* tools and materials — and now you demand that I pay for it?"

> Man is the handiwork of Hashem, said the Chofetz Chaim. Hashem has granted us our intellect, mouth, eyes, and the rest of our two hundred and forty-eight limbs and three hundred and sixty-five sinews. Hashem gave us the day and night as well.
>
> That being the case, how does man have the nerve — or the right, for that matter — to involve all of them in the transgression of *bitul Torah* (squandering time that could have otherwise been utilized for Torah study)?

~§ The Taste of Radish and Onion

A pauper had a wealthy relative who was about to marry his son to a girl from an aristocratic family. A wedding of such magnitude would surely require much preparation and even the pauper adequately readied himself for the great event.

"It goes without saying," thought the pauper, "that my relative will arrange a feast that is fit for a king. It is therefore worth my while to abstain from food and drink for two days before the wedding. This way, I will have an enormous appetite on the day of the affair and will be able to derive full benefit from the scrumptious delicacies that are sure to be served."

And so he did. He fasted for two full days, refusing to allow a morsel of food to enter his mouth. When evening fell on the day of the wedding, the pauper who felt faint stood by the window and peered out, as he wished to see if his wealthy relative's servants were knocking on his door in order to extend him an invitation. To his great anguish, however, he saw his relative's servants rushing to the homes of the city's distinguished residents, yet they bypassed his own.

"Please hurry, my dear wife," exclaimed the pauper. "In another moment, I will faint from hunger. Please prepare me whatever food we have in the house."

The devoted wife rushed and served her husband stale bread, a few onions, and garlic. She also managed to scrounge up a radish and placed it all before her unfortunate husband who literally devoured every bit of food that she served him.

After he was satiated and had *bentched* (recited the Grace After Meals), he suddenly heard a knock at the door. The wealthy man's servants had come to invite him to the wedding.

Embittered, the pauper walked to the wedding and sat at a table. For the first course, he was served baked fish that had been caught that very day. The fish was elegantly served on a silver tray and accompanied by a garland of vegetables.

The pauper tried a piece of the fish, yet the only thing he tasted was the radish that he had eaten prior to the wedding.

Next he was served tender roasted calf smothered in sweet gravy. Along with the main course came a side dish of baked potatoes and delicious mushrooms. The pauper tasted the delicacy and immediately grimaced — the taste of the garlic and onions that he had eaten in his home still lingered on his palate.

The pauper sat at the extravagant feast but did not taste another thing.

When the guests began to depart at the conclusion of the meal, the pauper overheard how they were lauding the amazing feast with praise, noting how they had not enjoyed such a meal in quite some time.

"Surely you are joking with me," said the pauper to the guests. "I also partook of the feast, yet I did not find it tasty at all." The men were astounded, until one of the wealthy man's servants put their astonishment to rest. "Do not be the least bit surprised!" remarked the servant. "I am the one who invited him to the wedding, and I saw how he had finished eating a meal that consisted of garlic, onion, and radish right before he came here...After such a meal — how did you expect these royal delicacies to taste?"

> Hashem gave us the Torah and *mitzvos* which are "sweeter than honey and drippings of the combs" (*Tehillim* 19:11), said the Dubno Maggid. In order to taste the amazing flavor of the holy Torah, however, one must approach *mitzvah* performance with a pure heart and soul. But if an individual has sated his soul with the bitterness of worldly temptations, how will he possibly experience the delectable taste of the royal delicacies of Hashem, the King of the World?

◆§ The King's Two Gardeners

A king possessed a large and exquisite garden which encircled his palace. There were two gardeners appointed to tend its care; one was an experienced horticulturist who was an expert at planting unique fruit trees as well as growing stunning flowers. The second was a villager who specialized in raising vegetables and herbs.

When summer arrived, the two gardeners came before the king, each one bringing with him a gift consisting of his finest crops and handiwork. The first one arrived with a basket filled with excellent-tasting grapes that were of very fine quality indeed. The small basket was decorated with beautiful flowers which emitted a pleasant fragrance as well. The second gardener brought with him a basket of choice vegetables that were not yet available in the city markets. The king was elated, granting each one a generous gift and praising their splendid handiwork.

Upon taking leave of the king, the horticulturist wished to celebrate with his friends. The villager desired to take part in the festivities as well, and asked if he could join them.

The vine-grower did not take kindly to the villager's request. "What business do you have with me?" he asked. "You and your ancestors have always been nothing more than simple farmers, yet I have been trained in the intricacies and wisdom of planting as well as grafting. I am not a simple villager like you are!"

"But the vegetables that I grew were accepted by the king just as your fruits were," said the villager. "That being the case, why are you any better than I am?"

"If you truly wish to know the difference between my work and yours," responded the expert, "wait several days. Then you will clearly see the difference."

Several days passed, until the marketplace was stocked with the new season's vegetables. The horticulturist then invited the villager to join him once again in bringing a gift from their produce to the king.

"This is not the time to bring the king such a present," responded the villager. "At the present time, anyone who wishes — be it a poor man or a wealthy man — can bring the king vegetables, as they are all available in the marketplace. Such a gift would be rather unremarkable."

"Perhaps now you understand the difference between us," said the expert. "You see, the produce that I grow retains its value throughout the entire year and is not readily available at any time. The same cannot be said about your produce, however, for its uniqueness is only momentary."

The same thing applies to this world, said the Dubno Maggid. In this world, items are valued by how rare they are and how difficult they are to attain. Copper, for example, which is easily obtainable, is worth far less than gold, which is quite rare.

The same cannot be said for the holy Torah, however — the more it is studied, the greater its value and significance. For to the extent that those who study Torah delve into its great depths of understanding, to that degree does their desire to learn the Torah increase!

◦§ A Valid Reason

A father bought his son a valuable watch in honor of his bar mitzvah and repeatedly cautioned him to take great care of the watch, lest it get damaged or lost.

The son's joy knew no bounds, and he promised his father that he would protect the watch from any potential mishap.

One day, the son crossed the bridge that extended over the river in his city. As he was walking across the bridge, a strong wind blew and caused the precarious bridge to shake to and fro. As the son held on to the guardrail, the watch slipped from his wrist and fell into the river.

The boy ran to his father and, in tears, related what had happened "Father!" cried the boy. "When I crossed the bridge above the river, a strong wind blew, and as I was holding onto the rail."

"Just tell me," interrupted the father, "do you have the watch or was it lost?"

"The watch," responded the son in utter humiliation, "is lost."

"If so," said the father, "of what significance is what occurred and *how* you lost the watch? What matters is that the watch is gone — what good will your story do?"

A Jew, said the Chofetz Chaim, is commanded to learn the holy Torah, as the verse states, "You should contemplate it day and night" (*Yehoshua* 1:8). However, various reasons and day-to day situations crop up and prevent an individual from fulfilling this requirement. Now, even though his excuses may be valid, at the end of the day — he has not learned Torah!

What good will his story do?

⊷ Eventually he Pennies Add Up

Two paupers dragged themselves from town to town and from village to village, knocking on doors and requesting charity wherever they went. Now, the townspeople they visited were by no means rich — but the Jewish residents took pity on them and their kindhearted nature prevailed. They gave the paupers copper coins, never allowing them to be turned away empty-handed.

The two paupers differed greatly in how they managed the money they collected. While one was accustomed to spending the money as soon as he received it, his friend saved each penny he collected, until, after quite some time, he had succeeded in amassing a paltry sum of coins. He would then purchase some merchandise with his money and sell it for a profit. He continued this practice for quite some time, until he become a wealthy merchant.

Even during the time that the one pauper's fortunes took a turn for the better, his long-time friend nevertheless continued to trudge along and collect copper pennies.

Every man has been allotted a certain number of years in this world, explained the Dubno Maggid, and these years are comprised of days and hours. A person must take care to conserve his time in this world and utilize it in order to learn Torah and perform *mitzvos*. By doing so, the hours and days which he has devoted to the service of Hashem will eventually add up, and he will ultimately be the recipient of overwhelming reward.

However, concluded the Maggid, if a person squanders his days with meaningless endeavors, when he arrives in the World of Truth he will be left with nothing.

ஃ *The Miser's Donation*

Word reached the residents that a massive legion of horsemen planned to conquer their city and plunder all of their possessions. An emergency meeting was convened between the leaders of the city and its sages, and they decided that they were left with only one option: they would have to collect a large sum of money, go out to greet the army, and present their offering. Perhaps the money would kindle a spark of mercy in the soldier's hearts, and they would agree to spare the people.

Due to the matter's severity, the leaders themselves went from door to door throughout the city in order to solicit four coins from each family member.

Their first stop was the home of one of the city's wealthier residents. His reputation as a miser preceded him, however, and he was infamous for his refusal to give even as little as a penny to charity.

Today the miser wore a different face, however. "Even though I normally do not give any donations," he said, "this time I will veer from my usual practice, as the matter is an important one indeed. I have but one question, though — why did you turn to me first?"

"It is specifically due to your usual reluctance to give," responded the communal leaders, "that we came to you first. You see, if we would have tried to collect from the other residents first, they may have refused to give, saying that we must wait — for perhaps salvation will arrive from another source. They might have claimed that the rumor was unfounded and that they would wait until it was verified. They could have come up with any number of empty excuses such as these as to why they did not want to give. But once they would hear," continued the leaders, "that even the wealthy miser contributed the requested sum — that would be a clear indication that there is no other option…"

The Ben Ish Chai, R' Yosef Chaim of Baghdad, quotes the Gemara (*Beitzah* 25b) which states: "Why was the Torah given to Israel? Because they are brazen!" The nations of the world are aware of the brazenness of the Jewish people and of the fact that they are reluctant to subject themselves to any manner of yoke. Yet if despite this attribute, they nevertheless agreed to accept the Torah and perform its *mitzvos*, it indicates that they saw and understood that the Torah is absolutely essential for the entire world and that it is impossible to live without it. Therefore they bent their heads and allowed themselves to be subjected to the yoke of Torah and *mitzvos*.

⮴ The Lost Tool

A ruler yearned to own an exquisite piece of jewelry so that he could arrogantly put it on display. He therefore invited a professional goldsmith to come to his home. He even provided the craftsman with his own personal working station. He placed gold and precious gems in front of him and ordered him to fashion a piece of jewelry, the likes of which had never before been seen. The ruler even supplied the goldsmith with every tool he requested; all in all, he was fully equipped to perform the task.

Some time later, the goldsmith approached the ruler and informed him that he had lost one of his most important and vital tools.

The ruler grew infuriated and shouted at the goldsmith, "Leave my home at once! Leave and never return!"

In a trembling voice, the goldsmith gathered the nerve to ask for an explanation. "But why?" he asked. "Are you expelling me from your home and rejecting my work simply because I lost an essentially worthless tool?"

"Not at all," answered the ruler. "The tool is inexpensive and has no more importance to me than an onion peel. But the fact that you lost it indicates that you have been deceiving me and eating in my home like a freeloader. For if you were truly working as you should have been," continued the ruler, "you would never have lost such an indispensable tool. If you have, it demonstrates that you have been sitting idly."

Said the Dubno Maggid, a man is required to study the Torah all the days of his life, in order to be constantly reviewing what he has learned lest he forget it. If he does forget what he has learned, it indicates that he is not learning as diligently as he should be!

✌§ The Reward for One Word

An embittered pauper walked dejectedly along the road. His house was lacking the most basic necessities, and he did not even have bread to feed his children. He simply ambled along, mulling over his miserable lot.

Suddenly, a sparkle caught his eye, and he was curious to discover what caused it. "Let me have a look," thought the pauper. "Maybe it was a coin that I saw shining."

He approached the area and was shocked to see a stone lying on the side of the road, glimmering brightly.

He picked up the stone and rolled it back and forth in his hand.

"I am going to take this stone to my friend the jeweler," thought the pauper, "and ask him if it is worth anything."

He made his way to the jeweler's store and entered carrying his newfound stone. The goldsmith began to examine it with his magnifying glass, checking it ever so carefully. Suddenly, he jumped as if bitten by a snake.

"Do you have any idea what you found?" shouted the jeweler excitedly. "This is no mere stone — it is priceless! Such a gem is beyond comparison and fit to be set in the emperor's crown!"

The jeweler immediately sent word to the emperor that someone had brought him an extraordinary stone of rare quality. The emperor, in turn, dispatched messengers to bring him both the stone and its owner.

The emperor examined the stone, and it found much favor in his eyes.

"How much money do you want for this stone?" the emperor asked the pauper.

"Your Highness," responded the pauper, "when I initially discovered this stone, I did not realize just how much it was worth. His Highness may therefore give me whatever he wishes."

The emperor granted him a huge sum of money for the beautiful stone, and from then on, the pauper was transformed into a wealthy man who never again tasted the bitter taste of poverty.

> Our holy Torah, said the Chofetz Chaim, is more precious than pearls, and is compared to a beautiful gem. However, we do not grasp the true value of the Torah, for at times we put our studies aside and engage in meaningless activities.
>
> We must know that Hashem, the King of Kings, grants anyone who learns even one word of Torah a limitless reward.

~§ A Vessel of Exquisite Beauty

An individual visited the mansion of a distinguished ruler and was overwhelmed by its sheer magnificence. What impressed him most were the beautiful sparkling vessels. Vessels as remarkable as these captivated all those who saw them, and the visitor was simply unable to tear his eyes away. The members of the ruler's household, on the other hand, did not pay the slightest attention to the beautiful vessels, as they had long grown familiar with them and were no longer spellbound by their appearance.

> This is not the case, noted the Dubno Maggid, when it comes to those who study the Torah. If one visits a place where there are individuals learning Torah, he will immediately sense just how beloved the holy Torah is to them.
>
> On the other hand, one who has never studied Torah nor ever tasted the sweetness of Torah — even one out of a thousand such individuals will not hold the Torah dear.

✌ The Palace

A story is related of a king who built an enormous palace befitting a great ruler of his caliber. The palace was spacious, and it was fortified as well, surrounded by a high wall and soaring towers. The palace itself consisted of hundreds of rooms and halls — it was as splendid an edifice as could be fathomed.

On one occasion, an individual whose vision was impaired passed the palace. To him, it appeared as if the palace was crooked … the towers looked bent over, as if they were ready to collapse, and one of the walls seemed to be leaning to one side.

The man began to shout, "My brothers, be careful! Evacuate the palace at once and save your lives!"

Some of the palace's residents were not very alarmed by his exhortations, as they saw with their own eyes that the palace was sturdy and standing tall, presenting absolutely no danger whatsoever. Yet there were others who did not even bother to check the palace's condition; they simply fled in a state of panic…

A wise man among them began to shout, "Doctor! Doctor!"

The frightened residents stopped running for a moment and asked in bewilderment, "A doctor? What good will a doctor do?"

"A doctor will be most helpful indeed," exclaimed the wise man. "For he will heal the ailing eyes of the man who shouted that the palace was crooked in the first place…"

> Our holy Torah, said the Chofetz Chaim, is similar to the fortified wall of a palace that has been built by the King of the World — Hashem. There are instances, however, when visually impaired individuals claim that the palace is crooked, staggering, and likely to collapse. As a result, they flee and distance themselves from the Torah. Yet there are many individuals who see clearly, realizing without a shadow of a doubt that the Torah is a mighty edifice that shall never crumble!

✎§ The Work Tools

A wealthy man donated an abundance of money to *tzedakah*. Once a week he had the noble custom of distributing funds in the following fashion: paupers from all across the land would line up outside his home. The wealthy man would sit at his table and, upon entering, each visitor would give a brief account of his trying predicament. Upon hearing their tales of woe, the rich man would put his hand into the drawer and remove several gold coins. To some he would give a great deal while to others he would give less.

On one occasion, a blind man was amongst the wealthy man's visitors. When it was his turn, he exclaimed, "I beg your forgiveness, sir, but it seems to me as if I am deserving of a more generous donation than all the other paupers. For I once earned my living polishing diamonds, and I made a considerable amount of money. But now I am blind and am unable to earn anything at all. Please have mercy on me!"

Something about the blind pauper's tale of woe did not ring true and made the wealthy man suspicious. He therefore requested, "Please bring me the work tools with which you used to polish diamonds. In this way, I will know that you are telling the truth!"

> In the World to Come, said the Dubno Maggid, all of the individuals who studied Torah and performed *mitzvos* will come to receive their reward. Among them, however, will be those who were not as scrupulous when it came to fulfilling the laws of the Torah. Such individuals will be told, "Present your work tools! Then we will see exactly what you engaged in throughout your life!"

Delve in the Torah and Delve in the Torah Again, for Everything Is in It

In a certain city resided an elderly miser who refused to spend even a penny of his money. His entire life had been utilized amassing money, and he had become an extremely wealthy individual. He was always fearful, however, lest the public discover that he was indeed wealthy and would take full advantage of his affluence, ultimately leaving him penniless. He therefore concealed his great wealth and hid all of his money inside the walls of his home.

It happened one day that the miser contracted what proved to be his final illness and shortly thereafter he passed away, leaving his home to a distant relative who was severely impoverished.

The poor relative lived in the house, completely oblivious to the fortune that was only a hands-breadth away, sealed within its very walls.

One day, the pauper happened to lose a particular item and in his search uncovered a small opening in the wall of the house. He stuck his finger into the wall and began to poke around, thus widening the hole; how amazed he was when he pulled out a chain of sparkling diamonds! He continued to widen the opening and was utterly astounded to discover a genuine treasure.

He checked inside the other walls in the house and found hoards of jewelry, gold coins, and chains laden with precious diamonds…

> The Dubno Maggid explained that Hashem concealed all of the world's wisdoms within the holy Torah. Through relentless toil and study, man is able to reveal more and more of the Torah and grasp, with Hashem's help, the other wisdoms as well, as *Chazal* state (*Avos* 5:26), "Delve in it [the Torah] and delve in it [the Torah] again, for everything is in it!"

◄§ The Stores in the City

A villager went to visit his friend who resided in the big city. The friend proceeded to give him a guided tour, showing him the city's most extraordinary sights.

First he brought him to the city's grain stores. Several of these had gigantic storage rooms that were literally bursting with sacks of wheat, rice, and sugar, and barrels of oil. Next, he showed the villager the city's garment and fabric shops. These stores were not quite as large as the previous ones nor did they have very much merchandise on their shelves.

Afterwards, the villager got a chance to see the silk stores, which turned out to be even smaller than the garment shops had been. The silver store that he was shown next was smaller yet, containing only two display cases. The gold store had but one display case, while the store which sold precious gems and pearls had none at all; the storeowner simply sat there holding his small sample case.

Upon returning to his village, the villager told everyone what he had seen in the city, saying, "I am so surprised how, in the center of the city, there is a store selling valuable jewels — why, there is barely any merchandise in it...The residents of the city would have been better off had the grain store been there instead."

Among the listeners was a city-dweller who, upon hearing the villager's words, erupted into a state of laughter. "You simple villager," he exclaimed. "Don't you understand? The more expensive the merchandise, the less of a supply there is. There are times when the cost of one exquisite gem will far exceed the cost of thousands of sacks of wheat!"

Individuals who study and support Torah are few in number, explained the Chofetz Chaim, but each one is like an extremely precious and expensive gem. For in the eyes of Hashem, there are times when one individual can be equal to one thousand other men!

◆§ Everything Is Contained Within it

A person would regularly shop in a certain store. One day, the storeowner glanced out the door and noticed his regular customer emerging from an adjacent shop.

The individual would not necessarily be hard-pressed to explain his actions. He could simply say that he entered the second store in search of merchandise that he could not obtain in the store where he usually shopped.

But if the first store carried precisely the same merchandise, how could the customer defend his actions? "On the contrary," the storekeeper would claim, "tell me exactly which product you were shopping for that you would have been unable to find in *my* store!"

> The same applies to the Torah, explained the Dubno Maggid. Everything is contained within the holy Torah, as *Chazal* state, "Delve in it [the Torah] and delve in it [the Torah] again, for everything is in it" (*Avos* 5:26)!
>
> Someone who wastes his time will therefore face the following claim: "Why was it necessary for you to graze in foreign pastures? What could you possibly have been searching for elsewhere which is not found in our holy Torah?"

◆§ The Torah of Earlier Generations

In a certain city lived a very wealthy man who earned his living selling grain wholesale across the land. On one occasion, he met a friend and related his concerns to him:

"It is certainly true," said the wealthy man, "that I have a multitude of employees and my business has spread into various branches. Nevertheless, I am not earning a great deal of profit as there is much competition, and my competitors expend much effort in trying to lower their prices in order to sell their merchandise."

Some time later, a great war erupted in the land and, once again, the wealthy man encountered his friend. "How has your business been faring during the war?" asked the friend.

"Wonderful!" exclaimed the wealthy man joyously, rubbing his hands together in a display of happiness. "*Baruch Hashem*, business has never been so good."

His friend was rather astonished. "Can business really be so profitable during wartime?" he asked. "Why, there is such a meager supply of grain to meet the demand!"

"That is precisely why I am prospering so," replied the wealthy man. "You see, before the war, customers came to me demanding excellent flour. They would examine my produce and, if the flour was not to their liking, they would simply go to another store. But presently," he continued, "there is a major shortage of flour; the customers therefore do not check it at all — they just grab whatever they can before there is nothing left…"

If such is the case with grain, remarked the Chofetz Chaim, how much more so is it true in relation to Torah and *mitzvos*. In previous generations, the Jewish Nation had great Torah giants. A person, concluded the Chofetz Chaim, should therefore not say, "What am I in comparison to the earlier generations, and of what value is my Torah study?" Such an individual is making a grave error, for in times such as these, any manner of Torah study and any *mitzvah* that one fulfills is considered "sought-after merchandise" and is very esteemed in the eyes of Hashem.

☙ Torah Returns to its Inn

A rabbi authored a *sefer* that was filled to overflowing with splendid novel Torah thoughts, and he wished to have it printed. He therefore gathered together his writings and traveled to the big city where there was a well-known printing establishment.

When he arrived in the city, he went to one of its inns, approached the innkeeper, and exclaimed loudly, "*Shalom Aleichem!*" He went on to state his name and from which town he had arrived and then continued, "I am visiting this city on the occasion of the printing of my *sefer*. I am therefore seeking a place to lodge for a period of three months, as this is the time required in order to print the *sefer*. I would be most pleased if you would allow me to stay at your inn."

The innkeeper was extremely perceptive, and he immediately understood that the rabbi was requesting to lodge at the inn free of charge. For if that was not his intention, why would he have commenced his speech with such appeasing words? Furthermore, why else would he have mentioned that he was a rabbi who had come to print a *sefer*?

"I'm sorry," answered the innkeeper, "but I will not be able to accede to your request. I am simply short of space at the moment. Try another inn."

The rabbi made his way to a different inn and relayed his request. Once again, he was turned away. The same thing happened at the third inn he visited, as well as the fourth…

Word of the rabbi's distress reached the ears of one of the city's residents. While he was by no means a wealthy man, he nevertheless looked for opportunities to perform acts of kindness for others. He therefore rushed over to the rabbi and invited him to lodge in his home for as long as he would like. In addition, he told the rabbi that he would fully provide him with all of his needs.

The rabbi remained in the city and printed his *sefer*. It was enormously successful and the rabbi grew quite wealthy, becoming renowned throughout the land.

Some time later, the rabbi visited the city once again, but this time he arrived in a magnificent coach that was harnessed to a pair of powerful steeds. All of the people in the city went out to greet him as his fame had spread far and wide. The moment he placed his foot on the ground, every one of the innkeepers and wealthy men of the city appealed to him to lodge in their houses.

"If you are truly generous individuals," challenged the rabbi, "then why did you not allow me to lodge in your homes when I first came here? Why did you turn me away?"

When Hashem desired to give the Torah to mankind, said the Dubno Maggid, He first offered it to the various nations of the world. They all rejected it, however, offering a variety of excuses as to why they could not accept it. But when the Torah was offered to the Jewish Nation, they accepted it, saying, "We will do and we will obey!" (*Shemos* 24:7).

Therefore, concluded the Maggid, in the future, when the reward that has been stored away for those who fear Hashem will be revealed to all, the gentiles will request to be given the Torah as well. Hashem will then answer them, "Why did you not "allow Me to lodge" in your homes when I first came here? Why did you turn Me away?"

ঙ্গ *On Condition to Fulfill*

There were once two sisters who married two brothers. One sister married a very wealthy businessman, and the other married a pauper.

One day, the poor sister went to visit the rich one. When she arrived at the magnificent palace where her sister lived, the poor woman was awestruck by its beauty and was simply unable to tear her eyes away. The palace contained large halls and parlors, floors were covered with expensive rugs, and the walls were hung with splendid portraits. In addition, dozens of servants dressed in special uniforms went about their chores quietly and were prepared to cater to their employer's every whim.

When they sat down to converse, the poor woman detected that her sister looked rather unhappy. "Why are you so sad?" she asked. "You have such a magnificent home!"

"That is certainly true," her rich sister replied. "My husband is indeed very wealthy and my home is extravagant, but my husband does not treat me nicely. He shows me no respect, and on occasion, even goes so far as to deride and denigrate me extensively.

"More than once," continued the rich sister sadly, "I have asked myself if my lot is truly better than yours. You may live in poverty, lacking a palace and servants, but at least your husband respects you and regards what you have to say."

There are times, concluded the Chofetz Chaim, when we adorn the sefer Torah in a beautiful silk casing and cap it with a shiny crown. We place it on a golden table and then return it to an ark that was hand-crafted by a skilled craftsman.

Yet all of these details are meaningless to the Torah if we do not hearken to its words. The Torah screams, "Remove all of this glamour from upon me! Just refrain from trampling me…"

There are times when it is specifically the poorer congregations — congregations unable to afford the cost of adorning the Torah in silk trappings — who accord the Torah great honor by adhering to its each and every detail.

Such poverty is a fitting honor to the Torah and is far superior to illusory splendor and the like.

⇜§ Man's Purpose

On the crossroads leading to the big city a merchant opened a store stocked with high-quality goods. It soon became apparent that few travelers were choosing to interrupt their journey and enter his store; rather, the majority of them hastened along the road towards the big city.

What did he do?

Adjacent to his store, he opened an inn where guests would be able to rest, as well as a restaurant that sold tasty delicacies. He placed a professional chef with a sterling reputation in charge of managing the inn and restaurant.

"I am not requesting anything from you," said the merchant to the chef. "Just go ahead and sell your delicacies, and do not pay me any money whatsoever. When travelers stop into your restaurant in order to partake of your delicious food, they will certainly enter my store as well."

One day, a group of unkempt-looking fellows visited the inn. After tasting the delightful cuisine, they decided to reside there for a number of days. While they helped themselves to a great deal of the food, they did not so much as enter the merchant's store. Seeing this, after several days of eating to their hearts' content, the merchant finally sent the guests on their way.

"Why are you kicking us out?" asked the surprised band of gluttons. "Did we not pay for the food?"

"You certainly did," responded the merchant. "But I derived absolutely no benefit from it whatsoever. The sole purpose of the restaurant is to draw customers into my store. You, however, filled your stomachs with a massive amount of delicacies and did not even step into my store. Your lodging in my inn therefore serves me no purpose — please leave and make room for someone else!"

> The Dubno Maggid said, Hashem bestows upon man a vast treasury of materialism from His goodness in order that man be able to engage in Torah study. Instead, however, man stuffs his stomach with these mundane delights and only occasionally steps into the *beis midrash*. His main purpose in life is relegated to secondary status, while that which is of secondary status is made primary.
>
> This is not the purpose for which Hashem created man!

✺ Choosing the Appropriate Profession

There are many professions in our vast world, noted the Dubno Maggid. There are professions which entail easy labor, yet others are more difficult. There are professions — such as diamond polishing — through which one can earn a lot of money, and others — such as a working as a blacksmith — that are far less lucrative.

Perhaps we would be tempted to ask the following question: Why doesn't every individual simply choose to learn a trade which will leave him unsoiled and reap him enormous profits?

The answer would be as follows: There is a great benefit accrued in learning to perform simple labor, for it is a skill which is inevitably held in heavy demand no matter what the place or time.

We see, therefore, that there is both an advantage and disadvantage vested in each and every profession.

The perfect scenario would be an individual whose trade commands a significant fee, yet he is also well versed in the skill of carrying out a simple task when the opportunity presents itself!

> The holy Torah, said the Dubno Maggid, is exactly like such an individual. On one hand, the Torah contains the deepest secrets, which only select individuals will be fortunate enough to grasp. Yet, on the other hand, every single individual is capable of studying the Torah's simple meaning and experiencing its sweetness!

⋐ What to Ask For

Two paupers walked along the street on a freezing winter day. They were dressed in tattered clothing and torn shoes, through which seeped a great deal of mud and rain without any hindrance whatsoever.

Suddenly, a magnificent coach passed by in which one of the wealthiest men of the city and his family were seated. They were all wearing warm fur coats, and sitting snugly on their heads were expensive hats. Between the lapels of the coats were valuable jewels which sparkled brilliantly.

One of the paupers let out a deep sigh. "If Hashem would just help me and give me a beautiful coach and precious jewels as well – how fortunate I would be…"

"You're dreaming about the wrong things, my dear friend," commented the other pauper. "You are requesting greatness and grandeur for yourself, but with your situation being what it is, you'd be better off wishing for a loaf of bread and a warm cup of tea."

We pray every day, remarked the Chofetz Chaim, "Please, Hashem, our G-d, sweeten the words of Your Torah in our mouth … May we and our offspring — all of us — know Your Name and study Your Torah for its own sake!"

We waste our precious time engaging in the trivialities of this world and we request to study Torah for its own sake! We must first enter the *beis midrash* and study Torah; only afterwards should we request that the Torah which we learn should be for its own sake!

✑ The Watch

A father had an only son whom he loved dearly, and subsequently catered to the boy's every request. When the son grew older, he very much wanted his father to buy him a watch. The father went to a professional watchmaker and asked him to fashion a stylish gold watch with an engraved casing. When he presented his son with the watch, the young man's joy knew no bounds. Now, the father was well aware of his son's spoiled nature, and he knew quite well that the lad would quickly grow tired of the watch. He therefore devised a clever plan. The father, in his wisdom, forbade his son to open the case. After some time had passed, the son indeed grew tired of the watch. Only then did the father permit him to open the case. When the son caught a glimpse of the delicate hands expertly crafted by the skilled watchmaker, he experienced a new feeling of elation over the watch. Some time later, the son once again grew tired of the watch. The father therefore opened the back of the watch and showed his son the fine wheel movements which operated it harmoniously. In this way, the son enjoyed the watch for quite a long time.

In His great love for the Jewish people, said the Dubno Maggid, Hashem desired that we rejoice in the precious gift that He granted us — the holy Torah. He therefore concealed within it a plethora of novel ideas that are revealed day after day, which constantly renew the experience of Torah study. The more an individual exerts himself in Torah study, the more he reveals these extraordinary novel ideas that serve to gladden his heart.

Part 11

Prayer

≈§ *Prayer Without Proper Focus*

A wealthy man had a dedicated servant who was at his service whenever he was needed.

On one occasion, the employer had to take a journey in order to tend to his many business matters, and he would be compelled to leave his home for several weeks.

He summoned his servant, gave him a long list of instructions, and said, "Please read this list each and every day, so that you do not forget to perform a single task from all that I have written here." The servant nodded his head in order to indicate that he understood.

The employer boarded the luxurious coach that was waiting outside for him and set off on his journey.

When he returned, he summoned his servant and asked him if he had followed his instructions.

"Yes, sir," answered the servant. "Each day, I read over the list that you wrote several times..."

"You fool!" shouted the employer in a voice that stung of rebuke. "Did I ask you only to read the list? My whole intention was that you would read the list and remember to fulfill that which I commanded you! Reading it alone is absolutely useless!"

> The same thing applies to prayer, noted the Chofetz Chaim. If an individual picks up a *siddur* and reads it without any *kavanah*, he is similar to the foolish servant...

≈§ *Praying Daily*

A king had a son for whom he provided fully. If the son was ever in need of anything, he would simply place a request with his father, who would lovingly give him whatever he needed.

One day, the son transgressed the will of his father. The king was furious and reprimanded his son, but it was to no avail — the son's disobedience persisted.

The king summoned one of his closest officers and said to him, "Generously provide my son with his each and every need."

The officer was absolutely bewildered by the king's instructions and asked, "Your Highness, why are you providing your son with his every need if he is does not travel the upright path?"

"You have not fully grasped my intentions," answered the king. "You see, as long as my son was acting properly, I wished to see him every single day. Therefore, whenever he required something, he would come to me; I would be happy to receive him and fulfill his requests. But now that he has veered from the proper path, even though I still love him, I do not wish to see him at all! I am therefore instructing you to provide him with all of his needs so that he will no longer come before me."

> Hashem, in His great love for us, granted us the privilege to pray before Him three times a day and, at any moment that we choose, to ask Him to provide us with all of our needs, even when we have strayed from the proper path. In His abundant mercy, He fulfills the verse, "You open Your hand, and satisfy the desire of every living thing" (*Tehillim* 145:16).

✒ With His Soul He Brings His Bread

The Dubno Maggid once offered the following parable:

A carrier of heavy loads — a strong and able-bodied individual — formed a partnership with a yeshivah student. The carrier would perform his labor and carry bundles, and give half of his earnings to the yeshivah student. The yeshivah student, on his part, would study Torah and give half of his reward to the carrier.

Some time later, the carrier approached the yeshivah student and proposed, "My friend, I would like to alter the conditions of our partnership. From now on *I* will sit and study Torah and *you* will lug the heavy packages..."

Thereupon, the thin mild-mannered young man went out to the marketplace in order to perform the strenuous work, while the carrier engrossed himself in the study of Talmud.

From such a partnership, noted the Dubno Maggid, one cannot expect to reap significant profits.

The Jewish people, he explained, acknowledge a total partnership between the body and soul. The body sustains the soul by providing it with its material requirements, while the soul contributes its share in spirituality. There are some Jews, however, who have reversed the partnership. The body becomes responsible for the spirituality and it therefore sways to and fro during prayers without any *kavanah* or thought. On the other hand, "with his soul he brings his bread" (see *Eichah* 5:9) — the soul assumes responsibility for man's materialistic needs, and during prayers his thoughts, therefore, center around business in the marketplace...Such a partnership cannot be expected to bear fruit.

⋅୫ *Preparation for Prayer*

When R' Avraham Mordechai Alter, the *Imrei Emes*, assumed the mantle of leadership of the chassidic dynasty of Gur, he ruled that prayer service would now be conducted in line with the halachic times of prayer, something that had not been the custom until that point.
The elderly *chassidim* approached the Rebbe and asked him, "What will happen to the extensive preparation that is required for prayer?"
"In response to your question," answered the Rebbe, "I will offer you a parable."

There was once a wealthy man who was accustomed to feasting on the delicious delicacies that his wife prepared for him each day. He would arrive at his home in the afternoon and wait quite a while before his wife served him the food that she had prepared.

"The waiting did not bother her husband in the least, for he understood that considerable preparation was required in order to produce such an outstanding repast.

"On one occasion, he waited for a long time, but instead of the usual scrumptious dishes, he was served bland, ordinary food.

"'Tell me, my wife,' asked the surprised husband. 'Why were you so delayed in preparing the food today? Why, this is ordinary food which does not require such meticulous preparation...'

"In the past," concluded the Rebbe, "prayer used to be vested with all of its kavanos and it therefore required a tremendous amount of preparation. In the present day, however, our prayers are unfortunately quite simple and therefore do not need as much preparation."

⁀ When Old Memories Are Rehashed

In a certain town lived a merchant who managed a small textile shop through which he earned a modest but steady profit. He eventually decided to move to the big city; there he would be able to open a large business and earn a hefty profit. And so he did.

One day, the merchant spotted an individual from his old town entering a different store and purchasing various goods. He approached him, placed his hand on his shoulder in a warm display of friendship, and said, "*Shalom Aleichem*! How happy I am to see an old familiar face! I beg of you, when you visit our city, make sure to stop into my store, and we can rehash old memories!"

The man gladly agreed, and the next time he traveled to the big city, he paid a visit to the man's shop. The two of them engaged in friendly chatter about days gone by. They enjoyed tea and refreshments, and the conversation carried on for quite some time.

When they concluded, the visitor rose, thanked his host, and went straight to the neighboring shop where he purchased whatever he needed.

Irate, the merchant pursued the visitor, and when he caught up with him, exclaimed, "Do you think that I wasted my precious time talking with you for no reason at all? I figured that we would converse a short while and then you would buy all that you needed from my store! Instead, you spoke for a long time and ultimately purchased your goods from my competitor!"

> We are the visitor from the town, said the Dubno Maggid, when it comes to praying to Hashem. We lift our eyes to Heaven and pray, "Enlighten our eyes in Your Torah, attach our hearts to Your commandments" (from the *Shacharis* prayer), and we immediately turn around and pursue the materialism of this world!

❧ Instill Understanding in Our Hearts

A wealthy merchant was walking through the city square and suddenly encountered a destitute pauper.

"Forgive me, sir," said the pauper, "but I have a huge favor to ask of you. A golden business opportunity has come my way, and it requires a modest investment of five rubles. While it may not be an extraordinarily large sum, I presently do not have one ruble in my pocket. It would be a tremendous *mitzvah* to loan me the sum of money, and when the business is successful, with Hashem's help, I will repay you."

"I will gladly loan you the money," answered the wealthy man. "But I do not have any cash on me at the moment. Please come to my house this evening at five o'clock, and I will give you the five rubles that you have requested." The pauper thanked the wealthy man profusely and went on his way.

That evening, the wealthy man made sure to be in his home at the designated time and even had the money prepared on the table. He waited for the pauper, but the man did not appear.

The next day, the merchant was walking in the street and once again encountered the pauper.

The pauper repeated his previous request.

"Did I not agree to lend you the money yesterday?" answered the wealthy man. "I even waited a long time for you to come, but you did not arrive. I will gladly give you the money; simply come to my home this evening."

The pauper expressed his thanks and went on his way.

That night was no different than the previous one. The wealthy man waited in his home at the designated time and even placed the money on the table, but the pauper again did not appear.

The following day, the wealthy man and the pauper met each other once again. The pauper repeated his request, but this time the wealthy man angrily censured the pauper, "You should be ashamed of yourself! Are you jesting with me? You do not want the money at all — you simply wish to waste my time!"

> We pray each day, remarked the Chofetz Chaim, "Instill in our hearts to understand and elucidate, to listen, learn, teach," "Enlighten our eyes in Your Torah, attach our hearts to Your commandments," and "Endow us graciously from Yourself with wisdom, insight, and discernment." Hashem, in His mercy, is prepared to grant us all that we ask for, but He makes one request of us, "Come to My home" – Come to the *beis midrash* and set fixed times for studying Torah, and I will give you the wisdom, understanding, and intellectual acumen that you crave. But we, with our multitude of sins, elect not to appear.
>
> The next day, we once again stand in prayer and repeat our requests.
>
> Are we not similar to the pauper who displayed so much *chutzpah*.

ᴥᔆ*The Request*

A poor young man from the village opted to travel to the big city and try his luck at earning a livelihood. At first he worked as an apprentice in a blacksmith's shop and after some time opened a small blacksmith shop of his own. He subsequently began to operate a small business, which ultimately became extremely successful. He accumulated more and more wealth, and was even appointed to be one of the king's most prominent ministers.

Despite his prominence, he never forgot his modest beginnings. One day he commanded his servants to harness his carriage, as he wished to visit the village where he had been born. Accompanied by an impressive entourage, he set out to visit his old village.

The news of his imminent arrival quickly spread, and all of the villagers stopped working in order to greet the distinguished visitor. Needless to say, it was quite a humbling experience to hear the minister's mighty steeds galloping into the center of town in a loud and thunderous fashion...

The minister alighted from his carriage and ascended the podium that had been set up many days earlier in his honor. With emotion-laden words, he addressed the capacity crowd: "My dear friends! I remember well my days of poverty and severe deprivation; on more than one occasion there were days when I was literally starving for bread...Now that I stand before you having achieved great prominence, I would like to bestow kindness upon each and every one of you. Let every man return home and write down a request on a piece of paper. Tomorrow, each one of you may present me with one request, and I guarantee to fulfill it!"

The excited crowd dispersed, each man quietly returning home — after all, it is not every day that such a golden opportunity arises. The following day, they presented the minister with their requests: One individual wanted a new home, another asked for a plow, and so on and so forth...

In the crowd was a pauper whose financial straits were horribly severe. The roof of his home leaked, there was no bread for his children, and he was up to his neck in debt. As a result, he was unable to decide what to ask for; what did he need the most?

Not knowing what to do and lacking any more strength, the pauper began to cry...

The minister approached him and asked softly, "My dear sir, why you are sobbing so? What is your request?"

The pauper related his dire predicament and said, "I simply do not know what to ask for; therefore I cry. If my sobs lead you to believe that I need a new home — it would certainly be true. If they lead you to think that I require money with which to pay off my debts — that would also be true. If you decipher my cries as a plea for bread in order to feed my little ones — that would also be absolutely true..."

> We pray to Hashem, "May Your ears be attentive to the sound of my pleas" (*Tehillim* 130:2). We simply do not know what to request first and therefore we wordlessly beseech him in a way that expresses all of our needs at once!

⋑ *Where Is His Focus Directed?*

A father was presented with a potential match for his daughter. The young man hailed from a distant city, however, and due to the distance and the fact that caravans arriving from there were few in number, all of the father's efforts to investigate the boy's family were in vain. But since he was reputed to be one of the finest young scholars around, the father decided to travel to his city and inquire about the boy's family and origins.

Upon arriving in the city, the father had doubts as to how to go about conducting his investigation. After all, he could not simply approach any individual on the street and begin to question him about the family, for perhaps he would be a close friend of theirs and laud them with false praises. He might even be the father of the young man himself!

He therefore decided to find out exactly where the boy's father prayed, for he made the following astute calculation: If he is a Torah scholar, then he will likely pray with the other Torah scholars in the city. If he is a merchant, he will certainly pray amongst other merchants. If, however, he prefers to pray with *amei ha'aretz* (individuals who are not knowledgeable in Torah learning), it is safe to assume that he is not going to be appointed *rav* of the city anytime soon...

> Each individual, said the Dubno Maggid, is capable of examining himself by discerning where he focuses his kavanah during prayers. Is his kavanah at its peak during the blessings of "You graciously endow man with wisdom," and "Bring us back, our Father, to Your Torah," or does he shed tears when he reaches the blessing of "Bless on our behalf...this year and all its kinds of crops for the best" and prays for his sustenance?

ৰু Small Jars*

A poor man had a large family, and he was so impoverished that he did not even have bread in his home to feed his young ones. When his oldest daughter came of age, his wife advised him to travel to his wealthy brother who resided in the big city; he would certainly take notice of his brother's sorry predicament, have mercy on him, and give him a generous donation.

Left with no other choice in the matter, the poor man consented to his wife's suggestion. He packed some stale bread into his knapsack and he set off on his journey.

The poor man traveled for many days and upon finally drawing close to his destination, developed severe pains in his feet. A passing caravan took him on board and quickly transported him to the city. Once there, his brother wasted little time and summoned the finest physician available. After a devoted treatment that carried on for a lengthy duration, the poor man recovered completely.

The doctor's fee was extremely costly, but the brother was glad to cover the entire expense.

"You are most fortunate," said the locals to the poor man. "for if you would have contracted your foot ailment in *your* city, you

---

* See Bereishis 32:25, Rashi there

would certainly not have received the dedicated treatment that you received here!"

"I am not fortunate at all," sighed the poor man, "for if I would not have contracted these pains, my brother would have given me money in order to marry off my daughter. But now that he has already spent such a substantial amount of money to cover my medical care, I do not have the heart to ask him for anything more…"

> We make a mistake, said the Dubno Maggid. When we stand in prayer, we should request that the *Beis HaMikdash* be rebuilt speedily in our days. For once it is rebuilt, we will automatically see an end to all of our misfortune. Yet, due to our rather small intellects, we ask only for an adequate livelihood.

ᴥᴥ§ *The Giver of the Gift*

A man received a gift from the king's treasury, and was granted enough money to comfortably support himself for the duration of the year.

Before he went to the marketplace each day to purchase his household necessities, he would make his way to the king's courtyard, stand there for a few moments, and only afterwards head to the marketplace.

"Why must you trouble yourself each day to travel to the king's courtyard?" asked his friends.

"Despite the fact that I take this money out of my own pocket," answered the man, "it is not truly mine; rather, it is a free gift from the king. In order to constantly recall this fact and feel gratitude towards the king, I am accustomed to spending a short while in his courtyard each day before I set out for the marketplace. In this way, my family and I remember from whom this kindliness has emanated."

> All of man's needs, said the Ben Ish Chai, R' Yosef Chaim of Baghdad, are provided for by Hashem, the King of All Kings,

Who mercifully sustains every single creature and concerns himself with their needs. Even though it may appear to an individual that he is sustaining himself with money that is coming out of his own pocket, he must remember that the money was given to him by Hashem. A man must therefore go to shul in the evening, morning, and afternoon in order to pray and beseech Hashem that He provide him with all of his needs. When man has accepted upon himself the yoke of Heavenly sovereignty, he will recall and feel gratitude for His abundant kindness.

◄§ A Boy's Weeping

A man was crossing the street when he suddenly heard a young boy weeping for his mother who had gone to the marketplace. There is a method by which this man can ascertain whether the mother just recently left the house or whether she has already been out for a long time: If the child is screaming loudly, "Mommy, Mommy!" this indicates that the mother has just recently left the home and her child hopes that she will hear his voice and return. But if the child is weeping softly, it is a sign that the mother has been gone for quite some time and her child does not expect her to hear his voice; he therefore emits a soft weak cry that can barely be heard.

The same thing applies to our prayers, commented the Dubno Maggid. Sadly, we do not beseech Hashem during prayer with all our might; rather, our prayers are simply uttered by rote, lacking any feeling. It is most certain that if a prophet would appear and inform us that the present moment is one when Divine compassion has been aroused and that Hashem would accept any request that we make, we would undoubtedly pray until our last vestige of strength has been exhausted.

This dismal state which we find ourselves in has been caused by the vast distance that has come between us and our Creator, as the verse states, "My God, my God, why have You forsaken me; why so far from saving me, from the words of my roar?" (*Tehillim* 22:2).

~§ A Favorable Request

A n individual was in desperate need of a favor from a friend of his. His friend enjoyed close ties with the government, and he needed him to speak favorably on his behalf. He therefore expended the effort to travel to his home, and he waited for nearly an hour until his friend returned from his business. When the friend arrived, he pleaded with him to fulfill his request, and reiterated several times just how important this matter was to him. When the friend finally conceded to the request, the man offered him heartfelt thanks and departed.

The friend carried out what had been requested of him, performing the favor for his longtime friend.

One day, he was walking in the street and met a different man who was an old acquaintance of his.

"Please do me a favor," requested the man, "and speak to the government on my behalf regarding a certain issue." The man agreed to perform the favor, but this time, he forgot the matter entirely and did not fulfill the request.

> The difference between the first instance and the second, noted the Dubno Maggid, is as follows: The first individual traveled a great distance and spared no effort to journey to his friend. Additionally, when he discovered that his friend was not home, he waited for him to arrive. The second individual, however, happened to encounter the man by chance and did not appear to have exerted any effort whatsoever to arrange an audience with him. This is why the man with the close ties to the kingdom likewise did not put forth any effort.

Our prayers are altogether different, noted the Dubno Maggid, when they are invested with effort and not simply uttered by way of habit.

·· In Former Years

One of the requests that we make during prayer is, "Then the offering of Judah and Jerusalem will be pleasing to Hashem, as in days of old and in former years." This supplication can be explained according to the following parable:

When two close friends present gifts to one another, each one accepts the token of friendship happily and contently. They do not examine the quality of the presents they received, and even if they would discover a particular flaw, they would never consider giving it back, as it was a free gift given with good will.

This would not be the case, however, if we were dealing with in-laws who promised to contribute a certain amount of money to the couple's dowry. If a discrepancy would be discovered in the amount that was given by either side, an immediate protest by the other set of in-laws would follow, as would a request to exchange the flawed gift for a perfect one.

The difference between the two cases is rather simple. When there is no requirement to give the gift, it will be pleasing in the eyes of the recipient even if it is not perfect or worth exactly as much as was expected. But if the gift is an obligatory one, this will not be the case.

In the generations of our holy forefathers, said the Dubno Maggid, prayer was not yet obligatory and was similar to a free gift. But as for us, we are bound by the requirement to pray, and Hashem is therefore extremely exacting when it comes to our prayers. We therefore beseech Hashem, "Then the offering of Judah and Jerusalem will be pleasing to Hashem, as in the days of old and in former years" — Even though they are lacking and deficient, let our prayers be pleasing like our forefathers' prayers of the earlier generations.

◄§ How to Ask

A son had managed to infuriate his father, who responded by expelling him from his home. The son wandered aimlessly around the land until he ultimately settled in a certain city. There he joined a group of beggars and lived with them.

Time passed and when the father's fury eventually abated, he longed for his dear son. He sat in his home for many days anticipating his banished son's return, but the son stubbornly refused to even consider returning to his father.

On one occasion, a merchant from the son's new city traveled to the father's city. At one point during his business transactions, he actually dealt with the boy's father as well.

Their conversation revealed that the merchant was quite familiar with the man's son, and when he realized that the father missed him dearly, the bewildered merchant asked him, "If you want to see your son so desperately, why don't you simply have him return to you?"

"If he would just request to return to me," answered the father, "I would welcome him with open arms."

"If it is dependent upon his request," said the merchant, "then I will act as his messenger and place a request in his stead."

"Your words are meaningless," replied the father. "You see, I specifically wish that *he* be the one to ask. In that way I will be sure that he regrets what he has done, and that he has forsaken his previous behavior. If he would send me a messenger, I would also forgive him and happily allow him to return to me. But you are here simply to engage in commerce, and you only met me by chance. Nevertheless, you have decided to place a request in my son's stead — is that the way to ask for forgiveness?"

If our primary desire during prayer, said the Dubno Maggid, would be to increase the honor of Hashem's great Name, and we would go to shul to pray and request, "And to Jerusalem, Your city, may You return in compassion" — we would be answered immediately. But due to our multitude of sins, our main focus during prayer is on materialistic things, and only in passing do we mumble our requests to increase the honor of the Divine Presence — is that the proper way to place a request?

ঙ্গ A Proper Appearance

A certain individual owed his friend a large sum of money, and when he delayed in repaying it, his friend demanded that he appear before a *beis din* (rabbinical court).

Despite the fact that he was well aware of his debt, the man searched for different plans and strategies that would free him from repaying it.

When he sought the council of his peers — who were just as "honest" as he was — they offered him the following advice: He should swear before the judge that he must care for his wife and young children, and that he simply does not have any money with which to repay the debt. "The judge will certainly believe you, and he will acquit you from repaying the entire debt," his friends assured him.

The man was overjoyed with the "wise" advice, and when the court date arrived, he donned the elegant clothing which he saved for special occasions, harnessed his magnificent carriage to four strapping horses, and prepared to set out for the courthouse.

"You fool," said his wife, "is this how you intend to appear before the judge? If you are dressed like one of the barons and arrive in such a beautiful carriage, how will you possibly be able to claim that you are destitute and unable to repay the debt?"

The man listened to what his wife had to say, and he realized that she was correct. He therefore donned tattered garments and asked his neighbor to loan him a rickety wagon that was harnessed to an elderly horse.

That is how he appeared before the judge.

So it is with our prayers, noted the Dubno Maggid. The level of Divine service which is demanded of us when we stand before Hashem in prayer is very great indeed. We must therefore appear before Hashem with a heart and spirit that is both broken and humbled. Amid feelings of shame we must beseech Hashem, all the while feeling anguish over our lack of recognition of what is required of us in our service of Him. But if one appears before Him with a proud and arrogant heart, how can he claim that he is not worthy of serving Him properly and in the manner that is demanded of him?

✎§ A House of Toothpicks

There are times when an individual stands in prayer, said R' Yisrael Ba'al Shem Tov, and asks Hashem to fulfill a particular request of his — but he is not answered. This person must know that his not being answered stems from Hashem's mercy for him. For while something may be of monumental importance in our eyes, Hashem knows that it would be to our detriment if we were to receive it.

This can be compared to a king's young son who was playing with toothpicks. He spent much time constructing houses, roads, caves, and bridges — all from toothpicks. One of the servants in the palace was not sufficiently cautious and stepped on one of the houses, reducing it to a pile of toothpicks.

The young prince ran to his father in a state of bitter weeping. "Father," cried the son, "just look at what that servant did to me — he destroyed my house!"

The king smiled but did not hasten to punish the servant, as he knew quite well that his son's "house" was not a house at all and that it was unnecessary to lament its destruction. For who knows better than the king just how many palaces and spacious properties are to one day be the lot of his son when he grows up? Compared to them, what is a house constructed of toothpicks truly worth?

☙ "He Is the Healer of the Brokenhearted"

In a certain city lived an expert goldsmith who was unsurpassed when it came to setting gems. Ministers and barons from all across the land would send him precious stones and pearls that he would set in place with the utmost precision and skill. He was eminently successful and earned a very substantial profit.

One day, the man broke his hand. He was no longer able to continue as a goldsmith and therefore set out to collect charity.

"It would not befit you to do such a thing," remarked those closest to him. "Should a skilled worker such as yourself, whose expertise was sought after day and night by all the barons in the land – now go and collect charity?"

"But what else should I do?" lamented the man. "My hand is broken, and I can no longer practice the trade that I formerly excelled in."

"What does that mean, 'you can no longer practice'?" asked his friends in amazement. "Go to a doctor and he will heal you — your hand will be as good as new!"

A person is obligated, said the Dubno Maggid, to spend the days of his life engaged in the study of Torah and the performance of *mitzvos*, and he must never let himself weaken in this area. There are times, however, when his heart offers him bad advice and lures him after meaningless endeavors. He must not heed this destructive council; rather, he must pray for mercy from the One Who is the Healer of the brokenhearted (see *Tehillim* 147:3) imploring Hashem, "Create a pure heart for me, O God, and a steadfast spirit renew within me" (*Tehillim* 51:12)!

⇜ Who Owes Who?

A merchant lost all of his money and was left penniless. Since he owed a great deal of money to a particular wholesaler and had no means of repaying his debt, he offered to work for the wholesaler free of charge instead.

The wholesaler, who knew the merchant to be an expert in his field and a very astute individual, happily agreed.

The merchant worked for the wholesaler, and his business absolutely flourished as a result of his productive labor.

Some time later, the merchant turned to the wholesaler with a complaint: "Why do I work so hard for you, yet I do not receive any payment whatsoever? Are you not ashamed to withhold the wages of a laborer?"

"Return home," answered the wholesaler, "and the matter will be settled."

The wholesaler summoned his servant and asked him to go to the merchant's house and collect the entire debt that he owed him.

"But his house is utterly bare," said the bewildered servant. "What then shall I collect from him?"

"I am well aware of this fact," replied the wholesaler. "But this man has forgotten the debt that he has accrued, and therefore claims that I should compensate him for his labor. I would therefore like you to go to his home and remind him of the large sum of money that he owes me…"

On one hand, said the Dubno Maggid, we sin against Hashem, Who bestows limitless kindness upon us each and every day. Yet, on the other hand, we pray to Him morning and night that He should provide us with all of our needs.

This is what is stated in *Yeshayahu* (58:1), "Raise your voice...proclaim to My people their willful sins, to the House of Jacob their transgressions."

ᮥᔥ *The King's Seal*

A king owned a beautiful signet ring that he used to imprint his official seal. Every letter or decree that he issued bore the seal of that ring and was irrevocable.

One day, he misplaced the ring and could not locate it. The entire palace searched for it, as it was rather disrespectful for the king's signet ring to be lying in the dust. They searched long and hard for the ring, but it was ultimately in vain — the ring simply could not be found.

The king issued a proclamation, stating that whoever found the missing ring would be granted a reward from the king's treasury.

Shortly thereafter, a young villager found the ring on the side of the road that ran through his village. It had transpired that when the king had gone hunting and had passed through the village's fields that the ring had fallen to the ground, and he had not taken notice.

The villager hurried to the palace holding the precious ring.

When he arrived at the palace, the royal guard initially wanted to prevent him from entering, but upon seeing the ring, they immediately opened the gates and ushered him into the palace. One gate after another was opened before him, until he reached the royal throne and stood before the king.

So, too, in regard to prayer, stated R' Yisrael Ba'al Shem Tov. When a Jew prays with *kavanah* (proper intent), he should know that he is carrying the king's seal along with him. His prayer will split apart the Heavens and open up gates, until its merit enables him to reach the Throne of Glory to stand before Hashem, the King of All Kings!

🦢 The Wanderer

A pauper walked along the road with his bundle slung over his shoulder. He was extremely thirsty, and his tongue was literally sticking to his palate, but he had no water with which to quench his thirst. Some time later, he began to experience pangs of hunger that grew so bothersome that he forgot all about his thirst.

He eventually reached his destination, and he entered the first house that he saw. It happened to be the home of one of the wealthiest men in the city.

It was mealtime when he entered the house, and he immediately noticed a table laden with a vast assortment of delicacies and delights, as well as outstanding beverages.

"If I request a modicum of food," thought the pauper to himself, "I will remain thirsty. But if I ask for something to drink, I will remain hungry."

So what did he do? He began to plead with his host to extend him an invitation to dine with him at his table. The wealthy man agreed, and the pauper ate until he was satisfied and drank until his thirst had been quenched.

> When a Jew stands in prayer, noted the Dubno Maggid, his heart is filled with a multitude of requests that he wishes to ask of Hashem. On one hand, he has spiritual requests, and on the other hand, he has material needs as well.
>
> So what should he do? He should beseech the Master of the World that He allow him to be like a son who sits at the table of his Father Who fully provides for him. In this way, he will lack nothing at all!

🦢 A Prayer for the Public

A group of men set out on a grueling journey. They scaled hills and mountains, trekked through fields and forests, and crossed rivers and streams. One day, they were crossing a weak bridge over a flowing river. Without warning, the bridge collapsed and several members of the group fell into the river.

Their companions tried to lift them out of the water, but they lacked the strength to do so. They decided to hurry to the closest residential area, there they would request assistance and even secure several lifesavers in order to save the drowning men.

The men rushed to the city with their friend's voices ringing in their ears, urging them not to tarry, lest a tragedy occur at any moment.

When they arrived, they spotted an inn that housed a restaurant displaying a wide assortment of delicious foods. Since they were extraordinarily hungry, they could not restrain themselves — they went inside, quickly sat down, and ate to their hearts' content.

One of them suddenly arose and exclaimed, "My dear friends, how can we sit here satiating ourselves, while our beloved peers are fighting for their lives in the roaring river? The water is freezing and their strength is waning — a catastrophe will take place if we do not rush to their aid!"

> How many of our Jewish brethren, said the Dubno Maggid, presently find themselves in an variety of precarious situations? For example, one is sailing at the heart of the sea in the midst of a raging storm, another is trekking through deserts, a third is ill and in need of Heavenly mercy, and a fourth lacks bread with which to feed his young children.
>
> How can it be that we sit peacefully and forget their suffering and anguish? We must recite on their behalf the prayer that our Sages composed, "Our brothers, the entire family of Israel, who are delivered into distress and captivity, whether they are on sea or dry land — may the Omnipresent One have mercy on them and remove them from distress to relief, from darkness to light, from subjugation to redemption, now, speedily, and soon — and let us say: Amen!"

ᴥᵹ Grab All That You Can

A parable is quoted in the Sefer Chofetz Chaim al HaTorah (*Parashas Va'eschanan*), which illustrates the importance of praying with the proper *kavanah*. Even when the *yetzer hara* attempts to distract an individual, he must nevertheless strengthen himself and refuse to allow his mind to be diverted from his prayers.

This can be compared to a young boy who was standing in the marketplace, holding a basket of apples that he was trying to sell.

He was suddenly approached by an individual who began to snatch the apples from the basket. The boy screamed with all his might, "Jews! Help!"

A wise man passed by and said to the boy, "Why are you screaming? Instead of merely screaming, you should also grab as many apples as you can, before this man succeeds in snatching all of the apples before you manage to grab any…"

Sometimes an individual stands in prayer, concluded the Chofetz Chaim, and the *yetzer hara* tries with all of his might to distract him in order that he should not be able to pray with *kavanah*. He may already be halfway through his prayers and not have concentrated on a single word.

It is worthwhile for a person to try and snatch a little bit for himself and pray the remainder of his prayers with great *kavanah*. For if he does not do so, he will be left with nothing for himself.

ᴥᵹ A Matter of Life and Death

A group of merchants entered an inn located near the crossroads. They asked the innkeeper to serve them food and drink, and knowing that his guests had the ability to pay, he hastened to set the table for them.

"What would you like to eat?" asked the innkeeper.

One of them answered, "I would like a good, thick meat broth."

"I would like to eat fresh fish," said another.

One by one, the merchants proceeded to order tasty delicacies, each one requesting the dish that he craved.

A weak voice was suddenly heard coming from one corner of the inn, "Please serve me bread, for I am starving!"

The guest who had made the request was a pauper who had happened to enter the inn at the same time.

The innkeeper left the group of merchants and quickly placed bread before the pauper.

"Should this pauper be served before us?" asked the merchants. "Why, we are ordering a massive feast, yet you prefer to serve him first?"

"You," responded the innkeeper, "are ordering delicacies for yourselves. This pauper, however, is asking for bread in order to survive. Who knows how long it has been since he has last had something to eat."

> There are times, said the Dubno Maggid, when individuals who pursue their cravings and lusts stand in prayer and make various requests in order to increase their assets and prestige in the eyes of the world.
>
> Then there is the individual who tearfully requests bread for his young children.
>
> Hashem will most certainly give his prayer preference and answer it immediately, for the man is pleading for his life and the lives of his children!

◆§ The Request of the King's Son

On one occasion, a prince angered his father, the king. Irate, the king banished his son from the palace without giving him a penny. His son wandered from city to city, collecting alms and barely managing to sustain himself.

When he grew weary of collecting charity, he made his way to the house of an elderly villager and offered to perform any form of labor that he desired, be it in the house or the field.

The villager took the young boy into his home, and the man was not disappointed. The boy worked with great vigor and performed any task that his master requested, whether it was working in the fields or tending to the animals. In exchange, the villager allowed the boy to board in his home, and he provided him with a meager meal as well.

One day, the villager died and his estate fell into the hands of his son. Trouble soon arose, however, as the son was a wicked man who increased the workloads of all of the villager's servants while at the same time decreasing their benefits.

Meanwhile, the king was in his palace in the capital city. He was sad and depressed over not having received any word of his son throughout the past several years, and not having any idea where he was or what he was doing. He therefore decided to travel around his kingdom and proclaim wherever he went that whoever had a request to make of the king or a grievance that needed to be settled was invited to come before him and state his claim.

Indeed, wherever the king went, long lines formed, consisting of the heavily burdened as well as feuding parties, in order to relate their troubles to the king.

The king's travels eventually brought him to the city in which his son resided. The son, as well, was among the individuals who lined up to speak with the king, and when it came his turn, he fell before the king and cried, "Your Highness! I work for a certain villager who forces me to do overbearing labor! I beg of you, order him to provide me with bread each day and not to oppress me so..."

The king fell on his son's neck and exclaimed, "Woe is me, that I must see you in such a state! Are you so heavily burdened that you have completely forgotten about your esteemed lineage? You are the son of a king, and your place is in the palace of kings. Instead of asking me for stale bread, ask me for permission to return to the palace!"

The Jewish Nation are the children of kings, said the Dubno Maggid. But the darkness of exile and the oppression we have endured have caused us to forget this fact. We therefore stand in prayer and request no more than a slice of bread.

We must beseech Hashem to renew our days as of old! (see *Eichah* 5:22).

ᥲᔥ *Where Is the King?*

All the people of the land obviously recognize their king. But when the king goes out to war, he is accustomed to disguising himself so as to not be recognized by anyone.

Even at such a time, the ministers and close company of the king who are constantly in his presence are familiar with his every movement, and even if he should change his attire, they will nevertheless recognize him with ease.

There is one way, though, that even the general populace can figure out where the king is located. Let them simply observe where there is the highest concentration of security — that is where the king can be found!

When an individual prepares himself to pray, said R' Yisrael Ba'al Shem Tov, the *yetzer hara* immediately intervenes in an attempt to disturb his *kavanah* and break his concentration. A person must know, however, that the obstacle that he faces clearly indicates that this is where the King is found! Hashem is close to all who call upon Him sincerely (see *Tehillim* 145:18).

It is incumbent upon one who prays to try with all his might to overcome the obstacle and reach the King.

A certain pauper was regularly supported by the generous donations of a wealthy man. One day, the pauper went to the wealthy man's house in order to receive his customary allocation. His desires got the best of him, however, and he began to covet a garment that he saw in the house. Eventually he stole the garment from his benefactor.

When the matter became known to the wealthy man, he grew irate and told the pauper in no uncertain terms that from that day on, he dare not step foot into his home ever again. Furthermore, exclaimed the wealthy man, the customary stipend was canceled indefinitely!

Without the wealthy man's assistance, the predicament in the pauper's home deteriorated, until he was no longer able to provide bread for his children.Left with no other choice, the pauper decided to take action.

He knew that each day the wealthy man would stroll through the forest that was adjacent to the city. One day, shortly before the designated time, the pauper went to the forest. He looked around and found a small cave; he then hid inside and waited.

When he heard the wealthy man approaching, he yelled loudly, "Please save me! Please take pity on me!"

"Who are you?" asked the wealthy man. "Approach me and I will help you to the best of my ability."

"This I cannot do," answered the pauper, "for I am embarrassed to show my face before you."

The wealthy man repeated his request several times, but the pauper refused to leave his hiding place.

"I am ashamed," said the pauper. "I am unable to leave this cave and face you, for I stole a garment from your home, and I am wearing it…"

> We stand in prayer, said the Dubno Maggid, and exclaim, "I called to you from the depths, Hashem" (*Tehillim* 130:1)! — We conceal ourselves in hiding places and cry out, "O Lord,

hear my voice, may Your ears be attentive to the sound of my pleas" — We are ashamed and humiliated to appear before You, Hashem, King of all Kings. Therefore be attentive to the sounds of our cries. Why are we ashamed? "If You preserve iniquities, O God, O Lord, who could survive (ya'amod)?" — We are clothed from head to foot in sin, and who could stand (la'amod) before You in such a manner?

ᵴ Like A Debtor

Chazal say (Berachos 34a) the following about one who does not have kavanah during his recitation of the first verse of Krias Shema: It is fitting to strike him with a blacksmith's hammer until he does have the proper kavanah!

This can be compared to a man who owed his friend a large sum of money. When he delayed repaying the debt, the creditor had him tried in beis din.

"But what should I do?" cried the debtor before the judges. "I simply do not have the money necessary to repay him."

The judges ultimately ruled that he was obligated to repay the debt in full. Since he lacked a portion of the money, however, he was required to return a small percentage of the debt each week, until he would finally have repaid the entire debt after approximately a year.

Now, if over the course of the year the debtor was unable to make one weekly payment it would be of little significance — for it is conceivable that the matter slipped his mind, or that he had incurred tremendous expenses that particular week. His lapse could therefore be overlooked.

But if he had already disregarded his responsibilities the very first week, this is evidence of outright negligence and a total lack of respect for the beis din's ruling — that would be not be overlooked quite as readily!

The same thing applies to prayer, said the Dubno Maggid. If a person suffers a lapse of *kavanah* in the middle of his prayers, it is still possible to view him in a favorable light and propose that the *yetzer hara* distracted him.

But if his *kavanah* has already lapsed by the first verse of *Krias Shema*, it is an indication of his utter disrespect, and it is therefore fitting to strike him with a blacksmith's hammer!

৺ঌ *The Visit*

An individual bestowed kindness upon the king, and the king wished to return the favor by giving him a gift from the royal treasury. However, the man did not want a gift; rather, he simply requested that the king personally come to visit him in his home.

The king acceded to the request and scheduled a day that he would pay the man a visit. He even sent him advance notice so that he would have ample time to prepare for receiving such an esteemed guest.

The designated day arrived and the king, accompanied by an elaborate entourage, arrived at the man's house. How great was his fury when it was discovered that the man was not at home...there could be no greater affront to the king's honor than that!

A man stands in prayer, said the Maggid, R' Yaakov Yosef of Polonoye, and begins with the morning blessings and *Pesukei D'zimrah*, which are songs of praise and adulation to the King of the World. With these prayers, man greets the King. When he reaches the *Shemoneh Esrei*, however, and the King wishes to enter his heart — the heart is filled with alien thoughts centering on nonsense.

Is there a greater affront to the honor of the King of the World than that?

✌ The Letters in the Box

An elderly wealthy man had a son who was an outright ignoramus. The father knew that when in a number of years his son would inherit all of his silver and gold, he would foolishly squander his entire fortune. He therefore took a large box and placed in it several letters containing words of approbation and pleas for help, customarily carried by individuals collecting charity. He then placed all of his money on top of the letter.

"At least," thought the elderly man, "my son will be able to take these letters and request some donations to sustain himself after he fritters away the inheritance..."

> Hashem, said the Dubno Maggid, established a *Beis HaMikdash* and a sacrificial rite for the Jewish Nation. Yet it was revealed before Him that the *Beis HaMikdash* would one day be destroyed. He therefore placed the thought into the heart of David *HaMelech* and the Sages to establish prayers for us, so that we would be left with a means capable of giving life to our souls.

✌ Answer Me Soon

In *Tehillim* it states, "Answer me soon, O Hashem, my spirit is spent; conceal not Your face from me" (*Tehillim* 143:7). To what can this be compared? To a sick, pain-ridden man whose suffering prevented him from eating or drinking. Occasionally, he would desire to eat something in order to sustain himself, but in a few moments he would lose that appetite as well.

One day, the man came to an inn, and when it was time to eat, he sat at the table together with the multitude of guests. He suddenly felt his appetite return; he therefore turned to the innkeeper and requested, "Please serve me first! If you delay, I will not be able to eat a thing!"

A man's heart, said the Dubno Maggid, is burdened by worries and countless other thoughts. Therefore, when he finally manages to free himself of these thoughts and he focuses his heart toward his Father in Heaven, he pleads with Hashem that He listen to his prayer right away, before his thoughts return to burden him once again.

Part 12

Repentance

❧ The Messenger and the Thief

A store that sold a wide variety of items opened in the center of the city. Scores of customers entered the store and walked around, feasting their eyes on the shelves crowded with a massive selection of goods. Indeed, business was faring extremely well.

Not all of the individuals who visited the store that day had pure intentions. Among the crowd was a sly thief who did not stop strategizing for a moment how he would steal the contents of the cash register.

After having observed the storeowner for an extended period, he discovered that at the day's end he would place all of the money in a large bag. This bag was then put into the hands of a trusted messenger who would hurry with the bag to the bank, where it would be placed inside a safe.

The thief thought and thought, trying to devise a precise plan, until he finally hit upon an idea.

On the road leading from the store to the bank was a shop in which were sold expensive suits, especially to the rich men of the city. Towards evening, the thief entered the suit store and said that he was the servant of a wealthy man who had sent him to purchase a number of suits.

"However," added the thief, "my employer does not have the time to come here and have the suits measured to fit him. He therefore sent me, his loyal servant, to perform the task. I must simply find an individual whose dimensions are similar to those of my employer's. If he tries on a suit and it fits, I will be able to purchase it."

"Fine," responded the storeowner to the odd request. "Show me an individual whose measurements match those of your employer's, and I will find a suit that fits him."

The thief and the owner of the suit store stood in the doorway searching for a suitable candidate to try on the suit. At that point, the thief spotted the messenger — carrying the precious bag filled with money — walking down the street.

"His dimensions," said the thief as he pointed to the messenger, "are exactly the same as my employer's."

The owner of the suit store approached the messenger and said, "Please sir, perhaps you would be willing to come into my store for a brief moment and try on a suit? It will not take very long at all, and your reward is guaranteed."

The messenger agreed and entered the store. There he tried on the expensive suit, and when he stood opposite the mirror to gaze at his reflection, the thief swiped the valuable bag and ran out of the store.

"Thief!" screamed the messenger as he set off in hot pursuit. He did not get very far, however, for the owner of the suit store grabbed him and said, "Absolutely not! First take off the suit and only then chase after him!"

The messenger removed the suit and made haste — but the thief had already disappeared.

> We are similar to that messenger, noted the Dubno Maggid. For we have been entrusted with a priceless treasure of Torah and *mitzvos* that we must bring to Hashem when we stand before Him on the Day of Judgment. The *yetzer hara*, however, devises various strategies in this attempt to entice us into engaging in meaningless endeavors; it as if he "dresses" us in these foolish pursuits.
>
> We are indeed able to pursue him, to fight him, seize him, and retrieve the valuable treasure that he stole from us. In order to do so, however, we must first remove the vile "outfit" in which he has dressed us.

◆§ In the Place Where Ba'alei Teshuvah Stand

Chazal state (*Berachos* 34b), "R' Abahu said: In the place where *ba'alei teshuvah* stand, *tzaddikim gemurim* (the purely righteous who have been untainted by sin) do not stand."

R' Itzele Blazer (Peterburger) offered a brilliant parable to explain *Chazal's* words:

There was a king who reigned over his entire kingdom with might and benevolence. On one occasion, the king wished to discover his subjects' true feelings regarding his sovereignty, and so he disguised himself as a beggar, and went out in the streets.

As he roamed the alleyways, he was assailed by a band of cruel thieves. They wished to harm him, but one of the thieves — a spark of mercy for the beggar having flickered in his heart — fiercely defended him against his attackers, even helping him escape to safety.

The king returned to his palace and, some time later, arranged a lavish *seudas hoda'ah* (lit., a feast of thanksgiving.), to which he invited all of the ministers and distinguished members of the kingdom. He also invited the thief who had saved him from the clutches of his cohorts.

The thief sat there in his simple attire and felt rather uncomfortable in the presence of the ministers who were dressed so elegantly. The ministers as well stared at the thief in utter bewilderment — what place did this lowly individual have at the king's feast?

The king noticed the puzzled expressions on the faces of the ministers. He therefore called over the thief and sat him down alongside him in a display of great honor. He then related to his guests what had transpired and how this thief had saved his life.

So too, concluded R' Itzele, in relation to repentance. The Torah states (*Hoshea* 14:2), "Return, Israel, unto Hashem your G-d." When an individual repents and becomes a *ba'al teshuvah*, he draws closer to Hashem like the thief who, through saving the king, repented and in effect anointed the king over the entire land. In a similar vein, when a *ba'al teshuvah* overcomes his *yetzer hara*, he an.oints Hashem King of the world as a result.

There can be no loftier plateau than this!

◄§ *The Tax Officials*

The commerce in a certain port city had escalated by leaps and
bounds. Many stores had opened and the merchants were conducting flourishing business. Since many ships arrived and set sail
from the city's port, a large smuggling ring flourished as well, with
sailors secretly smuggling goods into the city in an attempt to
evade the tax officials.

One day, the king finally decided to put an end to the smuggling.
He therefore commanded the tax minister to randomly dispatch officials accompanied by policemen to perform unscheduled
inspections of stores. If smuggled merchandise was found in their
possession, the storeowners would be fined and even sent to prison!

The merchants in the city heard about the new edict and were
very frightened. But since the profit in selling smuggled merchandise is very substantial, they assembled to devise a plan for
proceeding. They discussed various ideas, and they finally resolved to bribe one of the tax officers, who would inform them
ahead of time when the officials were coming to their city for an
inspection.

The plan was carried out and, indeed, prior to every inspection,
the bribed officer would inform the merchants, who would then
hurry to conceal their smuggled goods until it was safe to display
them once again.

Over time, however, some merchants began to make light of the
warning. They brazenly disregarded it, paid no heed to their friends'
warnings, and did not hide their smuggled merchandise. They even
went so far as to insult their friends, calling them "cowards."

One day, the officials arrived accompanied by police officers, and
all those who had belittled the warnings were hurled into prison.

> Many Jews are embarrassed about their sins, said R' Shimon
> Zevitz, rav of Pittsburgh, and as the Days of Judgment ap-
> proach, they hastily repent. There are those, however, who
> make light of the matter and do not take it to heart. When the

time comes, they stand before the Heavenly Tribunal, soiled from the sins in their possession!

◆§ Head Thief as King's Guard

Such is the way of the world, said the *Ohr HaChaim HaKadosh*, R' Chaim ben Attar: When a caravan travels from city to city and in the middle of its trip is assailed by a band of thieves that steal all of their belongings, the plundered turn to the king. The king then dispatches a troop of powerful soldiers who know precisely how to capture the thieves and return the stolen merchandise.

But what can be done if the chief thief is himself one of the king's guards? He will not allow them to approach the king and present their complaint … There is absolutely no hope in such a case!

If an individual, said the *Ohr HaChaim HaKadosh*, succumbs to the *yetzer hara* and allows himself to be dominated by it, the *yetzer hara* stands like a guard at the door and does not allow rebuke to have its impact.

◆§ Repentance Motivated by Love and Repentance Motivated by Fear

Repentance that is motivated by fear is on a lofty level indeed; if only we would merit to repent in such a fashion! Nevertheless, such an individual must be aware that he did not repent out of love for Hashem but, rather, out of fear of the subsequent retribution.

This can be compared to a legion of soldiers who were pursuing the enemy. The chase continued for many days, extending over mountains and through forests. One day, they paused to rest in the middle of a thick forest. The soldiers tied their horses to the trees, plucked some twigs, and lit a bonfire. They placed a large cauldron on the fire and cooked warm soup in order to revive themselves.

When the soup was ready to be served, the soldier who was manning the lookout station appeared and, in a panic, informed the soldiers that the enemy legion was approaching.

The fierce soldiers leaped onto their horses and galloped toward the enemy battalion in order to fight them.

There was a coward among them who did not rush to leave the pot of soup. He helped himself to a brimming bowl and even filled up his canteen with steaming-hot soup. He then nonchalantly mounted his horse and joined his battalion.

As he began galloping toward the battlefield, several drops of the boiling hot soup leaked from his canteen and splattered onto his horse. When the horse felt the scorching soup, it began to gallop out of control directly into the lines of the enemy brigade.

When the enemy spotted this brazen soldier heading straight into their lines, they were gripped by terror and dread, and began to run for their lives in a display of surrender. This lone soldier had tipped the scales of the battle!

His commander approached him and asked in astonishment, "I've known you for quite some time, and I am well aware that you aren't one of the bravest soldiers in the legion. So please tell me, what motivated you to display such incredible bravery by charging the enemy battalion all on your own? You deserve a medal of distinction from the king himself for such a heroic act!"

"Truthfully," admitted the soldier shamefacedly, "I am not the bravest of soldiers. Rather, a small amount of scalding soup dripped on my horse, and I was not able to control it as it stampeded into the enemy camp…"

"If that is so," responded the commander, "*you* do not deserve the honor and praise — your horse does!"

The same thing applies to repentance. One who repents out of fear should know precisely why he repented.

◄§ The Doctor's Advice

In a certain city resided a famous doctor who was known far and wide as an expert physician and healer of the sick.

His uniqueness lay in the fact that he did not cure his patients through medicines and bitter potions; rather, he knew how to determine with utmost exactitude which foods were making the patient ill. He would advise him to refrain from eating those foods, and the patient would recuperate.

On one occasion, a father and son visited the doctor because of the son's illness. The son was spoiled to the extreme, and when he heard the list of foods that he would no longer be able to eat, he grimaced and asked to leave at once.

"Listen to my advice," whispered the doctor to the father. "Take your son to a different doctor; he will prescribe for your son medicines which are as bitter as wormwood. When he tastes them, he will prefer to return to me..." And so it was.

> The Dubno Maggid explained that Hashem bestowed a great kindness upon us by showing us a path to repentance. But when a man chooses not to take this road, and instead hardens his heart and abstains from repenting, Hashem sends him various forms of suffering. When man tastes their bitter taste, he immediately repents wholeheartedly.

◄§ The Best Merchandise

In a certain city resided a wholesaler who would sell his merchandise to the city's merchants on credit. He was renowned for his kindheartedness and generosity, giving credit to whoever requested it and to anyone who had difficulty paying for his merchandise. On more than one occasion, he even turned a blind eye to a small debt that someone had incurred or to an individual who was late with payment.

One day, a competitor opened a store directly across from this kindhearted storeowner. The customers curiously entered in order to judge the quality of the new store, and they quickly realized that the prices were incomparably cheap.

Business is business, as the old adage goes, and the customers therefore did not think twice before purchasing all of their goods at the new store.

They soon discovered, however, that the new storeowner was not an honest fellow, and that the goods that he sold them were of poor quality and very undesirable.

Shamefaced, the customers returned to the first storeowner — their old friend — and asked him to forgive them for their most offensive behavior in the new store. They went on to request that he continue to sell them his excellent merchandise at a low cost as he did in the past and on credit for lengthy durations. Out of the goodness of his heart, the storeowner agreed wholeheartedly.

Among the customers were individuals who, after a short time, resumed purchasing their goods from the new store even though the merchandise there was of inferior quality.

When they returned to the storeowner a second time and requested to be given merchandise on credit, he refused.

Hashem has offered us the finest merchandise imaginable — Torah and *mitzvos*! In opposition, the *yetzer hara* opens its "store" and offers merchandise that at first glance appears beautiful and appealing, but after a while proves itself to be incomparably inferior. Anyone who has purchased it realizes that he has been ensnared, and he turns to beg for forgiveness from Hashem. He asks to once again be able to acquire Torah and *mitzvos*, and Hashem forgives him and pardons all of his sins.

But how can we come before the King if we ultimately return to purchasing "big bargains" in the store of the *yetzer hara*?

≈§ The Time Has Come to Repent

A wealthy man had a son whom he loved dearly. All his life, the son never lacked anything. His father fulfilled his every request even before it was articulated.

When the son grew older, he decided to prove to the public that he was capable of sustaining himself. He therefore left his father's home and moved to a different city, where he tried his hand at business.

The son's bubble burst rather quickly and the harsh reality soon settled in. His business was not faring well, and in a short time, he incurred a debt that he was unable to cover. He also began to experience the bitter taste of want.

In a bind, the son quickly sent an emergency letter to his father, imploring him to quickly send a sum of money that would enable him to keep his faltering business afloat. If his request would be refused, he wrote, his fate would be a bitter one due to his many creditors.

"My dear son," responded the father in a telegram, "I would certainly never deprive you of anything and will repay your loans. But if it is peace and quiet that you covet, return to me and I will support you as before."

> We must realize, explained the Dubno Maggid, that all of the evils which befall us are a sign from Hashem Who awaits our complete repentance!

≈§ The Pail at the Bottom of the Well

A man borrowed a pail from his neighbor in order to draw water from the well. As he was drawing the water, the pail slipped from his hands and fell to the bottom of the well. The man tried to retrieve the pail but his efforts were in vain. After a short while, he gave up and told himself that he would try to recover it at a different time.

The days passed by, and the trials and tribulations of the man's life made him forget completely about the pail.

Some time later, his neighbor requested that he return the pail. The man suddenly recalled the pail and he quickly ran to the well. With renewed vigor, he once again attempted to retrieve it. After much effort, he finally managed to pull out the pail, but it was now covered by moss and rust after the many days it had spent lying in the dampness. It was almost impossible to recognize that it had once been a pail.

> A person must take care and worry that he does not go through life entrenched in sin. For after a while, the sin begins to generate "moss" and "rust", and he no longer is able to recognize the path to repentance.

◆§ A Long Night

There was a minister who was particularly loved and respected by the king. The close relationship he enjoyed with the king evoked the envy of the other ministers, and, in their great wickedness, several of them decided to slander him.

When the king heard that his friend had wronged him, he dispatched his soldiers to have him imprisoned.

It was late at night when the soldiers arrived at the minister's home, and the minister was sound asleep in bed.

The powerful knocking on his door woke him up, and without the slightest display of respect, the soldiers dragged the minister to a dark dungeon and tossed him inside.

Shortly after gaining some clarity of thought, the minister once again fell asleep.

When he awoke in the morning, he forgot all about what had happened to him the previous night, and he thought that he was still in his bed at home. Not seeing even a ray of light, he naively thought that the morning had not yet dawned; he therefore turned onto his other side and fell back to sleep.

When he awoke a second time and noticed that morning had not yet broken, he was absolutely astounded. "How is this night different from all the other nights?" he asked himself.

The king, on the other hand, got up in the morning and desired to see his how his friend was faring. He went to the prison, approached the pit, and listened.

"Woe is me," he heard the minister lament. "When will the day break so that I can finally rise from my bed?"

"You fool," exclaimed the king. "Do you think that you are still lying in your bed? You have been thrown into a deep prison pit that is dark and damp! Instead of crying and pleading that the day should break, cry before me that I should take pity on you and release you from your imprisonment!"

When the *Beis HaMikdash* stood, said the Dubno Maggid, the entire Jewish Nation was aware of when they were required to repent. Whether it was through the prophecies and exhortations of the prophets, or the message of the crimson-colored thread which hung in the *Beis HaMikdash* on Yom Kippur which, if it did not turn white, caused the entire nation to break into sobs — the Jewish people understood what they were obligated to do. But now, due to our many sins, "He has placed me in darkness like the eternally dead" (*Eichah* 3:6), and we have no idea when it is a time of favor in Heaven. We are sunken on the bed of illusion, and we mistakenly believe that it is still night and not yet time to rise.

Hashem therefore says to us, "Return to Me...and I will return to you" (*Zechariah* 1:3) — return to Me at any time!

⤳ To Recognize the King's Greatness

A king was traveling along the road at the head of a huge entourage. Their journey led them to the edge of a field that was surrounded by a fence. Since they were pressed for time, the king ordered that the fence be demolished in order to facilitate their passing through.

The owner of the field was an ignorant and simple villager. He did not recognize the king at all nor he was familiar with royal etiquette. In his naiveté, he thought that the men who had broken the fence to his field were a team of hunters. His anger was kindled within him, and in a fit of rage he hurled stones at them; one of the stones even struck the king.

The field owner was immediately seized by the king's men and brought to trial. It did not take long for the court to reach a decision: The farmer was sentenced to death for his crime of rebelling against the king.

Seeing that the villager had absolutely no grasp of just how severe his act had been, the king had mercy on him and nullified the verdict. The villager would not go unpunished, however, as the king ordered him to clean the streets of the capital city.

The man was first instructed to clean the streets that were quite a distance away from the king's palace. Next he cleaned the areas immediately surrounding the palace, and ultimately the king's courtyard. With each area that he cleaned, the villager began to comprehend the enormity of the kingdom and just how mighty and awesome the king truly was. Having arrived at this understanding, it also dawned on him to what degree he had wronged the king and just how severe his infraction had been.

When he had concluded his task, he turned to the minister in charge and requested that he bring him before the king so that he would be able to entreat him and plead for his forgiveness.

A man who sins, said R' Yisrael Ba'al Shem Tov, does not have any conception of Hashem's greatness and therefore stumbles and sins on occasion. Had he understood the awesomeness of Hashem, the King of kings, he would plead and request forgiveness for his soul.

▶ One Who Says, "I Will Sin and Repent..."

In a certain city lived a wholesaler, who was patronized by all the merchants in his neighborhood. Out of the kindness of his heart, the wholesaler would sell them merchandise on credit.

One day, two merchants who had come to pay their debts stood in his store. One of the merchants arrived with a bundle of money in his hand; he paid his debt in full and left. But the second merchant approached the wholesaler with tears in his eyes and related that his store had burned down. In order to pay his debt, he continued, he had gathered together whatever he owned. As he finished speaking, he placed on the table a sack of pennies that he had managed to collect, as well as some vessels, charred clothing, books, and old clocks.

"The total value of these items," said the unfortunate merchant, "adds up to the amount of money that I owe you. I beg of you, please accept these items as payment for the debt."

The kindhearted wholesaler had mercy on the man and conceded to his request. He took the pennies, the old clothing, and the vessels, and erased the man's debt from his ledgers.

While both debtors repaid their loans, there is a very great difference between them. For if the first merchant will return and request merchandise, the wholesaler will immediately and happily give him all that he wants. But if the second merchant requests additional merchandise, it is doubtful that the wholesaler will comply.

> When an individual performs sincere, total repentance, noted the Dubno Maggid, regrets his past deeds, and makes a commitment to sin in the future — Hashem forgives him. But if a person wishes to repent simply to lighten the burden of sins that weigh so heavily upon him, and he lacks a firm resolve to totally abandon his sinful ways — this is not the repentance that is required of him!

A wealthy storeowner sought to hire an assistant who would be able to work in his shop. He looked into the matter and ultimately narrowed his choice to two potential candidates, both of them trustworthy: The first individual had worked for many years as an assistant in a large store, while the other had actually been a store-owner himself, but had since lost all of his money. He was now forced to hire himself out and work for other storeowners.

The storeowner chose the man who had lost his money.

"I specifically chose him," explained the merchant, "for there is a substantial difference between the labor that a hired worker performs for his employer and the labor which a storeowner performs on his own behalf. The hired worker does not expend any more effort than is absolutely necessary, and he simply wants to conclude his workday so that he can return home. This is not the case with a storeowner who works for himself; he works tirelessly, and feels neither hunger, thirst, cold, nor heat — rather, all of his interests are geared towards the success of his business. Furthermore, a hired worker never gives the business extensive thought; rather, he simply performs what is required of him. A storeowner, on the other hand, investigates a matter and ponders it thoroughly, arriving at an understanding as to how he can improve his business and increase his profits."

Chazal state (*Berachos* 34b): "In the place where *ba'alei teshuvah* stand, *tzaddikim gemurim* do not stand!"

In light of this parable, said the Ben Ish Chai, R' Yosef Chaim of Baghdad, we can understand *Chazal's* statement. A *ba'al teshuvah* is on a very lofty level for he knows and re-members well how he exerted himself in pursuing empty, meaningless endeavors. He is aware of the effort he put forth and the strategies he utilized simply in order to fulfill his warped goals. So now that he has merited returning to Hashem with all of his heart, he employs all of his abilities and strategies in the service of Hashem and fulfills all of Hashem's *mitzvos* with diligence and joy as well.

◄§ *Absolving the Debt*

In a certain city lived an extraordinarily wealthy merchant who sold a vast quantity of goods to the merchants residing in the small towns surrounding his city.

When it was time for the fair to be held, the merchant made it known that he intended to travel there in order to purchase new and outstanding goods. He therefore urged all those who owed him money to come and pay their debts.

Among those who owed him money was a merchant whose home had unfortunately burned down. All of his property had been consumed in the flames as well, leaving him penniless.

He was utterly distressed and humiliated at the thought of having to face the wealthy man. "How can I have the nerve to come before him empty-handed?" he asked.

"Just go to him," advised his friends, "and tell him the truth. There is nothing better than that!"

The merchant heeded their advice and journeyed to the wealthy man.

Sitting in the wealthy man's waiting room, the poor merchant was unable to restrain himself, and he broke into a fit of bitter sobbing.

The sound of the weeping reached the inner chambers of the wealthy man's heart, and he requested to know the reason behind it. Soon after, the merchant's story was related to him.

The wealthy man felt pity for the unfortunate merchant; when the man was brought in to him he embraced him and exclaimed, "Do not feel the least bit distressed. I hereby completely absolve you of your debt." He then tore the bill of debt into shreds.

The merchant thanked the wealthy man profusely and went on his way. The matter soon became known to the members of the community and eventually spread to the public at large as well.

Among those who heard about it was a crook who decided to deceive the wealthy man.

He traveled to the wealthy man's home, and upon taking a seat in the waiting room, began to wail loudly.

"What are you crying about?" shouted the wealthy man.

"I desperately need two thousand rubles," he cried. "I beg of you, please give me the entire sum."

"I am very sorry," answered the wealthy man, "but I am simply unable to give you such a large amount of money."

"But you absolved so-and-so from a debt of an equal amount," insisted the disappointed crook.

"You fool," said the wealthy man. "That individual owed me a great deal of money, and I knew that he did not have a penny to his name with which to repay me — what would I have gained had I not absolved his debt? Will I get my money back? That is why I forgave his debt. But as for you, I have absolutely no business with you — why should I acquiesce to giving you a sum of two thousand rubles? Should I give it to you simply because you are crying?"

> When a person repents, said the Dubno Maggid, sincerely regrets his misdeeds, and cries to Hashem that He forgive him for his iniquities — Hashem immediately forgives him. But if a foolish individual thinks to himself, "I will sin, repent, sin again, repent once again, and even cry over my sins afterwards" — his repentance will not be accepted!

✍§ On the Way to the Fair

A pair of individuals journeyed to the fair. One was a simple merchant who traveled in an old wagon that was harnessed to an aged horse that could barely manage to pull it. The other was a wealthy merchant who traveled in a magnificent carriage harnessed to powerful steeds that swiftly galloped along.

As the beautiful carriage quickly sped past the rickety one, the simple merchant's heart was filled with anguish. "How fortunate he is!" he thought to himself. "He will soon arrive at the fair and be able to engage in business; yet I...Who knows if my old horse will even be alive by the time we are halfway through this trip?"

In reality — although neither merchant was aware of this fact — the road they were traveling would not get them to the fair. It was an incorrect route that led in exactly the opposite direction.

Subsequently, the more the wealthy merchant hurried and his coachman whipped the horses, the farther they traveled from the fair. The simple merchant, on the other hand, was not harmed in the least by the slow pace at which his horses were traveling.

> A man who commits a transgression and knows that he has sinned, said the Dubno Maggid, is receptive to reproach and can easily repent. But if an individual is unaware that his deeds are flawed, he simply continues to move further and further away…

‌ Repentance Out of Love

> Chazal state (Yoma 86b), "Great is repentance out of love, for it turns sins into merits." Explaining the lofty level of repentance that is motivated by love of Hashem and why it is preferable to repentance motivated by fear of Hashem, R' Yosef Chaim of Baghdad quoted an extraordinary parable from the sefer Sha'ar Bas Rabim.

A thief decided to steal from the king's treasury, and he spent many days planning how he would dig a canal beneath it. Having done so, he would enter and fill his sacks with the array of treasures that lay within.

He ultimately devised a strategy and, one night, dug a ditch. His planning had not been exact enough, however, and instead of leading to the king's treasury, the canal led into the corridor adjacent to it. The thief entered the dark corridor and felt around, but did not find any riches whatsoever. Left with no other choice, he turned around and escaped before the sun came up.

That very same night, a different thief attempted to penetrate the king's treasury as well. He, too, dug a ditch, but unlike his counterpart, he managed to successfully enter the treasury and fill his sacks with the king's treasures. Before he took flight, however, he stopped for a moment and thought, "How could I be so brazen as to steal from the king himself? Why, I am obligated to honor him..."

The thief emptied his bags completely and fled to his home.

When day broke, the king's subjects noticed that there were two openings that were dug into the palace walls, but the ensuing investigation revealed that not a thing was missing from the treasury.

The king very much desired to know the explanation behind this strange occurrence; he therefore ordered that a through investigation be undertaken. Shortly thereafter, the king's police brought the two thieves before him, and the king interrogated them, asking them to explain their actions.

"I will not deny it," said the first thief. "I entered the king's treasury but did not find a thing. Since I feared that daybreak was near, I escaped in order to save myself."

The king responded by placing the thief in prison.

"I," confessed the second thief, "entered the treasury and even took whatever I could. Suddenly, however, I was counseled by my intellect and I understood that what I was about to perpetrate was a severe offense which was a slight to the king's honor. Out of love for the king, I therefore decided on the spot to abstain from this wicked deed."

When the king heard this, he sent the man home and even granted him many gifts...

> So, too, said R' Yosef Chaim, in relation to repentance. It is a great honor to the King of the World when a Jew repents out of love!

A wealthy man had a wonderful daughter who had come of age, and he therefore sought out a groom who would befit both his and her prestigious standing. He eventually found a young man who was a *ben Torah* and who possessed sterling character traits. The young man hailed from a family of paupers, however, and there was not a penny to be found in his father's home.

The wealthy man promised his son-in-law a beautiful apartment, fine vessels, and a large dowry. He was even willing to support him financially for many years; there was just one stipulation that he made with the boy's father — that he dress his son in nice clothing which was appropriate to be worn by the son-in-law of a wealthy merchant. After all, how could he be in the company of wealthy individuals and noblemen if he was dressed like a pauper?

The father-in-law withheld from spending money on bread, and, instead, sewed attractive clothing for his son.

When the day of the wedding arrived, the groom's family traveled to where it was to be held, and upon arriving, took up lodging in an inn.

The following morning, the wealthy man made his way to the inn and found his *mechutan* (in-law) and son-in-law sitting and weeping.

The sight frightened the wealthy man. "What happened?" he asked. "Why are you weeping?"

"Thieves came in the middle of the night," cried the son-in-law, "and stole all of the beautiful garments which my father had prepared for me for the wedding."

The wealthy man waved off the concern. "That's why you're crying?" he asked. "It will take me a moment to call the finest tailor in the city who will quickly sew you brand-new garments."

And so he did. It was not long before the tailor produced splendid garments befitting the son-in-law of one of the wealthiest men in the land.

After the wedding, the guests noticed that the groom's father was sighing.

"What's the matter with you?" they inquired in bewilderment. "Your son has merited being the son-in-law of one of the richest men in the land, and you — a simple blacksmith — are sighing bitterly?"

"Don't you know?" asked the poor *mechutan*. "Did you not hear that the clothing which I prepared for my son was stolen? That's why I am sighing!"

"You fool!" they exclaimed. "Be grateful to the thief who stole your clothing! He performed an act of kindness for you! We could just imagine the "stunning garments" which you sewed for your son...When your *mechutan* would have seen them, he certainly would have had something to say. As far as his wife is concerned, why, we don't even have to elaborate on what she would have thought...

"Your *mechutan*," they said, continuing to offer him words of comfort, "is well aware that you upheld your promise and sewed clothes for the young man; they were simply stolen. He will not have any objections whatsoever to the fact that it was he who sewed the fine garments for your son."

When a man, said the Dubno Maggid, fills up his "knapsack" — i.e., his days in this world — with *mitzvos* and good deeds, and his time to leave the world arrives, he will have to stand trial before the Heavenly Tribunal. At that point, various prosecutors rise against him and claim, "He performed this *mitzvah* only with the intention of receiving honor! He did not study this Torah for its own sake!" And so on and so forth; for every deed that a man performed, the prosecutors attempt to discover a flaw of some kind.

This is not the case, concluded the Maggid, with a *ba'al teshuvah*. When he repents, wholeheartedly regrets his prior deeds, and cries bitterly over his sins and about how he wasted his life with meaningless endeavors, Hashem personally turns all of his transgressions into merits.

Prosecutors will not have the ability to stake any claims against *mitzvos* such as these — *mitzvos* that Hashem personally granted to man.

◈§ The Level of a Ba'al Teshuvah

Two young brothers wasted away their days acting mischievously — one brother purchased food and drink, subsequently eating and drinking to his heart's content, the other naughtily ascended a table and promptly fell off, tumbling hard to the floor.

When the father heard about what his sons had done, he punished them and slapped them across their cheeks...

The father eventually felt pity for his sons, and in his desire to appease them, gave the first son one coin and the other son two coins.

Resentful, the first son turned to his father and asked, "Why did I receive only one coin while my brother received two?"

"Your brother," answered the father, "not only hurt himself when he fell off the table, but I slapped him across his cheek as well; he therefore received two coins. You, on the other hand, squandered your time eating fine delicacies. You ate and drank, but were ultimately punished. You therefore only received one coin."

A *ba'al teshuvah*, noted the Dubno Maggid, is on a lofty level indeed, for his suffering is twofold. His suffering was great when he sinned initially, and he recalls his previous transgressions when he subsequently repents. This, too, causes him great anguish and he weeps profusely over it.

Chazal have therefore stated (*Berachos* 34b), "Said R' Abahu: In the place where *ba'alei teshuvah* stand, *tzaddikim gemurim* do not stand."

❧ The Captive Prince

A king had two mighty and courageous sons. One day, the king went out to battle his enemies, and his two sons accompanied him as commanders in his army.

The sons fought with strength and bravery, until one of them was surrounded by the enemy and taken captive.

The king's son languished in the enemy prison, starving and deprived, and after an entire year, ultimately succeeded in digging a tunnel that enabled him to escape from captivity. The prince ran away, crossing over rivers and lakes, and trekking through forests and mountains. After a while, he finally managed to return to his father's home.

How great was the elation in the king's palace upon the prince's return. Elaborate celebrations were staged in his honor, and the king sat him to his right and showered him with gifts.

Without a doubt, this son's joy is ten times greater than a son who had never left his father's home.

> This is the identical happiness, said R' Yisrael Ba'al Shem Tov, that a person feels when he returns in complete repentance to his Father in Heaven. His joy is ten times greater than one who has never sinned, for only once a person has saved himself from sin can he truly perceive the taste of "captivity."

❧ The Valuable Collection

Over the course of many years, a villager collected silver and gold vessels as well as various types of jewelry, until he had amassed a very lovely and valuable collection. He feared storing such a precious collection in his home; he therefore turned to his friend who lived in the big city and requested that he guard the valuable treasure in his home. The friend readily agreed.

One day, thieves entered the friend's house and stole all of the valuables in his home, not even leaving a trace of the villager's precious treasure.

The friend sent a messenger to hurry and inform the villager that his treasure had been stolen. Upon hearing the bad tidings, he ordered the members of his household to harness the horses, and they set out to pursue the thieves on the road that was close to the village.

"Who said that the thieves are traversing this particular road?" wondered the messenger.

"Why did my friend dispatch you so urgently?" asked the villager. "My good friend is a very wise man; he did so only because he inferred from the thieves' words that they were set to flee along this route!"

> Hashem sends us many trials throughout our lives, said the Dubno Maggid. We must examine and scrutinize these tests and try to understand why they have been given to us. Our investigations will inevitably reveal that they are undeniable messages from Hashem that we must return in complete repentance!

⋙ Staking Claims

An individual leased a large tavern from the ruler of the city, and all of the gentiles and drunkards of the city would come to his tavern to drink whiskey. His lease was extremely expensive and he therefore owed a large sum of money to the ruler. The ruler requested that the bartender come to his palace on a particular day in order to pay his debt. The bartender sat in his home; next to him stood his wife and children. They stared at him as he counted his money in order to see if he had enough to pay the ruler — but he was still short a substantial amount.

The bartender turned to his family and in a fit of anger exclaimed, "When I stand before the ruler I intend to tell him exactly what I think of him! I mean, this is absolute robbery! There is no other city in which the ruler charges such high rental fees! One would think that my tavern is a melting furnace for gold…"

The bartender sat there listing off one claim after another, explaining why he was not required to pay such a hefty sum of money.

When the day arrived, the bartender made his way to the palace and entered the hall where the ruler was seated. The ruler was sitting on a magnificent throne, surrounded by servants dressed in glittering uniforms and armed soldiers awaiting his instructions. It was a scene that clearly proclaimed his glory and splendor.

The bartender stood trembling before him, and all of the claims that he had previously uttered with such passion and courage were all but forgotten; all that came out of his mouth was an apologetic stammer…

> The way of the wicked, said the Dubno Maggid, is to spend their entire lives in this world entrenched in sin, and their mouths are filled with deceit and excuses.
>
> Let it be known, concluded the Maggid, that when it comes time for them to stand trial before Hashem in the next world, fear and terror will befall them. They will stand there trembling and will not find the courage to stake any claims whatsoever!
>
> All of the claims that they uttered and used to delude themselves in this world are meaningless and pure folly!

◆§ The King's Messengers

The king's messenger summoned an individual to come to the palace at once. When the man saw that the messenger was wearing black garments and had an angry visage, he was immediately gripped by a feeling of terror, for perhaps he was destined to receive a punishment from the king.

There was a wise man standing nearby who soothed the man's anxiety. "What do you have to fear from the messenger?" he said. "He cannot do anything to you without a direct command from the king. Therefore, instead of being fearful and worrying, examine your deeds. If you know that you are free of any transgression, you would do well to hurry to the palace as the king commanded and hear what he has to say."

On another occasion, the king's messenger summoned a different individual to appear before the king. This time, however, the messenger was dressed in bright-colored clothes and wearing cheerful countenance as well. The man was overjoyed and he began to dance.

A wise man turned to him and said, "What do you have to dance about? Who really knows if this messenger is the bearer of good news or not? Do not be misled by the happy expression on his face; rather, think about whether you are truly loyal to the king. If you are, then the messenger is bringing you good tidings, but if you have sinned against the king, Heaven forbid, then evil has been determined against you..."

> A Jew should not judge himself, said R' Yisrael Ba'al Shem Tov, according to whether an event which befalls him is good or bad. Rather, he must constantly examine himself in order to know whether he is loyal to the King or, Heaven forbid, has sinned against Him.

❧ The Proclamation

A blind man's entire body was ailing, and he was lying on his bed, unable to move. A young boy assisted him and tended to all his needs. One day, the blind man heard sounds of a proclamation being announced throughout the city. He immediately summoned the young boy and asked him to go and hear what was being announced, for he wished to know if it was bringing the city's residents good tidings or perhaps informing them of impending danger.

"What difference does it make to you?" asked the boy. "It is certainly of great consequence to a healthy individual, for if the proclamation is about a *simchah* (festive occasion), then he will be able to participate in it. If it carries a warning of imminent danger, on the other hand, a healthy person must know how to prepare himself — should he wage war or perhaps go and appease the approaching enemy?

"But for you," concluded the lad, "the information is utterly insignificant. If there is a *simchah*, you will not be able to take part, and if there is looming danger, what will you do — get up and do battle?"

> The same thing applies to us, said the Dubno Maggid. We are full of sins, and when we rise to beseech the Creator of the World, we are left with nothing else to say but, "We have sinned!"

◦§ *Specifying the Sins*

Two paupers wandered together from city to city and from village to village collecting alms together. One of the paupers was physically fit, while the other was beset with illness, pains, and afflictions. Wherever they went, the healthy pauper warned his companion not to utter a word of his illnesses to the local residents; rather, he said, he should conceal them to the best of his ability, lest they both be driven away.

On one occasion, they arrived at an inn where a famous physician happened to be lodging at the time. The paupers approached the doctor and requested a donation.

The doctor took pity on them and instead of giving them money, offered to provide them with his services free of charge, if either of them were suffering from any particular ailment.

"Tell him," urged the healthy pauper. "Tell the doctor about your illnesses and do not leave out a single detail!"

"Why have you changed your mind?" asked the sick pauper in surprise. "Haven't you always told me that I should hide my ailments?"

"You fool," responded the healthy pauper. "Wherever we go, telling others about your condition can only be to your detriment, as the residents will avoid you and refuse to host you. But here you have an opportunity to be healed from all of your afflictions; you must therefore tell him everything and not omit a single detail!"

> Man, said the Dubno Maggid, is severely afflicted and full of sins. He must therefore refrain from being overly verbose when speaking to others. Yet when standing before Hashem, Who mercifully desires to forgive a repentant individual for all of his sins, an individual must not spare one detail, as this is a golden opportunity for him.

ۑۥ *The Goat*

A pauper purchased a goat and brought it back to his home. His wife was overjoyed, for she would now be able to provide her youngsters with milk. She therefore wasted little time, grabbed a bucket, and went out to milk the goat.

Much to her disappointment, the goat did not produce even one drop of milk.

The woman was very upset and began to weep.

"Do not be upset," said her husband. "The goat must be tired; allow her to rest a little bit, and place some straw and fodder before her. Afterwards it will surely produce milk for us."

> There are times, said the Dubno Maggid, when a person repents, regrets his sins, and even afflicts himself in order to procure atonement for his soul. He then immediately wishing to know if his actions took effect and if he was indeed forgiven.
>
> Hashem answers him, however, "Wait a little while, and we will see how the fasting and regret have affected you..."

A shepherd was in the meadow tending his sheep, and when he felt tired, he placed his head on the grass and dozed.

The sheep roamed to and fro until they found a breach in the fence. They entered the adjoining field where there was a lush, green meadow, and they grazed heartily. The fields, however, belonged to the ruler of the city, and when his servants spotted unfamiliar sheep grazing there, they confiscated the sheep and placed them among the ruler's flocks.

When the shepherd awoke from his slumber, he was surprised to discover that his sheep had disappeared. He investigated the matter and discovered what had transpired.

The shepherd thought about how he could appease the ruler.

"This has happened before," his friends told him. "Sheep entered the ruler's fields and ate from the good crop. But the owner of the sheep brought the ruler a sack of sugar as a gift, and he was forgiven."

The shepherd was elated and he, too, hurried and slung a sack of sugar over his shoulder. He then set out for the ruler's palace.

When he arrived at the palace, he was informed that the ruler had departed and would return the following day. He therefore placed the sack of sugar on the table in the ruler's chamber. From there, he went to the ruler's sheep pen and took back his sheep.

When the ruler returned home and heard what had happened, he became enraged and requested that the shepherd be brought before him immediately.

The shepherd arrived and stood trembling before the ruler.

"How dare you enter my home and then remove the sheep from the flock?" demanded the ruler.

"Forgive me, Your Highness," responded the shepherd in a frightened stammer. "I did just as my predecessor did; I brought you a sack of sugar and took the sheep…"

"You fool!" bellowed the ruler. "Do I need a sack of sugar? What is of primary importance to me are the pleas and supplications that your predecessor offered! When I heard his pleas, I forgave him, for I saw how he sincerely regretted what had happened."

We repent before Hashem, said the Dubno Maggid, and strike our chests reciting the *Al Cheit* as did our predecessors. But how do we fail to understand that it is the pleas from the depths of a broken heart that are of primary importance?

~§ The House's Cleanliness

A certain individual built himself a spacious home. First he went about hiring an architect, and requested from him that he draw a precise blueprint for the entire home. He wanted his home to be built perfectly, without leaving any spaces that could potentially allow wind to enter, carrying sand and dust from the roads along with it.

When the plan was completed, the man watched the builders ever so carefully, making sure that they did not become lazy and that the construction was carried out as planned.

When the house stood completed, the man moved his belongings into it. Among the many items that his neighbors saw him bring into his home was a broom in order to sweep up dust and sand.

"Excuse us, our dear neighbor," they asked him. "You have just built yourself a house without any spaces whatsoever. Why, then, do you need a broom?"

"Indeed," replied the man, "the house is entirely sealed from all sides. Despite these precautionary measures, however, it is inevitable that when individuals visit my home they will carry in dust and sand on their feet. I therefore need a broom; otherwise, my house will eventually be full of dust."

Hashem created man and placed a lofty soul inside his body, said the Dubno Maggid. He sealed the body, from all sides and put *mitzvos* and good deeds at each one of its openings

— each limb was given specific *mitzvos* that pertain to it alone — in order to prevent any "dust" from the trivialities of this world from entering. But he also gave us the opportunity to repeat — in case any "dust" comes in.

☙ *Two Bartenders*

Two bartenders resided in a certain village whose ruler leased them taverns located on opposite ends of the village. One day, the ruler summoned the two bartenders and pointed out that his ledger stated that each owed him a large sum of money. "How do you intend to repay your debts?" he asked them.

The first bartender asked the ruler to rent him the tavern for an additional year, in hopes that it would earn enough profit during that time to allow him to repay his debt.

The second bartender, on the other hand, requested to pay off his debt by performing various tasks in the ruler's home.

The ruler acceded to both their requests. The first bartender was sent back to his tavern, while the other one was presented with an array of tasks to perform in the ruler's estate.

One day, the first bartender met his friend and exclaimed, "You are most fortunate, my friend! By working daily, you are gradually repaying your debt. Yet I," he sighed, "am sunk up to my neck in debts that are rising above my head. Furthermore, in addition to my old debt, I have now accrued rental fees for another year as well…"

There is a sinner, said the Dubno Maggid, who adds one sin upon another and is sunken in his mire. Yet one who repents from his sin and sincerely regrets his actions purifies his past, and it is good for him in both this world and the next.

Part 13
Redemption

The phrase "I adjure you, O nations destined to ascend to Jerusalem…,"appears several times in *Shir Hashirim*. *Chazal* teach that it is telling us that Hashem has sworn the Jewish Nation not to force the *keitz* (conclusion of Jewish exile). Rather, the redemption will surely arrive in its proper time.

However, in *Yeshayahu* (60:22) it states, "I am Hashem, in its time I will hasten it," on which *Chazal* (*Sanhedrin* 98a) have expounded: Said R' Alexandri, R' Yehoshua ben Levi questions an apparent contradiction in the verse. On one hand, the beginning of the verse states that the redemption will come "in its time," — i.e., in its destined time — yet, on the other hand, the verse concludes, "I will hasten it," indicating that the redemption will arrive prior to its destined time. Rather, he answers, if the Jewish Nation merits, "I will hasten it," but if not, Heaven forbid, the redemption will arrive "in its time."

This can be compared to a guest lodging at an inn who went out to tour the city. When he returned to the hotel it was just after noon; he made his way into the hotel's kitchen and asked the cook to serve him lunch.

"The food is not ready yet," apologized the cook. "It is still too early."

Nevertheless, the man stubbornly persisted that he be served, and the meal was therefore brought to him.

The man grimaced when he tasted the food, as its flavor was rather odd — it tasted like it was uncooked …

"Did I not tell you?" sighed the cook. "But you forced me to serve you."

The next day, the cook exerted herself to go to the kitchen ahead of time and served the food earlier than usual. The man warily tasted the food, but this time it was delicious!

"I do not understand," remarked the guest. "Yesterday you served me before the scheduled time, and you told me explicitly that the food is not yet ready at this hour. Yet today you personally served me the food at the same time, and it tasted excellent."

"The difference is clear," said the cook. "Yesterday you rushed me and I wasn't ready to serve the food; today, however, I rushed myself and was therefore adequately prepared."

> When the Jewish Nation wishes to hurry the redemption, said the Dubno Maggid, it is not yet the proper time for it to come; Hashem has therefore made them swear not to do so. But if Hashem Himself wishes to hasten the redemption — there could be no more suitable time than that!

⋑ The Doctor and the Mighty Soldier

Two paupers were wandering from city to city, collecting charity. They were as different from one another as could be: one was tall, very strong, and in good health, while the other was thin, weak, and beset with illnesses from head to toe.

The healthy pauper derided his sick companion on account of his weakness and boasted to him about his strength and good health.

The unfortunate pauper was aggrieved over the daily barrage of insults, and he prayed in his heart that the day would come when a price would be paid for all the affronts he endured.

On one occasion, their roaming brought them to the capital city, where the king resided. Some time earlier, a tragedy had occurred in the king's courtyard: The king's physician, an expert in the medical field, had passed away. At the same time, the king's head guard, a very mighty warrior, had also left the world.

The king dispatched officers with instructions to search throughout the entire kingdom for individuals who would be suitable replacements. After a thorough search that lasted many days, an excellent physician was found who was an extraordinary expert in the art of healing as well as in concocting medications.

They also located a fierce soldier who was learned in warfare and a skilled combatant as well.

The king requested to test the two candidates and they happily agreed to prove their abilities.

"Bring me a sick man," said the doctor. "Even if he is extremely ill, I will heal him completely!"

"I would like just the opposite," exclaimed the mighty soldier. "Bring me as powerful an individual as you can find, and I will crush him like a gnat!"

The king's servants began searching and quickly found the two paupers...one, a mighty soldier, the other, a sickly individual.

The king's doctor took the ill pauper and extended him astoundingly devoted treatment, concocting a variety of medicines and creams for him. It was not long before the pauper was completely cured.

The king's head guard, on the other hand, thoroughly whipped the powerful pauper, and struck him soundly until he had to be brought to the hospital beaten and wounded.

> The Jewish Nation, said the Dubno Maggid, is presently entrenched in a bitter exile among the gentile nations who take pride in their strength and power. The Jews suffer persecution and denigration, but the complete redemption will soon arrive and Hashem will humble the haughty and elevate the lowly!

✑§ Participating in a Simchah

When a villager's wife bears him a son, it is customary to send wagons to the big city to bring his relatives as well as his invited guests to participate in the *bris milah* (circumcision). The host generally sends wagons according to his financial capabilities: If he is a wealthy individual, he sends large, spacious coaches just in case an additional person desires to partake in his *simchah*. If he is poor, however, he sends a small wagon to the big city, capable of seating only his nearest relatives. But if he is completely poverty-stricken, he sends only a lone donkey in order to transport the *mohel* (circumciser) alone.

> When the time for redemption arrives in the future, noted the Dubno Maggid, and we merit being redeemed on account of our good deeds, a large vehicle will be sent to gather all of the Jews who are dispersed throughout the four corners of the world. But if we are not deserving of the redemption, Heaven forbid, then the number of people who merit being redeemed will be much less, and only the worthy among the Jewish Nation will be gathered.

‎ؤ *The Custodian*

An elderly wealthy man had a young daughter. When he felt that his end was near, he summoned one of his trusted acquaintances and requested that he take extraordinary care and fully provide for his daughter after he had left the world.

"Indeed," said the elderly man, "I am leaving you with a vast amount of property, but do not use it to provide my daughter with her daily sustenance; for that, she must find work and earn a livelihood. When it comes time for her to marry, however, find her a suitable Torah scholar as a groom. You should pay for all of the wedding expenses and dowry from my money; the remainder shall be given to my daughter."

Some time later, the elderly man passed away, and his friend did exactly as he had been asked, guarding the money and leaving it untouched until the day of the wedding.

When the daughter grew older, she managed to find various jobs, but had a very difficult time earning a livelihood. After a while, her relatives turned to the friend and complained, "Just look at her face," they exclaimed. "Why, she has not had a satisfying meal in such a long time...please give her some of the money that you are safekeeping."

"This I simply cannot do," responded the friend, "for her father explicitly instructed me otherwise."

The daughter eventually fell ill and was bedridden. Her relatives, once again, turned to the friend and pleaded that he assist their relative — but, as before, he refused.

"I can only give her the money," he replied, "when she gets married."

"Look here," cried the relatives in bitter despondency, "her life is in danger. If you do not give her some money now, who will she marry when the day arrives?"

> Said the Dubno Maggid, all of the benefits that we will receive in the future when the redemption arrives are a result of the suffering which we endured in exile. It is much like a fruit from a tree — the longer it remains attached to the tree, the more it ripens. So, too, the longer our exile lasts and our suffering increases, the greater will our future benefits be!
>
> Yet we nevertheless cry and supplicate Hashem, "Why do You ignore us eternally, forsake us for so long?" (*Eichah* 5:20).
>
> The sufferings have increased and endured for such a long time that we barely have the strength to withstand them any longer.

৵৽ Preparing for the Feast

An individual returned home at the end of a difficult day tired and overwhelmingly hungry. He asked his wife to serve him bread and cooked food, as his pangs of hunger were quite severe.

"Please wait," said his wife, "and I will prepare you the scrumptious dishes that you so enjoy." The wife made her way to the kitchen and began to prepare the delicious food; however, the preparations stretched for quite some time...

"Forgive me, my dear wife," remarked the man, "but when do you think that the meal will be ready? I simply lack the strength to wait. A little longer and my soul will take leave of my body..."

"Wait just a little longer," responded his wife. "The food is not fully ready yet."

"How I long," said the man, "to receive delicacies that will be proportionate to the level of difficulty that there is in waiting for them..."

> The Jewish Nation, said the Dubno Maggid, is starving and thirsty for the benefits that will arrive with the eventual complete redemption. Hashem, however, requests that we not force the *keitz* (ultimate conclusion of Jewish exile), for our eventual benefits are perfected as the exile is prolonged.
>
> We therefore beseech Hashem, "Gladden us according to the days You afflicted us, the years when we saw evil" (*Tehillim* 90:15).

◄§ The Rich Man and the Drunkard

A rich man was walking through the city square with his son. He was wearing extravagant garments that were very costly. They were suddenly approached by a drunkard who went right up to the wealthy man and grabbed the lapel of his beautiful garment.

"You thief!" screamed the inebriated drunkard. "This garment is mine!"

"Indeed it is, my good friend," replied the wealthy man. "But do not suspect me of stealing it from your home; rather, your wife loaned it to me until tomorrow."

The wealthy man's answer appeased the drunkard, and he staggered away.

"Father," asked his son, "why did you answer him in such a manner? Why, this garment is yours — it has never been his!"

"True," he answered. "But why should I have entered into a debate with him? I therefore pushed him off until tomorrow; by then his sobriety will have returned, and he will be ashamed of the way he behaved. He will no longer whet his tongue against me with nonsensical claims."

In the future, said the Dubno Maggid, Gog and Magog will wage war against Hashem and His anointed. But, "He Who sits in Heaven will laugh, the Lord will mock them" (*Tehillim* 2:4) — Hashem will mock them, for their measure of sin will shortly be filled. "Then He will speak to them in His anger, and in His wrath He will terrify them" (*Tehillim* ibid.v.5)!

~§ From Mourning to Joy

A pauper may arrive in a city and go unnoticed by its residents, wandering to and fro but not finding a place to rest his weary body. But if the pauper is on the verge of collapse due to an illness he contracted, he will procure the assistance of the kind people of the city, who will do their utmost to support him and prevent him from expiring. Furthermore, even after he recovers and regains his strength, they will provide him with food and donations.

So, too, with the Jewish Nation, said the Dubno Maggid. The Jewish Nation is undergoing much suffering in their exile, and as long as they are able to endure, it is an indication that the time has not yet arrived for them to be redeemed. When they are ultimately threatened to drown in their afflictions, however, Hashem will immediately redeem them, as the verse states (*Yirmiyahu* 31:12), "I shall transform their mourning into joy and I shall comfort them and gladden them from their grief"!

~§ The Villager and the Teacher

A generous, kindhearted villager had an only son who was extremely beloved and dear to him. He wished to send his son to a renowned professor in the big city, so that the son would gain intellectual acumen. He traveled to the professor and the two of them reached an agreement: the professor would teach his son wisdom. The father agreed to provide fish and chickens, vegetables, wheat, and fruit, with which the professor's wife would prepare delicacies for his son. And so it was.

Out of the goodness of his heart, the father sent the son an adequate supply of food, and he even sent enough for the professor and his wife as well. They acted dishonestly, however, and took all of the delicacies for themselves, leaving the son with only stale bread and various leftovers. What is more, the professor pretended to be surprised, saying, "What's happened to your father? Has he lost all his money, or perhaps he has simply lost interest in his son?"

The son, however, knew his merciful father well, and he immediately grasped that the professor and his wife were stealing all of the choice food and leaving him with only the poorest quality.

Some time later, the son visited his parents' home. The father was frightened by the thin, pale appearance of his son.

The son related to his father all that had happened, and added, "I know, my dear father, that you are sending delicious food, but the professor and his wife are stealing it."

> Hashem, said the Dubno Maggid, generously sends the Jewish Nation His bounty and, for our sake, bestows the nations who persecute us with a profusion of good as well. But the nations of the world fill their vessels with the best of the bounty — and sustain us with only the bread of anxiety and water of sorrow.
>
> What is more, they open their mouths in surprise, asking, "Why does their Father withhold His goodness from them?" As the verse states (*Tehillim* 79:10), "Why should the nations say, 'Where is their G-d'"?
>
> In the future, their shame will be revealed before the multitudes!

eS Best Wishes

In a certain city resided two extraordinarily wealthy individuals, each of whom had a son. One of the sons was a brilliant Torah scholar and a pious, G-d-fearing man as well. He continued to strive and advance until he was appointed *rav* of the city.

His wealthy father was delighted upon his assuming the post, and he arranged a large feast in honor of his son, to which he invited all of the city's residents. Seeing the son's greatness, the towns-people wished each other similar good fortune, "If only we would also merit such a son who personifies both Torah and greatness!"

The son of the other wealthy man, however, was of low character and experienced one failure after another until he was found guilty of committing felonies for which he had to stand trial.

The trial was held and the son was found innocent on all counts; he was therefore sent back to his house.

The father was delighted with the trial's outcome and arranged a feast in the son's honor to which he invited his relatives and friends. But when this feast was held, no man wished his friend, "If only we would also merit such a son…"

A man who has been saved from a trying predicament, remarked the Dubno Maggid, does not wish the same thing upon his friend — his friend will forgo the predicament as well as the eventual rescue.

When Hashem redeems us from the suffering of the bitter and lengthy exile in the future, it will be a happiness of such proportion that all will exclaim, as it states in *Tehillim*, "Then will they declare among the nations, 'Hashem has done greatly with these. Hashem has done greatly with us, we were gladdened" (*Tehillim* 126:2,3)!

✑§ Guided in Miraculous Fashion

"In the future The wilderness and the wasteland will rejoice over them; the desert will be glad" (*Yeshayahu* 35:1)." This prophecy can be explained according to the following parable:

In a certain city lived two brothers; one was extremely wealthy, and the other was a destitute pauper. A third brother — an orator and *darshan* who would make his way through the various cities and towns to deliver sermons regarding Divine service — occasionally visited their city as well. Upon arriving in his brothers' city, he would customarily lodge in the wealthy brother's home.

On one occasion, he delivered a *derashah* in the city, and his passionate words found much favor with the community leaders. Immediately upon concluding his *derashah*, they approached him and informed him that from then on it would be their honor to sustain a Torah scholar of his stature. From that day on, they said, all of his food would be sent to him courtesy of the community's fund.

When word of this reached the poor brother, he rushed to his brother, the oustanding *darshan*, and invited him to be a guest in his home.

"Why have you not invited me until now?" wondered the *darshan*.

"Until now," responded the poor brother, "I have lacked adequate provisions for you, unlike our wealthy brother who merited having you as his guest. But now that your food is being provided by the community fund, why should you not be my guest? Are my wealthy brother and I not presently equal? You are a brother to both of us; you are our flesh and blood."

"The two of you are indeed equal," responded the *darshan*. "But I am accustomed to lodging in his house — why should I trouble myself to move into yours?"

"The reason that I requested this from you," answered the poor brother, "is rather simple. There is no doubt that the community fund will send you more delicious food than you actually require.

Therefore, if you were to stay in our wealthy brother's home, the leftovers would be thrown away and wasted. But if you lodge in my home, my family and I will enjoy the small amount of food that is leftover. Your stay in our home would provide us with a significant degree of pleasure..."

> In present times, said the Dubno Maggid, we receive our sustenance through natural means. An individual should therefore live in a populated area; for if he chooses to live in an area that is desolate and uninhabited, he will be unable to earn a livelihood and sustain himself. In the future, however, Hashem will guide the world in a manner that is not in accordance with the guidelines of nature, and all of a man's livelihood will arrive in miraculous fashion. That being the case, what difference does it make if one lives in a city or the wilderness? With regard to a miracle, every place is equal.
>
> Whatever is left over from the blessing which Hashem sends to man will benefit the wilderness as well. This is what the *Navi* means when he states that in the future the wilderness will rejoice and the desert will be glad.

❧ A Place Alongside the Table

In a certain city lived a wealthy man who invested a large sum of money in the *mitzvah* of *hachnassas orchim* (hospitality). His custom was to seat each guest according to his stature, and after a while his discerning eye was able to gauge the prominence of each guest.

On one occasion, he was host to an individual who was clad in regal attire. He therefore hurried and seated him at the head of the table, as befitted such an esteemed individual.

During the meal, the distinguished guests were served a dish containing meat that was plump and succulent. Those of lesser stature were served meat of a poorer quality, while the individuals who ranked after them received a bowl of ordinary broth. The lowliest amongst them were served a plate of vegetables.

When the well-dressed guest was presented with the plate containing the delicacy, he took a moment to smell it, in hopes of discerning what it was. He did not recognize the food, however, for he was not accustomed to eating such fine cuisine. He therefore opted for a different dish, taking a spoonful of vegetables and eating heartily.

Seeing this, his host approached him. "Please rise, my friend," said the host. "Perhaps you would be so kind as to sit at the end of the table…"

"Why are you humiliating the guest in such a manner?" asked his friends.

"Heaven forbid," answered the host. "I would never humiliate another person! I simply desire to provide each guest with his needs and with the food that he is accustomed to eating. Therefore, when I saw that I had indeed misjudged this individual, and that he prefers a dish of vegetables to a delicious meat delicacy, I changed his seat according to his stature."

The Dubno Maggid explained, Hashem fixed each nation its proper place according to its needs. To the Jewish Nation, He allotted a homeland in Eretz Yisrael next to the *Beis HaMikdash*. But when the Jewish people turned their necks to the holy Torah and extended their hands in order to take from the pleasures of the gentiles — Hashem exiled them to the gentiles' lands just as they desired.

When we will repent fully and Hashem's favor will be evoked, He will return us to our homeland and gather in the dispersed Jews from the four corners of the earth.

❧ The Amazing Musician

In a king's palace lived a skilled musician whose beautiful tunes amazed all those who heard them. The king very much enjoyed listening to the amazing melodies; he therefore built a special room inside the palace for the musician so that he would be always be in close proximity to him. Out of his great love for the musician, the king presented him with expensive garments like one of the princes.

One day, the king was informed that his beloved musician was a frequent visitor to the tavern where he would become drunk, just like the derelicts.

The king ordered that the beautiful garments that he had given him be confiscated, and the musician was expelled from the city in disgrace.

Realizing that he was destitute and that no individual would so much as take him into his home because they knew that he was repugnant in the eyes of the king, the musician took action. He took a blank sheet of paper and wrote a letter to the king, stating that he was regretful of the past. He asked for the king's forgiveness and even put in a plea for the future, requesting that he be reinstated to his former post.

The king wrote a letter in response. "You should know," he wrote, "that I did you no evil whatsoever; rather, my actions were inestimably good. For had I not confiscated all that you owned, you would have squandered it all in the tavern as drunkards are wont to do. You would then have been too humiliated to appear before me, as it is forbidden to come before the king in a garment of sackcloth. Rather, you would have fled and hid from me, and I would have decreed you a rebel to the throne…"

> With our wicked deeds, said the Dubno Maggid, we would have caused the Land to regurgitate us and the *Beis HaMikdash* to be destroyed. Furthermore, this would have thereby evoked inestimable wrath in Heaven.
>
> This is not the case, however, when it is Hashem, Who, in all

His glory, has personally exiled us among the nations and has destroyed the *Beis HaMikdash*. For then it is considered atonement for our sins and a conduit to bring about forgiveness, until we return to our Land and rebuild the *Beis HaMikdash*, speedily in our days.

ᴇᴈ *The Goldsmith and his Tools*

A skilled goldsmith renowned for his expert craftsmanship was in heavy debt and was forced to abandon his home and family and to travel far away.

He missed his loved ones dearly during his travels, and on more than one occasion let out a deep heart-rending sigh. One thought consoled him, however; that the day would come when he would return to his home and family, and provide them with a comfortable livelihood as he had in the past.

Some time later, the man indeed returned to his home and the joy was overwhelming. But when he approached his worktable and opened his toolbox, he discovered that over the years that he had been away his work tools had rusted severely and were completely ruined. Needless to say, they were no longer useable.

The more he looked around and observed the damage that had occurred, the more he realized just how sorry a predicament he was presently in…

The man broke out into bitter sobbing and exclaimed, "All the days of my exile, I was consoled by the fact that I would one day be restored to my former stature; but now I realize that such a thought was mere fantasy."

Hashem, said the Dubno Maggid, vested us with precious abilities so that we would be able to perform all of the *mitzvos* to perfection. But because of our sins we have been exiled from our Land, and our *Beis HaMikdash* has been destroyed. Languishing in our bitter exile, we are unable to utilize our abilities to serve Hashem. But it is, nevertheless, incumbent upon each individual to ensure that those precious abilities are not destroyed beyond repair, Heaven forbid.

◆§ A Tzaddik Decrees

A pair of neighbors shared a home and enjoyed a warm relationship with each other. Yet they were both beset by the same misfortune, as neither had merited having children.

The two of them decided to travel to a righteous rabbi and request a blessing for offspring; in the merit of his blessing, they would warrant Divine salvation. They heard about a great *tzaddik*, known far and wide, whose decrees were inevitably fulfilled by Hashem.

They traveled a great distance until they arrived at the *tzaddik's* home. When they entered his holy inner sanctum, they could not restrain themselves and broke into bitter sobbing.

After calming down slightly, they told the *tzaddik* the reason for their visit. He embraced them warmly and guaranteed that a son would be born to each of them in a year's time.

"But I have a request to make," said the *tzaddik*. "When your sons turn three years of age, with Hashem's help, bring them to me and I will bless them as well."

The two returned to their home, their hearts full of hope. In a year's time the *tzaddik's* blessing was fulfilled, as a healthy son was born to each neighbor.

When their sons turned three, the parents recalled the *tzaddik's* request; they therefore harnessed a carriage and journeyed to his city.

When they appeared before the *tzaddik* bearing their sons, he was most elated to receive them. He blessed the first son to grow to become a great Torah scholar, but he said that the second son would become a lust-driven individual who would not desire to learn a word.

The father of the second son was deeply aggrieved, but as that which is spoken cannot be taken back, they returned home.

When the children grew a little older and had already begun to learn with a *melamed*, the parents discovered that exactly the opposite had occurred, and the *tzaddik's* words had not been fulfilled. The first boy despised his studies and acted mischievously the entire day, while the second boy learned with amazing diligence.

When the first father observed the troubling predicament, he hastily traveled to the *tzaddik* to relate his distress. But upon simply entering the room, the *tzaddik* said, "Here he is, the father of the wise son!"

"It is not so, Rebbe," said the father sadly. "My son does not learn a word and my neighbor's son is diligent and studious."

"Impossible," said the *tzaddik*. "For I said that *your* son would be the wise one! Tell me about the boys and their actions."

The father related how he and his neighbor had hired a dedicated *melamed* who had the practice of persuading the children to learn by giving them various sweets. His son loathed the treats and threw them away, while the neighbor's son accepted them and learned well.

"It's just as I said," said the *tzaddik*, smiling. "You should know that when a child is young and does not understand the value of his studies, it is very difficult to get him to learn. We therefore tempt him with candies in order to motivate him to study. Now, one who is a lustful individual at birth — when he is tempted, he is drawn to study. Yet when he grows older, it is this very same lustful trait that distracts him from his learning. Your son, on the other hand, was born without this trait and therefore cannot be persuaded with sweets. When he grows older, though, he will grasp the true value of learning and will become a great Torah scholar!"

> The entire world, said the Dubno Maggid, desires the Land of Israel because of its goodness and positive qualities, and it was the quest for such goodness and pleasure that caused the Jewish Nation to sin, resulting in their being exiled from their homeland. But in the future, Hashem will redeem us and uproot the *yetzer hara* from within our hearts. At that point, our only desire will be to cling to His ways, and we will see the fulfillment of the verse (*Amos* 9:15), "I will plant them upon their Land and they will never again be uprooted from the Land!"

This volume is part of
THE ARTSCROLL SERIES®
an ongoing project of
translations, commentaries and expositions
on Scripture, Mishnah, Talmud, Halachah,
liturgy, history, the classic Rabbinic writings,
biographies and thought.

For a brochure of current publications
visit your local Hebrew bookseller
or contact the publisher:

Mesorah Publications, ltd

4401 Second Avenue
Brooklyn, New York 11232
(718) 921-9000
www.artscroll.com